# At the End
# of the Rainbow?

# At the End
# of the Rainbow?

## GOLD, LAND, AND PEOPLE IN THE
## BRAZILIAN AMAZON

*Gordon MacMillan*

Columbia University Press/New York

Columbia University Press
562 West 113th Street
New York, NY 10025

*Library of Congress Cataloging-in-Publication Data*

MacMillan, Gordon.
    At the end of the rainbow? : gold, land, and people in the
Brazilian Amazon / Gordon MacMillan.
        p.     cm. — (Methods and cases in conservation science)
    Includes bibliographical references and index.
    ISBN 0–231–10354–9. — ISBN 0–231–10355–7 (pbk.)
    1. Gold mines and mining—Brazil—Roraima.
2. Gold miners—Brazil—Roraima.   3. Yanomamo Indians–
Brazil—Roraima.   I. Title.   II. Series.
HD9536.B83B676   1995
338.2′741′098114—dc20                                      95-139
                                                                CIP

# Contents

## Contents

# Illustrations

## FIGURES

## TABLES

## PHOTOGRAPHS

# Illustrations

# Acronyms

| | |
|---|---|
| ALUNORTE | Alumínio do Norte (Aluminium Company of the North) |
| ANPOCS | Anthropólogia e Ciencias Sociais (Department of Anthropology and Social Sciences at the University of Rio de Janeiro) |
| ATPC | Association of Tin Producing Countries |
| BASA | Banco da Amazônia SA (Amazonian Bank plc) |
| BMF | Bolsa Mercantil de Futuros |
| CAPEMI | Caixa de Pecúnio dos Militares (Military Pension Fund) |
| CCPY | Comissão Pela Criação do Parque Yanomami (Commission for the Creation of a Yanomami Park) |
| CEDI | Centro Ecumênio de Documentação e Informação (Church Centre for Documentation and Information) |
| CETEM | Centro de Technologia Mineral (Centre for Mining Technology) |
| CIA | Companhia Industrial Amazonense (Amazonian Industrial Company) |
| CIDR | Centro de Informação de Diocese de Roraima (Information Centre for the Church of Roraima) |
| CIMI | Conselho Indigenista Missionário (Indian Missionary Council) |
| CIR | Conselho Indígena de Roraima (Indigenous Council of Roraima) |
| CODESAIMA | Companhia de Desenvolvimento de Roraima (Roraima Development Company) |
| CPI | Comissão Pro-Índio (Pro-Indian Commission) |
| CPRM | Companhia de Pesquisa de Recursos Minerais (Mineral Resources Research Company) |
| CPT | Comissão Pastoral da Terra (Pastoral Land Commission) |

| | |
|---|---|
| CS | Cultural Survival |
| CVRD | Companhia do Vale Rio Doce (Rio Doce Valley Company) |
| DNER | Departamento Nacional de Estradas e Rodagem (National Roadworks Department) |
| DNPM | Departamento Nacional de Pesquisa Mineral (National Department for Mineral Research) |
| DOCEGO | Subsidiary of CVRD |
| EDF | Environmental Defense Fund |
| ESRC | Economic and Social Research Council |
| FNO | Fundo Constitutional da Região Norte (Constitutional Fund for the Northern Region) |
| FNS | Fundação Nacional de Saude (National Health Foundation) |
| FUNAI | Fundação Nacional do Índio (National Indian Foundation) |
| FUNATURA | Fundação Pro Natureza (Foundation for Nature) |
| IBAMA | Instituto Brasileira de Meio Ambiente e Recursos Naturais (Brazilian Institute for the Environment and Natural Resources) |
| IBASE | Instituto Brasileiro de Analisés Sociais (Brazilian Institute for Social Analysis) |
| IBDF | Instituto Brasileiro de Desenvolvimento Florestál (Brazilian Institute for Forestry) |
| IBGE | Instituto Brasileiro de Geografía e Estatística (Brazilian Institute for Geography and Statistics) |
| IDB | Interamerican Development Bank |
| IMAZON | Instituto do Homem e do Meio Ambiente da Amazônia (Amazonian Institute for Man and Environment) |
| IMF | International Monetary Fund |
| INCRA | Instituto Nacional de Colonização e Reforma Agrária (National Institute for Colonization and Land Reform) |
| INESC | Instituto de Estudos Sócio-Econômicos (Institute for Socio-Economic Studies) |
| INPA | Instituto Nacional de Pesquisas da Amazônia (National Institute for Amazonian Research) |
| ISPN | Instituto Sociedade, Populaçaõ e Natureza (Institute for Society, Population and Nature) |
| ITC | International Tin Cartel |

| | |
|---|---|
| IWGIA | International Working Group on Indigenous Affairs |
| MCT | Ministério de Ciençia e Technologia (Science and Technology Ministry) |
| MEVA | Missão Evangelica da Amazônia (Evangelical Mission for the Amazon) |
| NDI | Núcleo dos Direitos Indígenas (Nucleus for Indian Rights) |
| NGO | Non-Governmental Organization |
| NRI | Natural Resources Institute |
| OEA | Organizaçaõ dos Estados Americanos (Organization of American States) |
| PAR | Projeto de Assentamento Rapido (Rapid Settlement Project) |
| PIN | Plano de Integração Nacional (National Integration Plan) |
| PNUD | Programa das Nações Unis de Desenvolvimento (United Nations Development Programme) |
| POLAMAZONIA | Programa de Polos Agropecuários e Agrominerais da Amazônia (Programme for Agro-ranching, and Agro-mineral development poles in Amazonia) |
| POLONOROESTE | Northwestern development pole |
| PR | Presidente do Republica |
| PR–SDR | Presidente do Republica–Secretária de Desenvolvimento Regional |
| PROVAM | Programa dos Valés de Amazonia (Programme of Amazonian Valleys) |
| RBC | Royal Bank of Canada |
| RR | Roraima |
| SCT | Secretária de Ciençia e Technologia |
| SEICOM | Secretária da Econômia, Industria e Comérçio (Economy, Industry and Business Secretariat) |
| SEPLAC | Secretária de Planejamento e Coordenação (Planning and Coordination Secretariat) |
| SEPLAN | Secretária de Planejamento (Planning Secretariat) |
| SI | Survival International |
| SPVEA | Superintendência da Valorização da Amazônia (Superintendency for Amazonian Development) |
| SUCAM | Superintendência de Combate a Malária (Anti-Malarial Superintendency) |

| | |
|---|---|
| SUDAM | Superintendência de Desenvolvimento da Amazônia (Superintendency for Amazonian Development) |
| SUPLAN | Secretária Nacional de Planejamento Agrícola (National Secretariat for Agricultural Planning) |
| TCA | Treaty de Cooperação Amazônica (Amazon Co-operation Treaty) |
| UDR | União Democrática Ruralista (Rural Democratic Union) |
| UNCED | United Nations Conference on Environment and Development |
| UNDP | United Nations Development Programme |
| USAGAL | União de Sindicato dos *Garimpeiros* de Amazônia Legal (Union of Amazonian *Garimpeiros*) |
| WHO | World Health Organization |
| WRI | World Resources Institute |

# Glossary of Brazilian Terms

| | |
|---|---|
| *aviamento* | system of debt peonage in the extractive economy, most prevalent during the Amazon rubber boom |
| *balsa* | floating raft upon which mining equipment is mounted for working river-bed sediments |
| *bamburrado* | struck it rich |
| *barranco* | plot of land in a *garimpo* to mine on; mining pit |
| *barrica* | measure of brazil nuts weighing 72–78 kilograms |
| *blefado* | skint, penniless |
| *caatinga* | thorny, scrubby vegetation typical of nutrient-poor sandy soils |
| *caboclo* | riverine dweller who usually lives off a combination of fishing, hunting, agriculture and extractavism |
| *conta própria* | work relationship in which the *garimpeiro*s organize their own catering and are considered to be working independently, not for somebody else |
| *dono* | 'owner'; for example, *dono de garimpo* means owner of the mine; *dono de máquina*, owner of a set of mining equipment, and *dono da pista*, owner of an airstrip |
| *draga* | large mechanized dredger |
| *farinha* | manioc flour |
| *fazenda* | cattle ranch |
| *fazendeiro* | rancher |
| *fofoca* | literally 'gossip', but signifies a rush of *garimpeiro*s to a particular site which rumours suggest is producing well. A *garimpo* can be described as being in *fofoca* when it is at the centre of a rush, usually in the immediate aftermath of a substantial find |

| | |
|---|---|
| *garimpagem* | informal-sector mining |
| *garimpeiro* | anybody involved in *garimpagem*; the term is used broadly to cover both those involved in the mineral extraction process itself, and the pilots, cooks or merchants who work in the *garimpo*s |
| *garimpo* | informal-sector mine |
| *meia-praça* | work relationship under which the *dono de garimpo* or *dono de máquina* engage their work-force; in both cases the *dono* provides food and employment for the workers who are paid with a percentage of the gold production |
| *(par de) máquinas* | a set of pumping equipment, for semi-mechanized mining |
| *pista* | airstrip |
| *posseiro* | squatter; somebody who lays claim to land that does not belong to them |
| *retentor* | mercury condenser |
| *roça* | plot of land devoted to food production |
| *sorte* | payment of management on a *fazenda* in which the manager receives a proportion of the new stock raised each year |
| *tapuio* | name given to the detribalized Indians who survived Pombal's Directorate Programme |
| *terra firme* | land that is not seasonally inundated by the rising water of rivers |
| *terras devolutas* | land that has no owner and therefore belongs to the federal government |
| *titulo definitivo* | the most secure land title |

# Preface

This book is about wildcat mining in the Amazon. In recent years both the place and the activity have entered the limelight. Television documentaries, newspaper reports and an array of magazine articles have brought us vivid images of the Amazon gold rush. But, this considerable media attention disguises a thin understanding of how and why events like this come about. For the truth of the matter is that very few long-term studies have been written on the subject. As a result, we are constantly informed by the press of particular happenings in Amazonia, but frequently lack more detailed explanations as to why they might have occurred. This situation can at best give rise to confused debate and at worse generate ill-informed policy.

The intention behind this volume is to provide a deeper insight into the causes and consequences of the Amazon gold rush. More specifically, I want to show how wildcat mining has been altering the course of development throughout the Amazon basin. The information and ideas on which this is argued are the product of four years of research into the informal-mining economy of Amazonia. Most of the data come from Roraima, Brazil's northernmost state, which leapt out of obscurity in the late 1980s following an invasion of the Yanomami Indian Reserve by approximately 30,000 prospectors. Despite serious attempts by the Brazilian authorities to evict the miners from this remote area, the gold rush persists. At the time of writing, violent clashes between the prospectors and Indians continue to mark the history of this highly destructive episode.

Prior to taking office in 1995, the Brazilian president, Fernando Henrique Cardoso, underlined his commitment to defend Indian land rights. Clearly, with the current pressures on groups like the Yanomami, this is a laudable goal. But while effective policing can certainly reduce illegal mining activity in Indian reserves over the short term, it is important to recognize that it rarely stops it altogether. Both the numbers of people involved and the size of the areas concerned are too big. Thus, a need also exists for longer term initiatives directed at the more fundamental social, economic and political forces that encourage people to invade Indian lands. While a falling price of gold and the new government's resolve to takle inflation both represent encouraging recent macro-economic trends in this respect, chronic social problems, not least of which are inequalities in land ownership, widespread poverty and a growing drugs industry, demand attention at a regional level.

Living in Roraima for 18 months afforded plenty of opportunities to explore the wider causes and effects of the gold rush. Some of this time was spent staying with gold miners, learning where they had come from, why they were there and being shown how the gold mines work. But most of it was spent with a wide range of other people who live in Amazonia: migrant farmers, ranchers, Indian groups, urban dwellers and riverine people. I was very interested to understand what impelled some of them to join the gold rush and risk the dangers of mining in the Yanomami Reserve, while others demonstrated a lack of interest in, if not disdain, towards the opportunities available in the gold camps. By looking at the influence of the mining boom on different groups of people and their livelihoods, I hoped to glimpse what forces were driving the rush, and see how they are currently reshaping Amazonian life.

The book is structured in three main parts. The first section provides relevant background and historical information. Chapter 1 outlines current understanding of gold mining in the Amazon, before introducing the social and geographical context of this study. Chapter 2 then looks at the history of mining in Roraima, focusing specifically on the 1987–90 gold rush on the lands of the Yanomami Indians.

The second section considers the impacts that this mining boom has on other Amazonian land-uses. Chapter 3 deals with its influence on smallholder agriculture offering an insight into the movements of labour attributable to the rush. In Chapter 4 the focus turns to capital flows as we examine the relationship between mining and ranching. The following chapter (5) looks at the response of Indian and riverine peoples to the changes brought to remote areas by the mining economy. Although many local people chose not to get directly involved in the gold rush, it did nonetheless alter their livelihoods significantly.

The third and final section considers these findings in their wider context. Chapter 6 assesses the political changes precipitated by the growth in the Amazonian informal mining economy over the 1980s. By gaining an insight into the forces that shaped the turn of events both in Roraima and elsewhere the structures which determine the allocation of Amazonian mineral resources are exposed. The penultimate chapter (7) looks at the environmental and social impacts of gold mining as it is currently being practised. Here, mercury pollution and other environmental consequences of mining are discussed together with social issues like the associated prostitution and drugs rackets. Finally, a brief look at the metal markets in Chapter 8 suggests that mining will continue to influence land development processes both in the Amazon and throughout the humid tropics over the foreseeable future.

# Acknowledgements

I am most grateful to the Economic and Social Research Council (ESRC) for funding this research and to the University of Edinburgh for providing the facilities with which to undertake it. I also thank the Royal Mail, the Scottish International Education Trust and the Edinburgh University Student Travel Fund for their assistance towards travel expenses.

I am particularly indebted to Peter Furley and David Cleary for their friendship as much as their advice.

In Brazil the following gave me invaluable help: Roberto Monteiro de Oliveira; Celso Morato at INPA (Instituto Nacional de Pesquisas da Amazônia), Boa Vista; Philip Fearnside, Bruce Forsberg and George Nakamara at INPA, Manaus; Alcida Ramos and Bruce Albert at the University of Brasília; Chris Uhl, Philippe Lená, Christian Geoffrey and Elizette Gaspar in Belém; Francisco Fernandes and Irene Portela at the University of Rio de Janeiro; Paulo Santilli and Nadia Farage at the University of São Paulo.

In Roraima I greatly appreciated the support and friendship of the Souto Maior family (especially Ana Paula and Bjorn), Frederico Caheté, Reinaldo Barbosa, Ari and Léda, Val, Ana-Luce, Yvonne, Oneron Pithon, Ednelson Macuxi, Marcão and Alvaro, Carlos Zaquini, Julio Martins, John Boyle, Aldecir, John Bradshaw, Daniel da Souza, Roberto F Da Silva, Chico Ceará, Senhor Nonato, and Umberto Mota. I will never forget the patience and hospitality of the Roraimense.

In the UK and USA I would like to thank the following for their diverse contributions to this work: Rebecca Abers and Alberto Carlos, Kenneth Taylor, Nigel Sizer, Liz Allen, Roger Moody, Liz Bondi, Jim Hine, Alan Campbell, Anna Sim and Lena, Anona Lyons, Jonathon Stitchbury, Nicola Exley, George Monbiot, Jane Rutherford, William Milliken, Fiona Watson, Tânia Sanaiotti, Chris Minty, Paulo Cesar, Monica Decanini, Ana Ashmole, Christoph Corves, Monica Wachowicz, Luiz da Souza, and Adrian Allan.

Above all, I would like to thank my parents.

*Ranching remains the principal cause of deforestation in Amazonia.*

# Chapter 1

# The Quickening Pulse of Amazonian Life

An impressive gold rush is sweeping across the Amazon. In 1992 a United Nations document exclaimed 'no other factor has produced as large a migration of people to the Brazilian Amazon in so short a time as gold-fever'.[1] The rush was sparked at the end of the 1970s when government plans to open up this mineral-rich region coincided with a sharp rise in the price of gold. During the following decade it was estimated that, in the Brazilian Amazon alone, somewhere between one million and 240,000 wildcat miners were directly employed in what is technically termed the 'informal-sector mining economy'.[2] In Brazil these informal-sector miners are known as *garimpeiros*, and at the time of writing there are probably about 300,000 of them working in hundreds of informal-sector mines (*garimpos*) scattered throughout the Amazon.

In fact, these figures are little more than informed guesses, as it is virtually impossible to quantify the exact scale of the rush. For example, the numbers above refer only to those directly involved in mining. But, for everybody employed inside the mines, there are at least as many again outside, whether they be bar owners, prostitutes or restauranteurs who depend on the mining economy indirectly for their livelihoods. This has led one authoritative source to suggest that as much as 30 per cent of Brazil's Amazonian population is directly or indirectly engaged in the mining boom.[3] Production data are equally elusive because smuggling is rife and only a fraction of the gold that is produced is ever officially registered. USAGAL (União de Sindicato dos *Garimpeiros* de Amazônia Legal), the Amazonian miners' union, believes that about 100 metric tons of gold are produced annually in the region's *garimpos*, but other

---

1.  IDB/UNDP/TCA (1992) p 38.
2.  The larger of these two estimates is given by the Amazonian Miners Union, USAGAL [Feijão and Pinto (1990) p. 1], and the smaller is a government estimate produced by the Department of Mineral Research (DNPM).
3.  IDB/UNDP/TCA (1992) p 37.

sources have suggested that even this figure may be conservative.[4] All of the indicators point to a major event in global mining history. Indeed, the Amazonian rush actually outstrips the Klondike and California gold booms of the last century, both in terms of production and the number of people employed.[5]

Thus, in a short space of time gold mining has become one of the principal catalysts for development in the world's largest remaining tropical rainforest. The socioeconomic changes associated with informal-sector mining are so strong that the activity has reshaped patterns of settlement and resource use in many parts of the Amazon. In fact the transformations are so marked that the whole emphasis of regional development has shifted. Since the 1970s specialist discussion has focused on the notion of an 'Amazon frontier', at which a peripheral peasant economy is gradually subsumed and integrated within an encroaching state-backed capitalist mode of production. This interpretation appeared to offer a relatively accurate explanation of events before the gold rush took off in the late 1970s. Up until this point regional development was largely the result of an intense 'struggle for land' played out alongside a network of newly constructed roads, the most famous of which was the Transamazonian highway. Conflicts arose when migrant farmers, who had either been allocated land in government colonization schemes or who had simply staked a claim to unoccupied landholdings, clashed with larger ranching or agro-mineral projects, many of which received government support in the form of tax breaks. The violence and deforestation, which marked this 'struggle for land', were most clearly visible in an arc stretching across the relatively accessible southern fringes of the Amazon from Maranhão and Pará in the east, through Goiás and Tocantins, into northern Mato Grosso, Rondônia and parts of Acre in the west. The northern states of Amapá, Amazonas and Roraima were virtually unaffected by what was seen as the 'Amazon frontier', precisely because they were too remote to attract venture capital in the same way as the southern Amazon did.

This picture began to change considerably as the gold rush gathered momentum in the 1980s. The huge amounts of public-sector funding invested in road building, ranching and agriculture, which had fuelled the expansion of the frontier, began to dwindle as

---

4. See for example Dourojeanni and Padua (1992) p 101, who suggest that the total sum may be three times this figure.
5. Cleary (1990).

soaring interest rates pushed Brazil's international debt over the US $100 billion mark. While the state-backed agricultural frontier faltered, people and capital were increasingly drawn to other sectors of the regional economy, the most attractive of which was the rapidly expanding informal-mining sector. Gradually, the quest for minerals came to supersede the 'struggle for land' as the principal force shaping contemporary patterns of settlement and resource use in Amazonia.[6]

This book takes a close look at how the development emphasis has shifted from the agrarian to mineral sector and considers the significance of this transition for the society and environment of Amazonia. Before starting, however, it is important to clarify a point of terminology. Although a recent study has described the gold rush as a 'mineral frontier',[7] this is not necessarily a useful turn of phrase. The word frontier is misleading when applied to the gold rush because it gives the false impression that a capitalist mode of production is encroaching upon a peasant or non-capitalist economy. The truth is that the economic and social relations of the Amazonian informal-mining economy are essentially non-capitalist. For while there are a handful of large corporate mining projects in the Amazon that can be described as capitalist, by far the greatest share of the region's output of gold and diamonds, as well as a large proportion of its tin ore, is produced by hundreds of thousands of *garimpeiros*. Not only do these miners work outside the capitalist economy, but their work relations are also totally informal; contracts are agreed verbally, incomes are not declared and no taxes are paid.

But there is another reason why it is inappropriate to apply frontier terminology to this situation. Use of the word conjures up an image of a development front moving gradually through the region transforming everything in its wake – a bit like a glacier. And though this might have had some relevance to the scenario in the 1970s, it has become an increasingly untenable concept. The mining sector is not dependent on the road network in the same way as the agricultural economy is, and so recent developments have not taken place along an easily identifiable front. Far from it, pockets of rapid social and economic change have sprung up throughout the region, in fact wherever valuable mineral resources have been discovered.

---

6. For a more detailed political–economic analysis of these processes see Cleary (1993).
7. Pereira (1990).

A map of the principal mining areas (Figure 1.1) reveals that some of the most significant goldfields are to be found in extremely isolated parts of Amazonia. It is in these remote areas, like the basin's northern watershed, that the impact of mining has been most keenly felt.

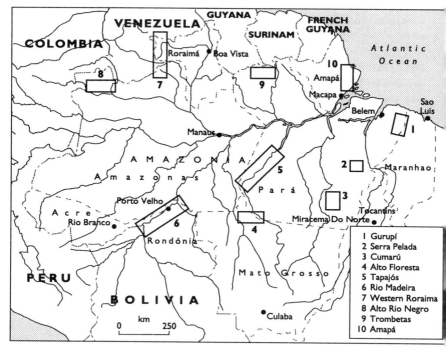

**Figure 1.1** *The Brazilian Amazon showing the principal gold producing regions*

Rather than offering a cursory and inevitably superficial glance at all these different places, much of the discussion in this book draws on recent events in the state of Roraima. Roraima is Brazil's northernmost state, covering a land area about the size of Britain. As Figure 1.1 shows, it houses one of the ten major gold producing regions in the Brazilian Amazon and, like most of the other sites marked, Roraima has a long history of small-scale mining, which gained a new impetus in the 1980s. The discovery of significant gold and cassiterite (tin ore) deposits on the Yanomami Indian Reserve brought the cutting edge of the Amazonian mineral boom to this remote area in 1986. By the end of the decade Roraima was producing an estimated 10 per cent of all gold extracted in the Brazilian Amazon.[8] Large numbers of people and considerable amounts of capital flooded into the state from all over the country, but the prosperity was unexpectedly short-lived. Government intervention seeking to prohibit access to the Yanomami Reserve, on which the illegal *garimpos* were situated, caused a sharp contraction of the local economy in 1990. The net result was a brief but very intense gold rush, which had a clearly defined impact on Roraima's social and physical landscape.

This provides a clear window through which to view the transformations that the gold rush brought to a remote part of the Amazon. With this in mind, I spent 16 months in Roraima (from October 1990 to March 1992) looking at how this boom in the informal-mining economy affected local people and their use of the land. The intention was to understand how a wide range of social groups responded to the rapid socioeconomic changes precipitated by the mineral rush on the Yanomami lands. In research terms, such a perspective scores what has become known as a 'double whammy' because it not only offers a privileged insight into the relationship between informal-sector mining and other land uses, but it also sheds light on a wider debate of global significance: 'One of the key potential contributions from social science to the conservation and development fields is in the analysis of local responses (by specific social group in particular ecosystems) to macro-level economic and political changes.'[9]

Thus, by considering the interactions between a range of social groups in a particular place, this book seeks to highlight the complex interrelationships between people and the land that characterize modern Amazonia. The emphasis is therefore on Roraima, but as the themes emerge information gathered from the state is discussed in relation to other events from different parts of the region. In this way we can identify the principal development processes at work throughout the Amazon, without divorcing them from the heterogeneous landscape in which they operate.

From the start, therefore, it is important to gain a clear understanding of the context in which the gold rush took off. Essentially we want to know what people did in Amazonia before the gold rush, and then see how this pattern has changed. Thus, the remain-

---

8. See Feijão and Pinto (1990) p 6.
9. Schmink (1992) p 2.

der of this chapter is devoted to introducing the three dominant Amazonian land uses, and tracing their historical development at both a regional and local level. Our attention will focus on what can loosely be termed Indian or folk management practices, ranching, and smallholder agriculture. Clearly, there are large parts of the Amazon that are not managed by anybody, and there are also areas in which other land uses, like hydroelectric reservoirs, industrialized mining and urban development dominate. But in the overall picture these activities are confined to relatively small areas, affecting no more than 2 per cent of the Brazilian Amazon's total land surface.[10] Logging is a slightly different case, which deserves a special mention, not least because the demand for timber is often perceived to be one of the principal agents of destruction in the Amazon. In areas rich in valuable hardwoods like mahogany, rosewood and cedar, timber cutting is undoubtedly an important development pressure.[11] Nevertheless, in most parts of Amazonia, including Roraima, sawn timber remains a secondary product derived from the clearance of forest for ranching and agricultural use. So, even though the picture may be changing in certain areas, these activities, together with mining, are still the main catalysts for Amazonian development and the timber industry tends to follow in their wake.

## INDIGENOUS LAND-USE PRACTICES

Indian groups are the only original Amazonian land users and their management techniques have evolved in relation to the local environment over the longest period of time. As a result, indigenous land-use strategies are so well adapted to local ecosystems that their impact is often indistinguishable from the legacy of nature herself. The full extent of Indian management is consequently poorly understood and its influence on the distribution of certain tree species and soil types is only recently becoming apparent.[12] Far from being a uniform rainforest, the vegetation types of the Amazon basin include dense montane forests, semi-deciduous

---

10. While no precise data are available on areas covered by cities and industrial mining projects, Fearnside (1991a) p 16 does provide some information on the size of areas inundated by hydroelectric reservoirs.
11. This is certainly the case for parts of Rondônia and Pará. For a more detailed discussion of the regional timber industry see Uhl et al (1991), as well as Johnson and Cabarle (1993).
12. For an excellent discussion of this consult Posey and Balée (1989).

woodlands, thorn scrub and, as is seldom appreciated, vast expanses of savannah with varying degrees of tree cover. It appears that some of these vegetation types are actually anthropogenic, suggesting that the floristic diversity of the Amazon owes itself in no small part to thousands of years of indigenous management.[13]

The extent to which native strategies alter the environment are further illustrated by the management practices employed by the Kayapó Indians of Pará. Researchers have shown that this group's stewardship not only improves soil fertility, but also facilitates the expansion of the forest into areas of savannah.[14] The important point made by these and other studies is that indigenous peoples have developed extremely sophisticated management techniques, enabling them to support considerable populations on nutrient-poor soils over thousands of years.[15] It has been argued that these practices actually enhance, not degrade, the fertility and biological diversity of ecosystems.

Even though the land uses employed by indigenous peoples are extremely diverse, a number of common elements may be identified.[16] Essentially, Indian land-use practices combine a variety of different activities such as fishing, swidden (slash and burn) agriculture, hunting and gathering within an overall management strategy. The importance of each activity varies seasonally and from place to place. It is not surprising therefore that anthropologists often see the migratory behaviour of Indian groups bearing a direct relation to their management of a dynamic resource base. But perhaps more significantly, the social organization and cosmological beliefs of certain groups actually regulate patterns of resource exploitation.[17] All this evidence suggests that the indigenous peoples of the Amazon have developed management systems that are finely tuned to the complexities of local ecosystems.

Despite the aptitude of these practices, there has been a gradual decline in the area of Amazonia subjected to Indian management.

---

13. Balée (1989) estimates that anthropogenic forests of palm, bamboo, brazil-nut, and liana, together with forest islands, and caatinga vegetation comprise at least 11.8 per cent of the Brazilian Amazon.
14. Anderson and Posey (1989).
15. Much of the relevant archeological evidence supporting this statement has been provided by Roosevelt (1992).
16. Clay (1988) and Eden (1990) both provide overviews of indigenous management practices throughout the Amazon basin.
17. For migration see Moran (1989), for social/cosmological regulation of resource exploitation see Ribeiro and Kenhiri (1989).

This trend dates from 1492, when the first Europeans set foot in South America, and continues to the present day. It is due to a sharp contraction in the size of native populations resulting from both the introduction of old world diseases and violent clashes with European settlers. The number of Indians in the Amazon basin has fallen from over seven million in 1492 to a current population of between 1 and 2.5 million.[18] In the Brazilian Amazon alone, there are about 213,000 Indians representing less than 2 per cent of the total population (17 million). Having once been the region's sole occupants, ownership of land by indigenous people is now restricted to officially designated Indian reserves encompassing only 1.6 per cent of Amazonia's five million square kilometres. Many of these reserves are located in nutrient-poor upland areas (*terra firme*) and, although these represent the original homelands of some groups, many other tribes have migrated to them from more fertile flood plains, having been displaced by European settlers during the colonial period.

The history of Roraima's Indian population is illustrative. Throughout the eighteenth century slave traders raided the numerous Arawak and Carib-speaking tribes who inhabited the open savannahs in the upper reaches of the Rio Branco. Carmelite missionaries from Airão (then called Santo Elias dos Tarumas) and Manaus (then called Fort Barra), considered Roraima's grassland tribes to be 'easily tamed' and for this reason they sent numerous slaving expeditions into the area. Their unfortunate captives represented a particularly important source of labour to the Carmelites during the first half of the eighteenth century. This is because their access to other groups in the headwaters of the Rio Negro was blocked for many years by the aggressive Manao tribe who lived at the current site of Barcellos.[19] Although the Amerindian slave trade was outlawed in 1750, reforms pioneered under the Marquis of Pombal's Directorate Programme (1757–99) proved no less damaging to the native population. This act withdrew the control of indigenous welfare from missionary groups and entrusted it to a number of state-appointed directors. These directors were charged with overseeing a network of villages which had been established throughout the Amazon to house its captive native population. Far from being benevolent patrons, the directors frequently exploited

---

18. IDB/UNDP/TCA (1992) p 27.
19. See Hemming (1990a), and Farage (1991) who provides a more detailed and exhaustive account of the early occupation of Roraima.

their authority and were only too ready to employ brutal measures when dealing with the resultant unrest. One such incident in the early 1790s led to the deportation of Roraima's captive Indian population. The native residents of all six villages that had been established along the Rio Branco were transferred to other director-ate settlements hundreds of kilometres away on the Solimões, Madeira, and Amazon rivers. A few years later a further rebellion occurred as the Carib-speaking Paravilhana and the Arawak-speaking Wapixana confronted the director of their village. The Portuguese responded with a punitive expedition, during which numerous Indians were slaughtered on the shores of the Rio Branco at a site that became known as bloody beach (Praia de Sangue). This was the final act in a series of violent incidents that left Roraima vir-tually depopulated by the start of the nineteenth century.

Atrocities of this nature were by no means restricted to the Rio Branco, and consequently the Indian population of contemporary Amazonia differs greatly from that of the seventeenth century. The Carib-speaking Paravilhana and Sapará tribes, which inhabited the savannahs at that time, have completely disappeared from Roraima. The disruption was so great that even the societies that did survive the intervening years were profoundly altered by the experience. Such is the case with the Macuxi and Wapixana who occupy the grassland plains of northern Roraima. With 12,000 members, the Carib-speaking Macuxi are now the largest group in Roraima, while their traditional adversaries, the Wapixana (Arawak), have a total population of about 5000.[20] As both groups have had such a long history of contact with colonial society, most of their members now speak Portuguese. The Wapixana and Macuxi are integrated into the local economy and large numbers of them currently reside in the state capital, Boa Vista.[21] Those who remain on the plains typically subsist on fishing, hunting and prac-tising swidden agriculture. Many of them, particularly the young men, choose to supplement their incomes by engaging in waged employment on the surrounding ranches, or in the local diamond *garimpo*s.

A marked geographical division between the northern savannah plains and the remaining forested area strongly influenced the human occupation of Roraima during the colonial period. Many of

---

20. Hemming (1990b).
21. See Ferri (1990) for an interesting discussion of Indian migration to Boa Vista.

the indigenous groups that lived on or fled to the upland (*terra firme*) forested areas were untouched by eighteenth century missionaries, who tended to restrict their activities to the flood plains and savannah. One such group was the Yanomami, Roraima's best known tribe, who inhabit the densely forested watershed dividing the Orinoco in Venezuela from various tributaries of the Rio Negro and Rio Branco in Brazil. The Brazilian Indian agency, FUNAI (Fundação Nacional do Índio), estimates that out of a total population of 20,000 Yanomami, there are 9000 living on the Brazilian side of the national border in Roraima (7000) and Amazonas (2000).[22] Because of their isolation, the Yanomami had very little interaction with non-indigenous people until a new phase of Amazonian land development, dating from the 1960s, brought them and other forest dwelling groups into contact with the rest of Brazilian society. This, in conjunction with the gold rush under study, is simply the latest step in a 500-year history of highly destructive contact between Amerindian and Old World societies.

## FOLK STRATEGIES: *CABOCLOS*

Contact with the Indians in Amazonia gave rise to a distinct folk culture, which was born from the collapse of Pombal's Directorate Programme at the end of the eighteenth century. By settling indigenous peoples in villages, the directorate effectively created a new detribalized Indian known as the *tapuio*.[23] In the aftermath of the directorate programme, these disfranchized survivors of the Indian tribes, many of whom were of mixed blood, dispersed along riverine areas to live in fragmented settlements. While adopting predominantly subsistence livelihoods, they also extracted various forest products and traded them along an extensive network of riverine commerce. They were the first generation of *caboclo*s, the Amazon's backwoodsmen, distinguished from their truly Indian relatives by mixed blood descent, limited commercial activity and a dispersed settlement pattern. *Caboclo*s came to inhabit the same

---

22. Yanomami is a generic term refering to groups who speak languages that have a common root – Yanomama. Even so, there are linguistic and cultural variations between different Yanomami villages. On the basis of these, anthropologists distinguish between the Sanuma, Yanomam (Waika), Ninam or Yanam (Xiriana, Xirixana, and Jawari) peoples. Migliazza (1978).
23. For a more detailed study of *caboclo*s see Ayres (1992) and Parker (1989).

flood plains from which their ancestors had been displaced by the Portuguese. In general terms, therefore, they have evolved land-use practices appropriate to the riverine ecosystem, while the remaining Indian groups have confined themselves largely to managing inaccessible upland areas.

The Amazonian riverine economy was transformed by the rubber boom of the nineteenth century. Initially, this brought a marked population increase to the region as thousands of northeasterners were drafted into remote parts of the Amazon to extract rubber. The majority of them left after 1916, when production from newly established plantations in Malaysia began to drive down the price of rubber.[24] Even so, large numbers of northeasterners did stay on and became incorporated into the Amazon's *caboclo* population through miscegeny.

The rubber boom also altered the economic basis of the riverine extractive economy, as a new work relation emerged linking the *caboclo* through debt to river traders. Typically, a trader advanced the necessary food and equipment to the *caboclo* for the extraction of certain forest products. In order to service this debt the *caboclo* was obliged to sell the extracted produce to the same trader, who usually set such unfavourable prices that it was virtually impossible to repay the original credit. More goods would be advanced for the following season's work and in this way the trader maintained control over the *caboclo*'s labour through a system of debt bondage.

Vestiges of this work relation (known as *aviamento*) still exist throughout rural Amazonia, particularly in states like Acre and Amazonas, where the extractive economy remains comparatively strong. Having subjugated thousands of workers to conditions of semi-slavery during the rubber boom, the *aviamento* system is currently far less coercive than it once was. Certainly its influence is waning along the lower reaches of the Rio Branco and its tributaries. Here, many of the *caboclo*s are still indebted to their traders, but declining prices of the principal extracted products discourage the latter from advancing further credit.

In Chapter 5 we shall consider how the gold rush has affected the livelihoods of Indians and *caboclo*s. Clearly, the land uses practised by these two social groups are completely different. *Caboclo*s typically manage seasonally inundated forests in the flood plains, while

---

24. This was a severe blow to Brazil, not least because the Malaysian plantations were established with seed that had been illegally smuggled out of the Amazon by the British botanist, Henry Wickham.

Indian stewardship is generally, but by no means exclusively, associated with *terra firme* areas supporting either forest or savannah. Even so, broad similarities do exist in the strategies on which these different management practices are based. In essence, they combine a variety of subsistence activities, which are supplemented by a modest cash income derived from production for, and employment in, the market economy. It is particularly important to understand how such strategies are affected by wider socioeconomic changes because they are frequently at the root of land-use systems that exploit the natural environment without destroying it.

*Road building in the 1970s unleashed a wave of migration into Amazonia.*

# RANCHING

Amazonian beef producers tend to be either traditional rural oligarchies, urban entrepreneurs, capitalized colonist farmers, or corporate entities. The origins of the first group date from the seventeenth century and their domain extends across the most accessible *terra firme* savannahs of Amapá and Roraima, as well as the inundated grasslands of the Ilha de Marajó and the lower Araguaia. This first wave of ranching was therefore restricted to the areas of savannah that extended naturally across a third of the Brazilian Amazon. The other categories of ranchers are more recent arrivals, having entered the region from the late 1960s, when government road-building programmes and fiscal incentives attracted investment in the Amazonian ranching economy. For the most part they established ranches on the forested areas of *terra firme* and planted artificial pasture for beef production. During the 1970s the growth of these more capitalized enterprises was closely associated with the expansion of the 'Amazon frontier' discussed above. This growth of ranching in the basin's southern and eastern fringes was itself sustained by the emergence of intensely speculative land markets along new highways.

The resultant incursion of ranching into forested areas has been both rapid and widespread. This has made ranching the principal cause of forest destruction in the Brazilian Amazon throughout the 1970s and 1980s. A study of regional deforestation from 1966 to 1975 found that ranching accounted for 38 per cent of forest loss, colonist agriculture for 31 per cent, road building for 27 per cent, and timber cutting for a relatively small 4 per cent.[25] Destroying the forest reduces biodiversity, releases carbon dioxide and other greenhouse gases into the atmosphere and causes soil degradation. It is therefore not surprising that a World Bank ecologist described ranching as the most ecologically damaging of all Amazonian land-use types.[26]

Regrettably, the detrimental impacts of ranching are not restricted to an exclusively environmental sphere. The activity has provoked violent land conflict in certain parts of Amazonia, most notably in southeastern Pará, Tocantins, and parts of Maranhão. Research in the eastern Amazon shows that one cow hand is

---

25. IBDF figures cited by Hall (1989) p 145.
26. Goodland (1980).

usually employed for every 250–850 hectares of ranch land.[27] But, under agricultural production, the same land could support many more people – an entire colonist household could subsist on 50 hectares. Thus, the expansion of ranching tends to cause land conflict, especially when peasants are evicted from their holdings in areas where access to land is already impeded. This is exactly what happened in southern Pará during the 1970s and 1980s. Here, squatters squeezed off the land by the expansion of corporate ranching were denied access to alternative holdings by the local elite's tight control over local forests, which are well endowed with valuable brazil-nut trees.[28]

The ranching economy in the northern Amazon generates all the same problems. But because it is less capitalized and because there has been less pressure on the land in this area, deforestation and land conflict are not currently of the same scale as that observed in the southern Amazon. The situation in Roraima is illustrative. In 1780 the state's first ranches were established by the Portuguese army on the northern savannah plains. During the course of the following century, beef production became the principal non-indigenous land use in Roraima, replacing extractivism (which can be loosely defined as the harvesting of rainforest products such as game, fish, fruits, nuts, timber, resins, oils, etc). Thus, the earliest Portuguese settlements, such as Fort São Joaquim (1776), were sustained by the beef economy and, to this day, ranching remains an important vehicle for regional occupation. In spite of the savannah's acidic nutrient-poor soils and highly seasonal rainfall, it is very attractive to ranchers. For not only does it represent a huge area of free grazing,[29] but, perhaps just as importantly, it is inhabited by an attentive indigenous labour force. An extensive ranching system has evolved to exploit this situation profitably, requiring minimum investments in either capital or labour. A local phrase candidly expresses the benefits that accrue to cattle breeders under these circumstances: 'In Roraima the rancher does not create the beef herd, it is the herd that creates the rancher.'

Although extensive beef production lies at the heart of this savannah economy, ranching is itself often practised in conjunction

---

27. Hecht (1982).
28. For a more detailed discussion of land conflicts in this notoriously violent area, known as the 'Poligino das Castanhais', see Hine (1991).
29. These savannahs cover 440,000 square kilometres or 19 per cent of Roraima's land surface.

with informal-sector diamond mining. Since 1912, diamonds have been extracted, together with small quantities of gold, from the alluvial deposits of the principal rivers that flow through these grasslands – the Maú, Cotingó, Suapí and Quinó. A handful of politically-influential extended families have traditionally dominated both activities and the Macuxi Indians have provided them with the necessary labour to do so. As a result, the profits from diamond mining have often been invested in ranching, facilitating the expansion of the ranches across the traditional homelands of the Macuxi. Complex interactions have evolved between ranching, mining and indigenous land uses on the plains, which are regulated by a peculiar set of social and economic relations between the ranching-cum-mining elite and the Indian population.

Managerial skills are contracted through a system called *sorte* (literally meaning luck), under which the rancher pays the overseer a set percentage of annual livestock production. This is typically a quarter of the new born calves, although on some ranches the ratio falls to a fifth.[30] On large ranches, this may amount to a substantial revenue, but from this income the manager is obliged to employ local cow hands, who are usually Macuxi, to undertake the daily tasks. In contrast, this labour is usually contracted on non-monetary fixed wages, receiving, for example, a pair of reproductive cows or a horse for each year of service. A manager often works for a rancher until he has gained a sufficiently large herd from the *sorte* system to establish his own independent ranch nearby. By constantly spawning new ranches in this way, the *sorte* system has been instrumental in expropriating savannah lands from its native inhabitants.

Ranching in the southern part of the state has a very different history. The recent expansion of the activity into this forested area follows a pattern that is common to Amazonia as a whole and stems from highway developments in the 1970s under the Plano de Integração Nacional (PIN). It is worth looking at the motives behind the construction of these roads because they totally transformed the geography and structure of the local economy.

The expansion of the highway network embodied geopolitics that sought to occupy remote parts of Brazil and integrate them within the national economy. A comprehensive survey of the Amazon's natural resources, called Projeto RadamBrasil, preceded

---

30. The *sorte* system originated in the northeast of Brazil. Its application in Roraima is described in greater detail by Rivière (1972), and Kelsey (1972).

a massive programme of road building in the region. Having recognized the considerable wealth of Amazonia's natural resources, the military government was keen to engineer their exploitation, fearful that neighbouring countries might otherwise claim them as their own. Roraima merited particular attention because the RadamBrasil survey had identified it as a mineral-rich state. The study noted the presence of radioactive materials and strategically important minerals such as columbite, tantalite, molybdenum, and ilmenite. Denying either Venezuela or Guyana a chance to covet this impressive geological wealth, Brazil set about developing the state.

To fulfil such objectives, the BR 174 highway was constructed between Manaus and Boa Vista and, shortly after its completion in 1977, work began on the ambitious Northern Perimeter highway – the BR 210. Both roads were driven into the heavily forested *terra firme* areas, which were the ultimate refuge of Roraima's Indian societies. The consequences were disastrous. Attempts by the Waimiri-Atroari to prevent the BR 174 crossing their lands in the early 1970s were countered by military intervention, which has been held primarily responsible for a dramatic decline in the tribes' population. Having boasted over 1000 individuals in the late 1960s, the Waimiri-Atroari numbered only 332 in 1983.[31] The Northern Perimeter highway (BR 210) cut into the lands of the Yanomami in the west and the Wai-Wai in the east, and although neither group suffered the violence inflicted upon the Waimiri-Atroari, they both experienced the introduction of old world diseases to which they had no natural resistance. The painful irony is that this disruption was caused by a 'road to nowhere', as financial constraints prevented this highway from running its intended course across the northern Brazilian Amazon from the Atlantic coast to the Colombian border. Over a decade later, its truncated arms still do not extend beyond Roraima to either Pará in the east or Amazonas in the west.

In 1974, a governmental initiative called POLAMAZONIA (Programa de Polos Agropecuários e Agrominerais da Amazônia, the programme for agro-ranching and agro-mineral development poles in Amazonia) directly linked the expansion of the ranching frontier to the new road developments. Just over half of Roraima was identified as an economic growth pole under this programme and funds were allocated to stimulate its expansion through the Amazonian

31. Baines (1991) p 75. Also see Carvalho (1982) for a detailed account of these events and history of the Waimiri-Atroari's contact.

development agency, SUDAM (Superintendência de Desenvolvimento da Amazônia). Although the programme outlined four principal objectives – to support the construction of the BR 174 and its associated colonization projects, to develop the ranching sector, to research mineral resources, and to expand trade with Guyana – only the first of these has been achieved with any degree of success. Some 20 years after the formulation of POLAMAZONIA, Roraima's ranching sector remains largely decapitalized; mineral resources are poorly mapped and trade with Guyana is minimal (though perhaps likely to expand given that a road between Boa Vista and Georgetown was completed in 1992).

The government was clearly unsuccessful in attracting capital into the state's ranching economy. Only six of Roraima's largest ranches received SUDAM grants and most of these were already in existence prior to the POLAMAZONIA initiative. Corporate finance was more easily drawn to the southern and eastern Amazon, where better communications linked the ranching economy to the principal domestic markets. This trend was not reversed by an INCRA (Instituto Nacional de Colonização e Reforma Agrária) directive in 1977, which established a 600,000 hectare ranching district to the north of the western branch of the BR 210 in the municipality of Mucajaí (see Figure 1.2). Although 247 plots of land (each of about 3000 hectares) were delimited under this scheme, only 34 names were registered as recipients, and, of these, only two individuals proceeded to develop modest ranching enterprises.[32] Instead, many ranchers were attracted to more accessible land available in the margins of the newly constructed BR 174 and BR 210 highways. In this way, numerous smaller ranching enterprises were established on amalgamated holdings originally intended for agricultural development.

## SMALLHOLDER AGRICULTURE

Agriculture in the Amazon has also been supported by government initiatives since the 1970s, in spite of being the second major cause of deforestation. Unlike cattle raising, however, agriculture does provide a livelihood for approximately three million Amazoni-

---

32. As it transpired, this inability to attract capital to the scheme pre-empted a potential land conflict, because an 800 hectare section of this ranching district overlapped with the intended Yanomami Reserve. Silveira and Gatti (1988) p 52.

ans.[33] Thus, the environmental costs of the activity are to some extent offset by the social benefits that derive from it.

*Following their inception, roadside colonization projects received little support from inefficient government agencies.*

Since the 1930s the Brazilian government has been distributing plots of Amazonian land to landless farmers. Among other reasons this was seen as an effective mechanism to defuse rural social tensions in other Brazilian states.

---

33. Richards (1992) p 2.

Source: adapted from Silveira and Gatti (1988) p 51

***Figure 1.2*** *Roraima – roads, principal colonization projects
and Indian reserves*

Such pressures are particularly intense in the northeast and
centre-south of Brazil,[34] and migrants have been flooding into the

---

34. Throughout this volume the 'northeast' refers to the states of
Maranhão, Piauí, Ceará, Pernambuco, Rio Grande do Norte, Paraíba,

Amazon from the areas since the 1960s to acquire land in government colonization programmes. Settlement projects have been established along the highways in all Amazonian states, with the largest numbers of colonist farmers currently residing along the BR 364 in Rondônia, and the Transamazonian highway in Pará. Migrant families are typically allocated 50–100 hectare plots of forested *terra firme* land, which are connected to the highways by dirt 'feeder' roads. Usually they apply minimal amounts of capital to grow rice, maize, manioc and a small quantity of beans among a wide variety of other cultivars, such as bananas, black pepper, coffee, and sugar cane.

In Roraima, a small number of colonization projects established by the state government agricultural secretariat in the 1940s and 1950s predate the more recent expansion of agriculture along the BR 174 and BR 210 (see Figure 1.2). The first three colonization projects settled a total of 270 immigrant families on fertile soil in the hinterland of Boa Vista. Notwithstanding these favourable conditions and the proven agricultural experience of the colonists, poor communications and inadequate health facilities led to a gradual abandonment of virtually all plots by the mid-1960s.[35] Despite the failures encountered in these early projects, many of the same problems continue to plague more recent colonization programmes in the state. This reflects a pattern observed not only throughout the Amazon, but also across many other parts of the humid tropics.

In 1975 the federal government land agency INCRA was established in Roraima to regulate land titling in the state and to administer the colonization of the BR 174 and BR 210 highways. INCRA was ceded a 100-kilometre swathe of land alongside the new federal highways in which to mark out, distribute and register landholdings for the incoming colonists. These later colonization schemes were located on poorer soils because fertile Alfisols cover less than 1.00 per cent of the state, and by 1975 virtually all of this good land had been allocated under previous state government settlement projects. So most of the INCRA programmes were situated on poorer Ultisols and Oxisols, which predominate both in Amazonia and Roraima.

By far the largest proportion of colonists arriving in Roraima originate from the Brazilian northeast. Even so, the composition of

---

Alagoas, Sergipe and Bahia. The 'centre-south' refers to Rio Grande do Sul, Paraná, Santa Catarina, São Paulo and Mato Grosso do Sul.
35. Silveira and Gatti (1988).

migrants in each settlement project is related to the date of the project's initiation. Settlements established before 1980 tend to be dominated by migrants from Maranhão. These include some of the more recent state government programmes like Alto Alegre (1978) and the earliest INCRA schemes created along the BR 174, like PAD Anauá (1979).

A small percentage of colonists from the Brazilian centre-south were settled in these early projects, and, although they still represent the minority of colonists in Roraima, their numbers began to increase after 1980. This was due to a process of secondary migration to Roraima by farmers who had been settled in Rondônia's POLONOROESTE project during the 1970s. Migrant households, originating predominantly in the northeast and centre-south, came to Roraima via Rondônia at the start of the 1980s. Many of them were allocated land along the eastern branch of the BR 210, which INCRA was settling at that time. A survey of households in this area found that 38 per cent of colonists had previously farmed in Rondônia and, more strikingly, that 62 per cent had moved three to five times prior to their arrival in the state.[36] Roraima therefore inherited a population of smallholders who had a long history of migration, suggesting that their customary response to difficulties was to move away from them.

Although it officially contravened INCRA regulations to allocate new land to families that had already abandoned or sold a plot, the bureaucracy that should have enforced this legislation was poorly applied at that time. This is because INCRA had adopted a new policy of rapid settlement as a pragmatic response to the previously slow procedure for allocating land. Unfortunately, this objective was achieved at the expense of the migrants, many of whom were settled in projects before the basic infrastructure had been assembled. Even so, the experience of migrants settled in these schemes was probably not dissimilar to those of households obtaining land elsewhere. People who had been given plots in the more organized projects found that the infrastructure they had been promised was seldom provided in full. In other areas situated outside the official colonization schemes, a growing number of migrants started laying claim to the land spontaneously, having received no government support at all.

This lack of assistance for colonists undermined the government's attempt to establish a dynamic rural economy in Roraima.

---

36. SUDAM (1984).

The problems encountered in attracting significant capital into the ranching sector during the late 1970s have already been noted, but they were exacerbated by a contraction in the agricultural economy itself during the early 1980s. Health care, education, credit lines, technical advice and transport facilities were all scarce, reflecting a widely recognized shortfall in Amazonian colonization. In response to low agricultural incomes, smallholders began to supplement their earnings by extracting brazil nuts from the forest, renting out small pastures for grazing and even migrating seasonally to Rondônia for the rice harvest.[37] Others abandoned or sold their landholdings and moved to informal-sector mines or nearby urban areas – particularly Manaus and Boa Vista. From 1980 to 1985 a decline in the area devoted to annual crops coincided with the rapid growth of Boa Vista, suggesting that these contractions in the rural economy were stimulating widespread rural–urban migration.[38]

In spite of the local government placing advertisements in the national press, the flood of colonists into Roraima never acquired the same proportions that were witnessed in Rondônia. During the 1970s the population of that state had increased from 111,000 to nearly 500,000 (an average annual growth rate of 15.8 per cent) and then doubled again to approximately one million in 1990.[39] Roraima's demographic boom is smaller in comparison and occurred about a decade later. The state's population doubled from a modest 40,885 to 79,159 throughout the 1970s and then surged during the 1980s at a rate of 9.5 per cent per annum to give a population of 215,790 in 1991. The government-backed colonization programme clearly contributed to this population growth, but it was the informal-sector mineral boom in the latter half of the 1980s that attracted by far the greatest proportion of migrants to Roraima over the decade. On average, 2400 migrants arrived each year during the height of the colonization programme.[40] In comparison, an estimated 40,000 people were directly involved in the 1987–90 gold rush, and many more worked in related activities. Thus, a conservative estimate, which recognizes that a proportion of this figure was already resident in the state and also accepts that the government census of agricultural migration may be incomplete, still

---

37. Ibid.
38. Abers and Pereira (1992).
39. Fearnside (1989).
40. Silveira and Gatti (1988) p 56.

suggests that the migratory pull of the gold rush was at least double that of the colonization programme.

# ON THE EVE OF CHANGE

This historical perspective shows that while Roraima experienced similar developments to those occurring throughout Amazonia, recent processes did not reach the same intensity as elsewhere. The state's geographical isolation from the principal markets of central and southern Brazil ensured that highway construction was not accompanied by the explosive land speculation and agrarian violence witnessed in Rondônia and Pará. By the early 1980s it was clear that the government's attempts to stimulate the rural economy through planned agro-ranching developments had largely failed. And few people would have believed that in the course of the following decade a spontaneous, informal-sector mining boom would achieve precisely that.

This then is the background from which the gold rush of the 1980s emerged. In the following chapter I look in detail at the rush itself and see why mining gained such prominence at this time. But before proceding it is worth recognizing the activity's historical roots. Far from being a new arrival on the Amazonian stage, informal-sector mining has been practised on a small scale throughout the region since the eighteenth century. Over this period, it has provided a livelihood for a whole range of social groups. Communities of escaped African slaves were Pará's most prolific *garimpeiros* during the last century, as were smallholders and plantation workers in the Gurupí of Maranhão. In Roraima we have seen that both the ranching community and indigenous residents of the savannahs have been enthusiastic miners since the early 1900s. The point is that, although informal-sector mining came to the fore in Amazonia during the 1980s, it is just as intrinsic to the region and its inhabitants as say rubber tapping or brazil-nut gathering.

# Chapter 2

# Indian Gold: The Rush to the Yanomami Reserve

The myth of El Dorado lured eighteenth century travellers across the savannah plains of the Guyana Shield in search of spectacular mineral wealth. Nonetheless, the geological resources of Roraima remained unexploited until diamonds were discovered in the sediments of the Rio Maú in 1912. Since then, a number of diamond *garimpo*s have been established along the rivers of the savannah, which drain from Mount Roraima. Small quantities of gold are recovered together with diamonds from all these mines, but for most of this century the price of the metal has been so low that, until the 1970s, it was regarded as an insignificant by-product of diamond mining.

The diamond economy was itself dominated by production from a *garimpo* established on the table mountain Serra de Tepequém in 1938. This mine expanded throughout the 1940s and 1950s, drawing labour from the more established mining areas along the rivers Maú, Cotingó, and Quinó of northeastern Roraima (see Figure 1.2). The westerly drift in mining activity from the savannah into the forest continues to the present day. From the late 1950s prospectors filtered up the rivers Uraricoera, Uraricáa and Ericó, establishing a number of small diamond *garimpo*s west of Tepequém, the most significant of which is Santa Rosa, dating from the mid 1970s.

Notwithstanding this long history of mineral extraction, Roraima's geological resources remain poorly understood. The Radam-Brasil natural resource survey provided the first geological maps of the state in the 1970s, published at the reconnaissance scale of 1:1,000,000. Although this level of mapping is insufficiently detailed to provide anything other than a crude indication of the principal deposits, it did suggest that Roraima's subsoil was of considerable economic value. Two principal findings of the RadamBrasil survey are relevant to this study because they have influenced the subsequent development of the state's mining economy.[1]

Source: IGBE/Gov do Ter Fed de Roraima (1981) p 12

**Figure 2.1** *Geological formations of economic significance in Roraima, and garimpeiro reserves*

---

1.   DNPM (1975) pp 101–7.

First, RadamBrasil noted that the origin of gold and diamonds is associated with the decomposition of the ancient Guyana Shield. More specifically, it mapped the geography of the Roraima Conglomerate (a type of greenstone belt), which is the secondary matrix of the original material, representing the mother lode of these two minerals. Its brief to prospectors was that gold and diamonds should be encountered in river sediments that drain outcrops of Roraima Conglomerate. Figure 2.1 illustrates the distribution of these economically-significant geological formations. Not only did this confirm that the older *garimpos* below Monte Roraima and Tepequém were on, or draining, areas of Roraima Conglomerates, but it also suggested that previously unexplored areas like the mountainous region around the Serra de Surucucús, showed potential. These western outcrops, which straddle the Venezuelan border, generated even more interest, as the RadamBrasil survey also noted that the quality of diamonds generally improves the further west the source material lies.

The second important discovery was geology favourable to the formation of cassiterite (tin ore) in the same area. A granitic formation around the Serra de Surucucús (henceforth referred to as the Surucucús granite) was identified as the source material here. The only problem was that both the Surucus granite and the unexplored areas of the Roraima Conglomerate lay in the heart of the Yanomami lands.

RadamBrasil itself warned that the presence of the Yanomami, as well as the inaccessibility of the area, demanded careful planning prior to any mining in the region. Nevertheless, it did recommend that prospecting for cassiterite should be focused on the headwaters of the Mucajaí, Parima and Catrimani river basins, all of which are inhabited by the Yanomami.

Having whetted the appetites of larger mineral groups with the RadamBrasil findings, the government anticipated that private investment would be ploughed into more detailed geological research under the PoloRoraima programme. However, it soon became apparent that few companies were prepared to survey such remote deposits, which lay within Indian land. By law, claims for mining concessions on indigenous reserves may be registered by the DNPM (Departamento Nacional de Pesquisa Mineral), but companies can only work in these areas with both the permission of FUNAI and the consent of the relevant Indian group. Notwithstanding the legal complexities of mining on Indian lands, geological surveying in remote parts of Amazonia is sufficiently expensive, and risky, to dissuade investment. Thus, companies that hold registered claims, both in and beyond Indian reserves, often do not research their geological potential. Frequently the mineral rights for these speculative claims are upheld only after *garimpeiros* have discovered economically significant deposits on them.

As a result, private-sector investment in geological surveys within Roraima has been minimal, even though 197 claims to the state's subsoil are registered with the DNPM, covering a total 1,927,831 hectares.[2] Most mineral companies preferred to work in Pará and Rondônia, where RadamBrasil had identified more accessible deposits lying outside Indian reserves. This paucity of private investment in Roraima ensured that virtually all the subsequent geological mapping in the state was undertaken by the government. The Companhia de Pesquisa de Recursos Minerais (CPRM), the DNPM's research subsidiary, published three substantial geological surveys between 1975 and 1985,[3] but even these failed to stimulate the anticipated flows of private capital into the state's mining sector.

Consequently, Roraima's mineral resources came to be exploited almost entirely by the informal sector, and a greater knowledge of the state's subsoil is currently retained in the minds of *garimpeiros* than is available in any published documents. The *garimpeiros* responded immediately to the RadamBrasil findings, establishing a cassiterite *garimpo* on the Serra de Surucucús by 1975. But the working life of this mine was short-lived. Within a year FUNAI had expelled its population of 500 miners, arguing that the health and welfare of the Yanomami were prejudiced by the mining. In spite of this incident, there was growing interest in the Surucucús cassiterite deposit. The Companhia do Vale Rio Doce (CVRD), which had a registered its claim to the site, received permission from FUNAI to research the geology of the area in 1979. The survey published by its technical subsidiary, DOCEGO, is one of only a handful of geological research projects ever financed by the private sector in Roraima. The DOCEGO report confirmed the existence of a 15,000 ton deposit of high-grade tin ore (71 per cent) at Surucucús. But the CVRD advised the DNPM to declare Surucucús a national mineral reserve on the grounds that the economic benefits of developing the site at that time did not outweigh its potentially damaging impacts

---

2. Gama de Silva (1991) p 282.
3. These were the Projeto Rio Branco (1984), Projeto Molybdenum (1978), and Projeto Catrimani-Uraricoera (1982).

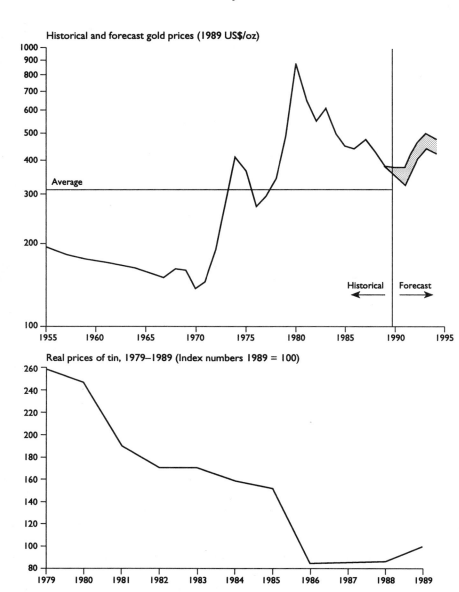

Sources: gold data: *Mining Journal* 1991, p 17
tin data: Crowson 1992, p 278

***Figure* 2.2** *The changing price of gold and tin*

on the Yanomami. Responding to the CVRD's apparent disinterest in developing its claim, the DNPM transferred part of the Surucucús site into the hands of CODESAIMA (Companhia de Desenvolvimento de Roraima), the state government's development company. However, FUNAI continued to thwart subsequent endeavours to extract tin from Surucucús by both CODESAIMA and *garimpeiros*. José Altino, the head of USAGAL, was responsible for one of the most daring attempts to develop the site. In 1985 he was jailed briefly for spearheading an unsuccessful invasion in which 60 *garimpeiros* arrived in five aircraft and tried to claim the cassiterite-rich Surucucús plateau by force. Despite the interest in this cassiterite deposit, it was gold, not tin, that opened up the Yanomami lands. Indeed, following these events, the Surucucús deposit remained virtually untouched until the end of 1987, by which time thousands of *garimpeiros* were already mining gold within the Indian reserve.

## THE SYMPTOMS OF GOLD FEVER

As the price of gold climbed steadily during the 1970s (see Figure 2.2) Roraima's *garimpeiros* began to emphasize gold extraction over diamond mining. Because most of the deposits they mined yielded both minerals, it was not a difficult transition to make. The *garimpo* of Santa Rosa, which had played an increasingly central role in local mining since its inception in the 1960s, was responsible for the state's first sizeable gold production. Even though Santa Rosa was situated within the then proposed Yanomami Reserve, the state government commissioned CODESAIMA to extract gold there at the beginning of the 1980s. In the course of the following decade this conflict between the objectives of state government and FUNAI ensured that few effective attempts were made to reduce the social impacts of gold mining, which frequently occurred in close proximity to indigenous communities.

The Maiongong and Xiriana, who lived upstream of Santa Rosa along the Uraricoera, Uaricáa and Ericó rivers, were probably the first Indian groups of western Roraima to come into contact with *garimpeiros*. Initially, they encountered diamond prospectors who had been venturing up these rivers since the 1950s, and in subsequent years the same people taught them how to mine alluvial gold. The Xiriana were not only quick to seize the commercial opportunities offered by gold mining, but they also passed the technology on to other Yanomami communities. In the early 1980s, a party of Xiriana from the Uraricoera basin visited the Yanomami villages of the Couto de Magalhães, a tributary of the river Mucajaí, to teach their relatives how to extract gold manually. The modest quantities of gold the Indians produced were traded in Boa Vista, often by FUNAI employees, for hammocks, pans, fishing hooks, knives, and other useful items to which the Yanomami would otherwise have had only limited access.[4]

While the Yanomami were learning the basics of gold mining, pressure was mounting for the closure of the Santa Rosa *garimpo* and in March 1982 federal law GM/015 (of 9 March 1982) was passed, forbidding access to the proposed Yanomami Reserve. As the authorities clamped down on the mining operations, many of the displaced *garimpeiros* returned to the agricultural economy. They either went back to plots of land they had previously owned, or they acquired land in recently established colonization projects, such as Apiaú (founded in 1981), Confiança (1982), and along the eastern area of the BR 210 (1982) (see Figure 1.2). Typically they worked in agriculture during the wet season and mounted prospecting trips into the Yanomami Reserve during the agriculturally-unproductive summer months. So, from the early 1980s colonist farmers with mining experience from the Santa Rosa *garimpo* started working small manual deposits along the rivers Catrimani and Apiaú (most notably along its tributary, the Rio Novo) on a seasonal basis. There were approximately 600 *garimpeiros* working in this area during the summer of 1985, some of whom had already come into conflict with local Yanomami villages.[5] By 1986, the influx began to gain momentum following the discovery of a sizeable gold deposit at the *garimpo* of Cambalacho in the head-waters of the Apiaú river (number 73 in Figure 2.3).

All the ingredients were present for the start of a mining boom. Many of them relate to wider processes that had been shaping events throughout Amazonia during the early 1980s. The unprecedented rise in gold prices was only one of various factors that contributed to the explosive growth of the regional mining economy. The existence of extensive alluvial gold fields that could be mined with very rudimentary technology proved just as significant. A pivotal role was also played by the road building programme of the previous decade. The highways not only improved access to remote parts of the Amazon, but the migration stimulated by the

4. For a detailed account of these events see Lazarin and Vessani (1987), and Ramos, Lazarin and Gomez (1985).
5. CCPY (1985), and (1989) p 39.

roads themselves and by the associated colonization projects also provided the necessary labour for the rush. Furthermore, the political climate was particularly favourable, as the new interest in mining offered a further vehicle with which to fulfil the government's mandate of regional occupation and economic growth.

Within this context, two occurrences further boosted gold extraction in Roraima. Declining production in the *garimpos* of Pará (notably Cucá, Tucumã, and the Tapajós) during the mid 1980s encouraged many small miners to look towards other sites for work. Roraima was particularly attractive because its dry season coincides with the wet season elsewhere in Amazonia. Thus, miners from Pará and Rondônia could maintain production throughout the slack months by migrating to the northern Amazon on a seasonal basis. Having discovered the potential of Roraima's gold fields, many of them stayed. Those with more capital arranged transportation of their mining equipment to Roraima while simultaneously negotiating a plot of land on which to work.

The convergence of labour and capital on the fledgling gold fields was fuelled by macro-economic changes in 1986. As Figure 2.1 illustrates, the price of gold started to rise again at this time, which significantly, coincided with a period of recession in other sectors of the regional economy. Gold mining became increasingly attractive during the late 1980s as Government incentives for ranching were reduced and the urban economy simultaneously underwent sharp contractions inflicted by the '*Plano Cruzado*'. This financial strategy of 1986 was an attempt by the Sarney government to reduce hyperinflation through freezing wages and introducing price controls. As the squeeze was felt, labour and capital fled to the informal-mining sector where tax-free incomes, paid in hard currency, were available.

## THE SCALE OF EVENTS

An increasing number of people migrated to Roraima from 1987 and the flow had acquired flood-like proportions by the start of 1988. Local newspapers reported that 200 migrants a day were entering the state and, although no precise figure exists, it is estimated that between 30,000 and 40,000 people were directly employed in Roraima's *garimpos* during the following three years. As *garimpeiros* spend a proportion of their time (and money) in Boa Vista between mining trips, the numbers engaged in mining at any one instant could be as little as 50 per cent of this figure. For each person involved directly in mining, many others were dependent upon the economic opportunities that accompanied the boom, so that the employment it generated was extremely far reaching. Almost all population growth was confined to Boa Vista, which was the principal logistical base for the rush.

Even so, very little is known about the people who were drawn to this and other mining booms in the region. To date, the most comprehensive survey of Amazonian *garimpeiros* is provided by Pereira who interviewed 168 miners in six of Pará's *garimpos*.[6] He observed that although people came from all over Brazil to mine in Amazonia, the regional *garimpo* workforce is dominated by migrants from the Brazilian northeast; 76 per cent of the people he interviewed originated from that region, with 60 per cent coming from the state of Maranhão alone. Roraima's mining workforce appears to follow this pattern closely. In August 1991 I interviewed 66 *garimpeiros* entering a rush in the headwaters of the Jatapú river in the southern part of the state. Of these, 53 (78 per cent) originated in the northeast and the majority were from the state of Maranhão (40 respondents or 61 per cent of the sample).[7] While it is probable that the composition of the gold-mining workforce varies slightly between localities, evidence from different parts of the Amazon confirms that it is dominated by migrants from northeastern Brazil.[8]

The Jatapú interviews give some indication of the migratory routes through which *garimpeiros* arrive in the state. A small number of the most experienced respondents had worked in the Tapajós in the late 1970s, but they were drawn to Serra Pelada and the other *garimpos* of southeastern Pará (notably Cucá and Tucumã) in the early 1980s. A large number of migrants were absorbed into the Amazonian mining economy at that time and the majority of the *garimpeiros* interviewed at Jatapú fall into this classification. As the productivity of these gold-fields declined in the mid 1980s, the larger part of the workforce moved to northern Mato Grosso (around Alto Floresta) and the Tapajós. A smaller number went to

---

6.  Pereira (1990).
7.  The total breakdown is as follows; (n=66) Maranhão (40) Ceará (6), Paraná (4), Pernambucco (3), Goias (4), Pará (2), with one representative from each of the states of Paraiba, Minas Gerais, Bahia, Mato Grosso do Norte, Roraima, São Paulo, Rio Grande do Sul, and Santa Catarina. Of the *garimpeiros* interviewed in the Jatapú survey, 85 per cent had worked in the Yanomami Reserve; this sample can consequently be read as broadly representative of the earlier influx to western Roraima.
8.  Coy (1991) p 4; Cleary (1990).

Rondônia, either extracting gold along the Rio Madeira, or mining cassiterite in Bom Futuro. And a handful scattered across the northern Amazon, working in northern Amapá (on the Oiapoque), and the Cabeça do Cachorro region of Amazonas (Rio Uaupés) (see Figure 1.1).

The Roraima gold rush appears to have drawn its workforce from all of these areas, with the majority coming from the gold fields of northern Mato Grosso and the Tapajós. A smaller, but nonetheless significant, fraction came from Rondônia. *Garimpeiros* in Boa Vista note that there was a degree of segregation between these two groups. In general, the Rondônia workforce veered towards the Uraricoera river, where mining was principally by equipment mounted on floating rafts (*balsas*), while those from the Tapajós/ Mato Grosso dominated the Mucajaí, Apiaú, and Catrimani rivers, where land-based mining prevailed. This reflects the differences of origin in the mining techniques of different *garimpos*, for extraction on the Tapajós tends to be land-based while on the Madeira it is predominantly riverine. But the distribution also suggests that *garimpeiros* prefer to work alongside people they already know. Relocating is an expensive and risky operation, particularly if equipment is being transferred. These risks and expenses can be reduced if trusted friends exist in the new *garimpo*; they will lend money and equipment, facilitate the acquisition of a labour force, explain the local geology and help negotiate a plot on which to mine.

At this point the distinction between 'professional' and 'temporary' *garimpeiros* should be recognized. Mining is the principal form of employment for the former. Temporary *garimpeiros* are those whose primary employment lies outside the mining economy, often in smallholder agriculture, ranching, or in the urban informal sector. They tend to be opportunists, spending short periods in the *garimpo* to supplement their income from other sources. Although many of the temporary *garimpeiros* may work seasonally in *garimpos* over a number of years, and thereby acquire considerable mining experience, they have not made the same commitment to the activity as their professional counterparts. Professional miners usually reinvest a larger percentage of their revenue in the activity by purchasing equipment and financing prospecting trips. Even so, no hard and fast rules can be made, and much of the initial prospecting for the Roraima gold rush was undertaken by experienced temporary *garimpeiros* with landholdings in the state's colonization projects. In broad terms, one can think of a core of professional miners providing much of the air support, mining equipment and prospecting expertise, being complemented by a large number of temporary *garimpeiros*, who probably represented the majority of the labour force.

Production estimates of the Roraima rush are variable, but USAGAL believe that 36 metric tons of gold, worth approximately US $540 million, were extracted in the state between 1988 and 1990. The largest proportion of the metal would have passed through the hands of Boa Vista's numerous gold dealers, of which only 33 are officially registered. Generally, they traded it on to more powerful companies and financial institutions in Rio de Janeiro or São Paulo, from where much of it would probably have left the country. Enormous opportunities for smuggling existed and attempts to police it were derisory. On one of the rare occasions that agents of the government's tax office (the Receita Federal) inspected the cargoes of light planes at Boa Vista's airport, they confiscated 30 kilograms of gold in one day.[9] To put that in perspective, only 15 metric tons of gold were ever registered by the same department during the boom years from 1988 to 1990.[10]

## STATE SUPPORT FOR THE RUSH

Following the invasion of Cambalacho, the intensity of mining in the watershed of the Apiaú river increased as smallholders walked the two-week long trail from the Apiaú colonization project to seek

---

9. *Folha de Boa Vista*, 24 November 1988.
10. Even so, this accounts for over 40 per cent of USAGAL's estimated production, which seems very high given that contraband was the norm. A closer look at the figures suggests that total production during the Roraima rush might have been considerably higher than USAGAL's estimate of 36 tons. In 1988, when USAGAL estimated a peak production of 14 tons, the Receita Federal registered only 1.3 tons, which is equivalent to 12 per cent of total production. However, the following year USAGAL believes that gold production declined to 11 tons, while the Receita Federal processed documentation for the increased amount of eight tons, representing 72 per cent of total production. The figures for 1990 are 11 tons produced (USAGAL), of which six were registered, giving a registration rate of 55 per cent. As there is no evidence that the authorities succeeded in cutting down on levels of contraband, it is highly unlikely that over half the total gold production was declared to the Receita Federal in these ultimate two years. If it is assumed that only 40 per cent of production was officially registered in 1989/90, which represents a more plausible figure, then the USAGAL estimate of total production can be increased by 13 tons to 49 metric tons, with a total value of US $735 million.

out new deposits. By July 1987, Manuel Luiz, a farmer from Alto Alegre, had crossed the watershed and discovered a gold-mining operation belonging to the Yanomami in the middle reaches of the Mucajaí basin. Its owners were absent at the time, and so Manuel claimed the site, christening it the *garimpo* of Novo Cruzado. Accounts differ over what happened next. It has been suggested that the Yanomami who returned to the site a few days later came into immediate conflict with the intruders. But some *garimpeiros* argue that a working relationship was established with the Yanomami owners and violence only broke out when this agreement subsequently collapsed. Whatever the case, a clash ensued which left four Yanomami and one *garimpeiro* dead.[11] The Yanomami had reportedly expelled miners from that area on three previous occasions, and relations between the two parties were increasingly violent. But although this was by no means the only incident of its kind, it did prompt both FUNAI and the state governor, Getúlio Cruz, to threaten the closure of these clandestine mines. The first plan to remove the *garimpeiros* (known as Operation Roraima) was launched in September 1987, but its complete inefficacy simply demonstrated a lack of political will to tackle the problem with conviction. Consequently, the *garimpeiros* became increasingly aware of the authorities' reluctance to curtail mining activities in the Yanomami Reserve.

In fact the government and the armed services were not only loath to intervene in the burgeoning rush, but they actually endorsed it. A military project known as *Calha Norte* (literally meaning northern trench) provided the infrastructure that greatly facilitated the *garimpeiros'* access to the Yanomami Reserve. This project was formulated in 1985 and encompasses all Brazilian territory lying north of the Solimões and Amazonas rivers (24 per cent of the legally defined Amazon). The initial phase of *Calha Norte* ran from 1986 to 1990, and it sought to increase the occupation of the northern Amazon by stepping up the military presence in this area. Among other specified objectives, the project aimed to improve the transport and energy network, to attract new settlers and investment as well as to define an appropriate Indian policy. Not surprisingly therefore, the most polemic aspect of the *Calha Norte* project concerns its impact on the local Indian groups. As one observer has noted:[12]

---

11. *Folha de Boa Vista*, 12 August 1987.
12. Albert (1992) p 52.

> The rationale for *Calha Norte*, as a project for 'bringing poles of development into the interior' under military control, revolves around a strategy to reduce Indian territories in order to facilitate the access of large-scale mining companies and placer-mining groups to the deposits located in these lands.

Events at the airstrip of Paapiú provide a candid illustration of this. Paapiú (number 50 on Figure 2.3) is located beside the Couto de Magalhães river, which is a tributary of the Mucajaí at the centre of the region's gold fields. The airstrip was originally constructed in the early 1970s by Protestant missionaries, Missão Evangelica da Amazônia (MEVA), who went to the area on short evangelization trips to catechize the Indians. A permanent presence at Paapiú was not established until 1981 when FUNAI built a post next to the airstrip, which was itself extended in 1986 by the Brazilian air force under the *Calha Norte* project. Tenente Mota, a military policeman charged with overseeing the airstrip, became aware of the gold deposits that the Yanomami were working manually nearby and immediately recognized the considerable mineral wealth of the area. Informing other miners of his discovery, the Tenente organized a group of well-armed *garimpeiro*s to fly into Paapiú and invade the airstrip in December 1987. The Airforce made no attempt to expel the invaders and FUNAI subsequently abandoned its outpost at Paapiú in 1989 leaving the *garimpeiro*s with unrestricted use of the airstrip. The strategy paid dividends for Tenente Mota, who, having negotiated with a local village leader, João Davi Yanomami, established his own *garimpo* in the vicinity.

Following this incident Paapiú became a small settlement in the heart of the Yanomami Reserve, which serviced some of Roraima's most productive *garimpo*s. Within five hours' walk of the airstrip, Vando Preto, a smallholder from the Apiaú colonization project, had discovered a spectacularly rich deposit, which earned both him and his partner over 100 kilograms of gold each.[13] Between the sites lay the Igarapé da Caveira, which also became a heavily mined area next to which lay the *garimpo*s of Chico Ceará, Mestre Pedro, Jonas Dias, Rangel, and Dudu (numbers 46, 38, 51, 53, and 52 in Figure 2.3). Thus Paapiú not only yielded access to a strategically important auriferous zone, but its opening up also defined a new

---

13. *Correio de Garimpeiro*, December 1988.

political climate of support for the illegal activities of the *garim-peiro*s.

It is not hard to see why this happened, for the gold rush enabled the military to fulfil some of the principal objectives enshrined in the *Calha Norte* project. The strategists were seeking to promote the integration of western Roraima with the rest of Brazil, and the 'living frontier' of *garimpeiro*s moving into this area helped them achieve this goal. In supporting the rush the military saw an opportunity to further its own geopolitical agenda, though clearly at considerable cost to the local Indian population:[14]

> They [the military] decided to absorb and attempt to control the dynamic *garimpeiro* frontier in the Yanomami area, in spite of its considerable ecological and social costs, thereby furthering the fundamental objectives of the *Calha Norte*; the economic and military occupation of northern Amazonian frontier space to the detriment of its Indian populations.

For this very reason the gold rush gathered momentum under an increasingly sympathetic political climate. Potential objectors to events within the Yanomami Reserve, including anthropologists, health teams and missionaries, were expelled from the area in 1987. This embargo, which lasted until 1990, prevented interested third parties from closely monitoring the impacts of the gold rush on local people. The gold rush itself gained further support with the appointment of the two subsequent governors of Roraima, General Klein and Romero Jucá, both of whom vigorously defended the *garimpeiro*s' occupation of Indian lands.[15] In this way, a flagrant breach of the Brazilian constitution was deemed politically acceptable by both the federal and state governments.

## DISCOVERY OF THE ALTO MUCAJAÍ GOLD FIELDS

At the end of 1987, the *garimpeiro*s were well established in the headwaters of the Apiaú, Catrimani, and Couto de Magalhães rivers. But large areas of the Yanomami Reserve still remained to be explored and considerable sums were being reinvested in prospecting expeditions. The following account shows how the *garimpeiro*s

---

14. Albert (1993) p 43. My translation.
15. Klein governed from 12 October 1987 to 16 September 1988. Jucá's period in office extended from 16 September 1988 to 1 August 1990.

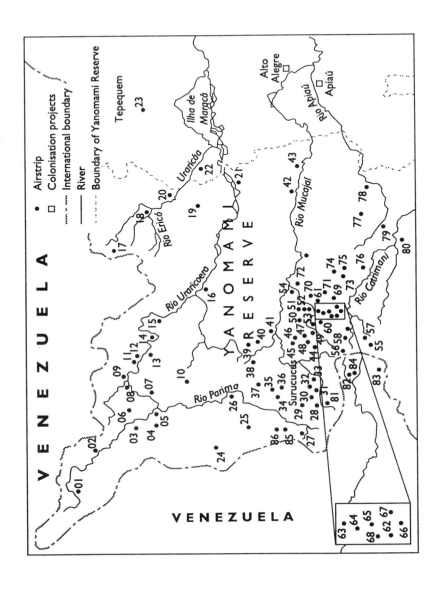

Sources: Map compiled with data from CCPY, SUCAM, FAGAR, INPE 1992

*Figure 2.3* *Map of the airstrips used during the 1987–1990 gold rush in the Yanomami Indigenous Reserve*

## List of the airstrips marked in Figure 2.3

The name of the airstrip is given first and where the name of the owner is different it is given in brackets afterwards (? = owner not known)

01 Auaris (MEVA – Calha Norte)
02 Olomai (MEVA)
03 Vitalino
04 Junior Brefo
05 Fazenda Parima (Gaucho Animal & Vivi)
06 Nossa Senhora Aparecida (Roberta)
07 Jovair
08 Paulo Alceu
09 Luiz da Agropecuaria (Luiz & Olimpio)
10 Chico Jacare
11 Quincas Bonfim
12 Raimundo Pau Grosso
13 Macuim (Eloi Viana)
14 Rangel II
15 Waikas (FUNAI)
16 Palimu (MEVA)
17 Surubaí (?)
18 Ericó (FUNAI–Calha Norte)
19 Osvaldo II
20 Nova de Santa Rosa
21 Osvaldo
22 Santa Rosa (Gov of Roraima)
23 Tepequém (Gov de Roraima)
24 Santo Antonio (?)
25 Fogo Bravo (Antonio)
26 Xiriana (Mineraçaõ Xiriana)
27 Tomé Mestrinho
28 Pedro Jacaranda
29 Pupunha
30 Oliveira

31 Jeremias
32 Tarzã (Chico Malária)
33 Baiano Formiga
34 Americanos (MEVA– abandoned)
35 Surucucús (FUNAI– Calha Norte)
36 Docego (CVRD)
37 Picão
38 Mestre Pedro
39 Gaucho Chapeu Preto
40 Paulista
41 Raimundo Nenêm II
42 Missão de MEVA (FUNAI)
43 Baixo Mucajaí (FUNAI)
44 Rubens
45 Fernando
46 Chico Ceará
47 Mestre Pedro
48 Caveira I (Adão Neguinho)
49 Caveira II (Adão Neguinho)
50 Paapiú (FUNAI– Calha Norte)
51 Jonas Dias (J D Carneiro)
52 Dudu
53 Rangel
54 Senzala
55 Nova do R. Neném
56 Bibiano
57 R. Neném
58 Bibiano
59 Novo Cruzado (Marcelo)
60 Comunidade (Osmar

& Jurema)
61 Alexandre
62 Biano Marcelo II
63 Valmor
64 Raimundinho (Robertinho)
65 Baiano Marcelo
66 Aroaldes
67 Calistro
68 Buri
69 Nova do Marcelo
70 Gaucho Animal (Cesar Greigar)
71 Marcelo
72 Mineraçaõ (Antonio Rogério)
73 Cambalacho (Alex & Robertino)
74 Botinha (Galdino Antonio)
75 Vando Acreano (Chico Ivanísio)
76 Helio
77 Rio Novo (Gov of Roraima)
78 Nova do Apiaú (?)
79 Apiaú (Gov do Roraima)
80 Cristovão
81 Banana (?)
82 Constituinte (?)
83 Sadam Husein (?)
84 Rainha de Inajá (Dicão)
85 Atatais (Lauro Texeira)
86 Parima (José Altino)

undertook this geological research using light aircraft to support prospecting in very remote areas. Although mining techniques vary somewhat between different parts of Amazonia, a number of common work relationships do apply. For this reason, the central characteristics of a *garimpo*'s genesis and development, illustrated in the case study below, are broadly representative of *garimpagem* as practised throughout the Brazilian Amazon.

*Miners at work. The jet of water blasts into the gold-bearing sediments, which are then pumped up and passed over a sluice box outside the pit.*

Daniel is the owner of a 1200-hectare ranch situated alongside the BR 210. He came to Roraima in 1986 when his construction company in Brasília fell victim to the economic contractions induced by the *Plano Cruzado*. The difficult financial situation facing small ranchers prompted him to enter the *garimpo* of Novo Cruzado in October 1987, even though he had no previous experience of *garimpagem*. By January 1988 he was working manually in Vando Preto's newly established *garimpo* and, within a month, he had borrowed a set of two-way radios, pooled his gold earnings with those of four partners and organized a prospecting team from Baiana Marcelo's recently constructed airstrip at Novo Cruzado (no 59 on Figure 2.3). While Daniel coordinated the expedition from his base at the airstrip, his partners spent two months testing the sediments of the streams and tributaries in the upper reaches of the river Mucajaí.

After a month the prospectors needed resupplying, so they cleared a patch in the forest with a chainsaw, which they carried with them. Passing their rough location over the radio to Daniel, they arranged an airdrop at a set time the following day.[16] Daniel bought the necessary goods and chartered a light plane to fly over the area at the designated time, being guided to their location by a column of smoke from a fire they had lit in a corner of the clearing. Once overhead, Daniel dropped the supplies after checking that their sign of a blue and red hammock laid out in an 'L' shape was visible in the clearing below. This precaution ensured that he did not inadvertently drop their provisions to any of the numerous other prospecting teams working in the area.

The team had good luck and, like many other finds along the Mucajaí, they were led to a gold-rich site by a Yanomami whom they had befriended in the forest. Being unaware of the historical events that introduced mining to the Yanomami communities in the Mucajaí, the *garimpeiro*s believed that missionary groups working in the area had taught the Indians to extract gold for the benefit of their religious institutions. The find was made on Easter Saturday 1988 and was named the Grota de Tarzã after the nickname of one of its discoverers. Having each invested 800 grams of gold in prospecting, the partners would recover 40 kilograms a head from the site. Two members of the group stayed to start mining the richest deposits manually, whilst the other two made a direct route back to the airstrip at Novo Cruzado. Simultaneously, Daniel, having been informed of the discovery over the radio, borrowed some gold and organized a further airdrop of necessary supplies to the infant *garimpo*.

---

16. For example, at 7.00 a.m. six days' walk up the left bank of the Mucajaí above the Melo Nunes river.

This behaviour attracted the attentions of other *garimpeiro*s at Novo Cruzado, a number of whom accompanied Daniel and his two partners on the eight-day walk back to the Grota de Tarzã. Having discovered the site, the partners are automatically recognized as owners (*donos*) of the new *garimpo*. In accordance with this position, they allocate the incoming *garimpeiro*s plots of land to mine manually.

Gold mining in alluvial material is very simple. A wooden sluice box is constructed and lined with sacking. Horizontal wooden bars, known as riffles, are placed across the sacking, and the gold-bearing material is passed over the whole contraption with large quantities of water. This itself will retain a percentage of the gold particles, but rates of recovery are greatly improved by the use of mercury. As mercury amalgamates with gold, its increased weight lodges more effectively in the sacking and behind the riffles of the sluice box. The use of mercury and the issue of mercury pollution are discussed in greater detail later on, but for the time being it is important to understand a little about the way in which mining is organized.

Some of the earlier arrivals were engaged by Daniel and his partners in a working relationship known as *meia-praça*. Under *meia-praça* the owners (*donos*) of the *garimpo* supply the incoming *garimpeiro*s with food and a plot of land to mine in return for half the gold they (the *garimpeiro*s) extract. During the first four months of the Grota de Tarzã, 400 people were working manually in gold extraction, of whom only 30 were engaged in *meia-praça* work relations. The rest mined under a different work relationship, literally 'at one's own expense' (*por conta própria*). The distinction rests more on the provision of food than anything else, but it does affect the distribution of gold income among the workforce. *Garimpeiro*s working 'at their own expense' are responsible for their own catering arrangements, but are nonetheless obliged to give 40 per cent of their gold production to the owners of the mine (*donos de garimpo*) as payment for the plot of land they have been allocated. However, in remote *garimpo*s, such as those of western Roraima, the *donos* have a monopoly over the supply of all goods, which they then sell at considerable prices to the *garimpeiro*s. On the whole, basic foodstuffs in the *garimpo*s, such as sugar, salt, rice, beans and manioc flour, all cost three to four tenths of a gram of gold per kilogram (US $4). Luxury items were more expensive; a can of beer was half a gram, while a pack of six batteries for a radio, or a packet of cigarettes would each cost one gram. This constituted an important source of revenue for Daniel and his partners, along with the taxes they levied on gold production. From their income, they not only contracted gunmen to police the *garimpo* and extract their dues, but they also had to resupply the site by air at a cost of 200 grams of gold per airdrop.

Once the most easily accessible deposits had been exploited manually, the *donos* ceded their right to construct an airstrip to a mutual friend called Chico Maláría. In August 1987, with his partner, Chico invested about four kilograms of gold to finance the construction of the airstrip, which took 20 labourers 45 days to complete. For every plane or helicopter that touched down on the strip, Chico and his partner charged the standard ten grams of gold landing fee. From this income alone they became rich, for throughout the summer months the *garimpo* regularly received over 30 flights a day. The completion of the airstrip also acted as a springboard for further prospecting, but even before it had been commissioned, a number of important finds had been made in the vicinity. Groups that had been prospecting near the site at the time of Tarzã's discovery rapidly focused their attentions on the surrounding area. Baiano Formiga passed the site four days after its discovery and, within the week, had struck gold nearby. The principal *garimpo*s of the Alto Mucajaí, such as Jeremias, Pedro Jacaranda, and Popunha were all established in a similar way during this period (numbers 31, 28 and 29 respectively in Figure 2.3).

The construction of an airstrip in a *garimpo* is a mixed blessing to the *garimpeiro*s, for while it greatly facilitates the transport of people and provisions, it also heralds the arrival of machinery that may replace a large proportion of the manual workforce. Under semi-mechanized production, teams of five to six people (including a cook) are employed to operate a set of diesel-fuelled pumps. The jet from one of the pumps is used to blast into the sediments which are then sucked up by a large tube connected to the other pump. The recovered material is then passed over a sluice box to separate out the gold in exactly the same way as in manual extraction. In fact, Daniel had airlifted the first such set of equipment into the Grota de Tarzã by helicopter over a month before work had begun on the airstrip. Although it cost over two kilograms of gold to install the machinery in this way, it allowed him to exploit some of the most concentrated deposits before the mine was opened up to other more capitalized *garimpeiro*s. Before the airstrip was built, the diesel required to fuel Daniel's machinery had to be supplied by air drops.

To survive the impact it was injected into large gas canisters, more commonly used as containers for domestic cooking fuel. On completion of the airstrip the *donos* installed a further seven sets of mining pumps. They also sold off two large patches of land to two wealthy individuals called Bigode de Cavalho and Zé Bigode, each of whom managed ten sets of the same equipment on their plots. The *garimpo* therefore employed between 166 and 196 individuals on 28 sets of machinery, in comparison with the 400 who had worked there manually.

Under the manual regime the *garimpo*s often have to close during the wet season, when heavy rainfall fills the mining pits, but the seasonal nature of the activity is reduced once pumping equipment has been installed. *Garimpeiro*s often weigh up the benefits of this extended mining calendar against their changing economic prospects. For while employment on the machinery still offers reasonable wages, the best opportunities for striking it rich undoubtedly lie in the very early manual workings at recently discovered sites. Besides, conditions are often healthier before machines are introduced to a site. Semi-mechanized production tends to create ideal breeding grounds for the anopheles mosquito because it increases the area of standing water in the *garimpo*. For these reasons alone, non-capitalized *garimpeiro*s often prefer the harder option of manual work in the earlier stages of a *garimpo*'s life to subsequent employment as machine operators.

The changing work relations incurred by the adoption of semi-mechanized production are also an important consideration in this equation. Generally, the individual *garimpeiro* receives a lower fraction of the total gold extracted mechanically, but because a far greater volume of material is being processed, wage rates do not necessarily fall. The six person crew operating a set of mining pumps share 30 per cent of the gold recovered from the operation. The remaining 70 per cent goes to the owner of the equipment (*dono de máquina*), from which the running costs and catering expenses are deducted. A set of the same mining pumps may also be mounted on a raft (*balsa*) to extract gold from river sediments. A team of four divers rotate two-hour shifts, sucking up material from the riverbed with a vacuum-pumped hose. Their return for undertaking this more dangerous work is a 40 per cent share of the gold production, split between them. Again, this leaves the owner (*dono de balsa*) with the remaining larger portion, from which catering and operating expenses are deducted. In both situations, *garimpeiro*s are effectively engaged under the *meia-praça* arrangement, in so far as their food and accommodation are supplied by the owner of the machinery.

Thus, the economy and society of the *garimpos* are organized according to well-established work relations. In Amazonian terms, these are unusual in two ways. First, they give *garimpeiros* an exceptional degree of autonomy. Because members of the work-force are not tied to the *donos* by debt, they consider themselves self-employed and free to move between jobs. Secondly, while the majority of *garimpeiros* receive a reasonable income paid in hard currency, a small elite (the *donos*) may become exceptionally rich.

## THE DRIFT TOWARDS VENEZUELA AND THE EXPANSION OF TIN PRODUCTION

Prior to the completion of Chico Malária's airstrip, Amadeus, one of the team to have discovered the Grota de Tarzã, resolved to continue prospecting. He was paid his share of the profits by his partners and invested some of this money in a ranch in Pará. Amadeus then undertook a five-month long prospecting trip along the Venezuelan border around the base of the Surucucús plateau, and along the Parima river, which drains the upper reaches of the Uraricoera basin (see Figure 2.3). Although he was not fortunate enough to uncover a second large deposit, his journey is interesting because it traces the path of the developing *garimpos*. The *garimpeiros* drifted into the headwaters of the principal rivers in search of the source material of the secondary deposits they were mining. This movement into the watershed brought them into the area most densely inhabited by the Yanomami. But while this in itself increased pressure from Indian rights groups for government intervention in the gold rush, the *garimpeiros* gained new political adversaries when they crossed into Venezuela and started to mine in the upper reaches of the Orinoco catchment. As this frontier is not clearly defined, the Venezuelan government reacted aggres-sively to the construction of various *garimpo* airstrips, notably Sadam Hussein, Constituinte, and Rainha de Inajá (numbers 83, 82, and 84), along the border. Tensions heightened in January 1992 when the Venezuelan National Guard shot down a light plane that was servicing these *garimpos*.

Concern about the activities of Roraima's *garimpeiros* was moun-ting simultaneously from other quarters. One significant develop-ment during the latter part of the gold rush relates to the increased production of cassiterite (tin ore). Due to its density, tin ore is extracted gravimetrically, using the same technology employed in gold mining. In 1987, *garimpeiros* working gold in the Alto Mucajaí usually discarded cassiterite on account of its comparatively low value-to-bulk ratio. Subsequently, however, *donos de garimpo* started to buy the mineral at cheap prices from *garimpeiros* (from both manual and mechanized production) and to transport it back to Boa Vista whenever space was available in any returning aircraft. By 1989, a number of *garimpeiros* working around the Surucucús plateau had begun to specialize in cassiterite production. Typically the tin ore was dried and stockpiled in Boa Vista before being sold to freelance intermediaries, who negotiated with larger companies such as Paranapanema and Best Metals and Solders. These middlemen usually arranged road transport of the mineral to Manaus or the south of Brazil.

The high costs of transporting tin ore and the limited number of potential buyers ensured that cassiterite (unlike gold) was handled mainly by *donos de garimpo*, pilots or dealers. Not surprisingly therefore, an oligopoly rapidly emerged over the production of the mineral. According to cassiterite dealers in Boa Vista, two ventures, backed by different sources of multinational capital, started extracting and transporting large quantities of tin ore from Surucucús towards the end of 1989. The *donos* of these two operations came to dominate tin production, airlifting tons of the mineral in DC3 aircraft from airstrips over a kilometre in length constructed in the Yanomami Reserve. In both cases, they stockpiled the ore on ranches between Alto Alegre and Boa Vista before passing it on to their creditors as repayment for their initial loans.

The increase in cassiterite production was of great concern to the Association of Tin Producing Countries (ATPC). The ATPC aims to maintain a high and stable price for tin on the world market by encouraging its members to accept production quotas. World tin prices plummeted by 60 per cent between 1985 and 1990 (see Figure 2.2) following the collapse of the International Tin Cartel (ITC) in October 1985. By the end of the 1980s, the ATPC was struggling to restrict production in the face of a contracting world market as the industrialized countries entered recession. Prices were further driven down in the early 1990s, when the United States of America released over 13,000 tons of strategic tin reserves, which it had built up during the Cold War, onto the world market.

*A Yanomami village near Paapiú. The plastic sheeting has been acquired from nearby gold camps.*

Although Brazil is only an observer at the ATPC discussions, she does accept a voluntary production quota and has come under increasing pressure from the association to control informal-sector tin production in Amazonia.[17] Indeed, the tin trade was in such a precarious state during the late 1980s that the prospect of high quality Surucucús cassiterite flooding onto international markets was accredited with depressing world tin prices in the second half

---

17. The pressure on Brazil to restrict informal-sector tin production is clearly noted in ATPC (1991).

of 1989.[18] Clearly, it was the larger producers, such as the huge Brazilian national Paranapanema,[19] that had most at stake, and so they too began to lobby the government for the closure of the *garimpo*s in western Roraima.

## THE CONSEQUENCES FOR THE YANOMAMI

Tragically, the direct impacts of this gold rush were absorbed by the Yanomami, one of the world's most isolated indigenous groups. They had little resistence to malaria and to other diseases, like tuberculosis, which the *garimpeiro*s helped to transmit in this part of the Amazon. As a result, the Indians died in their hundreds. Between 1988 and 1990, an estimated 15 per cent of the Yanomami population died.[20] While disease accounted for the largest number of fatalities, the death toll was exacerbated by conflicts between *garimpeiro*s and the Yanomami. A lawyer for the CIR (Conselho Indígena de Roraima) has specific records on the murders of 14 Yanomami between 1987 and 1992,[21] but these are certainly conservative, for many violent incidents that took place in this remote area went unrecorded. As it is taboo in Yanomami society to mention the name of the deceased, it is very difficult for outsiders to know exactly how many people were killed in these conflicts. Having said that, the death toll of one particularly savage episode, which hit the headlines of the international press in August 1993, was established. Armed *garimpeiro*s murdered 19 men, women and children in two separate attacks on the village of Haximu. They mutilated the bodies of their victims with machetes before incinerating them.

It is particularly disturbing that, as soon as the gold rush started in 1987, the Brazilian government prevented health teams and anthropologists from entering the Yanomami Reserve. They were not allowed back in until the end of 1990, by which time government intervention had considerably slowed the gold rush. A concerted attempt to provide emergency health care was made in the following year, although logistical difficulties, inconsistent funding and poor co-ordination reduced the efficacy of the project (known as the Yanomami Health Project). In essence, the provision

---

18. DNPM (1990).
19. Paranapanema is one of the world's largest tin producers, responsible for 13 per cent of global production in 1987. Andrade (1989).
20. FUNAI/CIMI/INESC/NDI (1991) p 2.
21. CIDR (1992).

of health care to the Yanomami in their hour of greatest need can be summarized as 'too little too late'.

The welfare of the Indians was also prejudiced by the environmental degradation accompanying the gold rush. Hunting became increasingly difficult in the vicinity of the principal mining centres, for game was both shot by the *garimpeiros* and scared off by the mining activity. Habitat destruction itself should be qualified as mining is not directly responsible for widespread deforestation. While trees are removed to gain access to deposits, the concentration of work in confined sites ensures that the total areas deforested are small, particularly when compared to other land uses in Amazonia. Nevertheless, virtually all the vegetation is stripped from areas of intensive mining and, as this is usually along streams, localized water courses are totally transformed. The churning of river sediments not only pollutes the drinking water, but also disrupts the reproductive cycle of fish – an important source of protein in the Yanomami diet.

It is possible that these physical alterations may be ameliorated over a relatively short term following the termination of mining activity. However, mercury contamination of the aquatic ecosystem could continue for decades. The use of mercury is common to all types of gold-mining technology employed in the *garimpo*. As well as placing mercury in small reservoirs within the equipment, *garimpeiros* often mix the metal with gold-bearing sediments in the mining pit (*barranco*) itself. Essentially they try to ensure that the two metals have combined before they start recovering them. This is because it is much easier to trap the heavier gold-mercury amalgam in a sluice-box than it is to capture pure gold. The miners periodically stop washing the sediments over the sluice boxes to recover their haul. The riffles are removed, and the gold–mercury amalgam lodged in the sack lining of the sluice box is swept down into a metal prospecting dish. The gold miners then place the contents of the dish into their T-shirt and squeeze off any excess mercury, which is then poured into a storage bottle and retained for future use. The gold–mercury amalgam is then tipped back into the prospecting dish, where it is heated (usually with a blow torch) so that the mercury vaporizes, leaving only the gold.

In this way the mercury enters local watercourses either directly through spillages from the sluice-box, or as rainfall when the vapour is condensed out of the atmosphere. Initially it accumulates in stream and river sediments in an inert metallic state, but it is subsequently transformed into an organic form through a process known as methylation. This process is generally accelerated in acidic waters, which have high rates of conductivity. Having undergone this transition, the organic mercury may be absorbed by aquatic biota and accumulates in the food chain, typically attaining highest concentrations in the tissues of predatory fish and caiman.

While mercury vapour is inhaled directly by the *garimpeiros* and gold traders who do the burning, surrounding communities are often contaminated by consuming fish from the polluted rivers that drain the mining areas. The symptoms of mercury contamination are in many ways similar to those of malaria, thus complicating its diagnosis. These include trembling of the extremities, headaches, poor vision and, in extreme cases, unconsciousness and death. Analysis of hair samples from 162 Yanomami in 1990 recorded above-average levels of mercury from villagers living around Paapiú and Surucucús.[22] But no samples exceeded the World Health Organization's maximum permissible concentration of 6 μg of methyl-mercury/g of hair. Although these values are relatively low compared to mercury levels recorded in the older mining areas of the Amazon (such as the *garimpos* of the Tapajós and the Madeira basins), it is wrong to assume from these initial findings that mercury contamination will not pose health problems to the Yanomami in the long term. Before the full implications of mercury discharges on the health of the Yanomami can be accurately assessed, a detailed study of their dietary habits is required (to provide data on levels of mercury uptake), as is accurate information on the degree to which the aquatic ecosystem is already contaminated.[23]

The changes mentioned above refer to the physical effects of the gold rush on the Yanomami, and can be measured. But their impact on the Indian's social organization and cosmology is much more difficult to comprehend. The Yanomami, in common with many indigenous peoples, believe that spirits dwell in the natural environment around them. Because of this, the detrimental physical consequences of the gold rush extend into the spiritual world. As Davi Kopenawa Yanomami explains:[24] *Xawara*, a spirit manifest as a vapour, is released from the subsoil during mining and is responsible for the ill health that afflicts both the Yanomami and the *garimpeiros*. Ultimately, *Xawara* threatens to undermine the

---

22. Castro et al (1991), see also Malm et al (1990).
23. Personal communication with Bruce Forsberg, 1991.
24. This is paraphrased from an interview published in *Ação Pela Cidadania* (1990).

protective spirits, *Hekurabe,* which support the sky and preserve the forests. The consequences of continued mining are apocalyptic for both the Indians and *garimpeiros* alike, as the demise of the *Hekurabe* heralds the end of the world.

## GOVERNMENT INTERVENTION SLOWS THINGS DOWN

Even though domestic and international pressures were mounting for the expulsion of the *garimpeiros* from the Yanomami lands, laws were passed that legitimized their activities within the area. The inter-ministerial decree 250/88 of 10 November 1988 reduced the proposed Yanomami Reserve from eight million hectares to 2.4 million hectares, composed of 19 separate islands. The area surrounding these isolated Indian reserves was designated a National Forest, within which *garimpeiros* were free to operate. Two subsequent presidential decrees, signed on 25 January 1990 and 16 February 1990, went one step further by designating three areas withn the recently established National Forest specifically for *garimpagem*. These were the three *garimpeiro* reserves of Uraricoera, Uraricáa-Santa Rosa, and Catrimani-Couto de Magalhães, which are marked on Figure 2.1. Although these were created to appease strong lobbying by *garimpeiros*, the impressive gold fields of the Alto Mucajaí, as well as the tin ore deposits of Surucucús, lay outside these areas. Even so, the miners started to shift their operations into the designated reserves, where a number of *donos* made heavy investments in prospecting, constructing airstrips and installing equipment. Encouraged by the government's legal recognition of their work, they aimed to secure a major share in what appeared to be a promising future.

The situation changed dramatically in March 1990, shortly after Fernando Collor de Melo replaced José Sarney as president of Brazil. He immediately revoked the decrees signed by his predecessor and, in a blaze of publicity, declared his resolve to expel the *garimpeiros* from the whole area originally proposed as a Yanomami reserve (9.4 million hectares). Operation Free Forest (*Selva Livre*) was implemented and teams of federal policemen were ordered to destroy the clandestine airstrips and remove all miners from the area. Temporary *garimpeiros* were the first to be squeezed out by this action, and they mostly returned to their alternative forms of employment. However, a large number of professional *garimpeiros* stayed on, repairing the damaged airstrips the police had blown up.

Ironically, this intervention actually increased the economic opportunities for many *garimpeiros*, particularly those who owned sets of pumping equipment (*donos de máquinas*). This is because the monopoly exerted by the owners of the mines was effectively destroyed when their airstrips were dynamited. Thus, *garimpeiros* who continued working in these areas were no longer obliged to pay landing fees or buy mining rights off the *donos de garimpo*.

Towards the end of 1990, a more convincing phase of Operation Free Forest was implemented and federal police forces started to destroy the motors of any mining equipment they encountered in the *garimpos*. This crippled many of the remaining operations, but, more significantly, it drained the momentum of the gold rush, which had been sustained by a rapid reinvestment of earnings in prospecting and equipment. Some of the more resourceful *garimpeiros* avoided this action by moving further south within the Yanomami Reserve to mine around the Pico de Neblina in northern Amazonas or by drifting west into Venezuela, although the Venezuelan National Guard was also trying to evict them from that side of the border. Nevertheless, a large number of professionals did leave the reserve, principally heading for the diamond *garimpos* on the savannah of Roraima and Guyana, as well as returning to the gold fields of the Tapajós and Alto Rio Negro.

In spite of its forceful intervention, it is questionable whether the government will fully succeed in halting mining within the Yanomami Reserve. Throughout 1992 there were approximately 2000 people working in the area at any one time and this number had risen to an estimated 11,000 by early 1993.[25] The government's inability to prevent this reinvasion illustrates the power of the socioeconomic pressures that currently fuel informal-sector mining in Amazonia. If there are no significant political changes in the immediate future, the number of *garimpeiros* working in western Roraima will probably continue to fluctuate in response to the intensity of police vigilance, the price of gold, the time of year, the cost and availability of fuel, and variations in other sectors of the regional economy.

## THE BROADER CONTEXT

The Yanomami gold rush is sometimes regarded as an exceptional chapter in contemporary Amazonian history. But there is nothing

---

25. *Financial Times*, 20 February 1993.

unusual about either the conflicts with Indians or the government intervention, which are its hallmarks. Throughout the region *garimpeiro*s have exploited deposits on Indian lands. In this respect, the Kayapó of Pará, the Waiampi of Amapá, the Uru-eu-wau-wau of Rondônia and the Tukano of Amazonas have all shared similar experiences to the Yanomami. Regrettably, it is likely that the invasion of Indian lands will continue as the region's relatively accessible gold deposits are either mined out or allocated to the formal mining sector. Clashes between private companies and *garimpeiro*s also ensure that Roraima's *garimpo*s are not exceptional in provoking government intervention. A similar response restricted production in Pará's Serra Pelada in 1983, and in Rondônia's massive cassiterite *garimpo* of Bom Futuro in 1991. In both these cases, the rights of *garimpeiro*s to exploit the deposits were being contested by the formal mining sector. The point is that, while the Yanomami gold rush does reflect many idiosyncracies, it is nevertheless quite representative of informal-sector mining as practised throughout Amazonia.

With this in mind, the government's inability to stop the rush is particularly significant. The very phrase 'gold boom' gives the misleading impression that mining is abandoned when a natural cycle comes to a close. But historical evidence and contemporary events prove that this is not the case. For example, mining continues to thrive in Roraima's diamond *garimpo* of Tepequém, even though its boom days terminated half a decade ago. There is a tenacity here that is seldom recognized, but which is nonetheless reflected in other activities. Perhaps the most obvious parallel is to be found in rubber, which continues to be extracted 80 years after the rubber boom ended. Just as significantly, rubber tappers are still visible as a distinct social category on the Amazonian stage. The suggestion is that neither *garimpeiro*s, nor their trade, will simply disappear when the heady boom days pass. Far from it, they will continue to fulfil a role, albeit a less conspicuous one, in the diverse social and economic landscape of Amazonia.

The remainder of this book considers how the Yanomami gold rush affected the course of development in this part of the Amazon (the state of Roraima). By looking at how different groups of people participated in the rush, we see how *garimpagem* and its protagonists fit into their regional context. But this is not simply a case of slotting pieces of a jigsaw puzzle neatly into their designated spaces. Rather, a much more organic scenario arises from the complex social and economic interactions of modern Amazonia. Any hard edges to our jigsaw pieces are rapidly eroded as we witness considerable flux between a wide range of social groups and a diversity of livelihoods. The objective here is not to define and categorize the different actors in the theatre, but to interpret the relationships and interchanges between them that ultimately create the play.

# Chapter 3

# Just Keep on Digging Away: Smallholder Agriculture and Gold Mining

*The smallholders' lot.*

This brief history of the Yanomami gold rush highlights the significant role played by smallholders in exploiting local mineral resources. Here, our attention will focus more closely on this relationship between agriculture and mining in Amazonia. It is an important subject to explore. Because the two activities are frequently interlinked in the livelihoods of colonist farmers, migration to the *garimpos* can not be divorced from the wider agrarian context in which it occurs. Having recognized that this is the case, we can then begin to question whether the Brazilian government is able to reduce migration to the Amazon's *garimpos* through appropriate changes in agricultural policy.

As we noted earlier, there are now three million smallholders living in the Brazilian Amazon. But, even before they arrived, the region's agriculture was already being strongly influenced by the government's desire to expand the mineral sector. This is because the highways along which the colonists were settled were themselves planned in relation to the mineral deposits that had recently been identified by the RadamBrasil survey.[1] In this way large numbers of migrant farmers came to live either next to, or on top of, substantial mineral deposits. In Pará, the colonization projects of Marabá, Tucumã and Altamira, are all situated beside major gold fields, as is the Alto Floresta settlement scheme in northern Mato Grosso. Even so, gold is not the only mineral to be found next to the colonization project areas. At Ariquemes in Rondônia, farmers have been given land rights next to the massive cassiterite mine of Bom Futuro, while further north, where the BR174 intersects the border between Amazonas and Roraima, the planned agricultural community of Presidente Figueiredo lies beside another huge deposit of the same mineral.[2]

Although the planning of the highways ultimately favoured the participation of smallholders in the mining economy, it is difficult to argue that this was the government's intention right from the outset. Far from it. The state initially saw the corporate mining sector as the main vehicle for developing the Amazon's mineral potential. Clearly, had it been realized, this capital-intensive approach to mining would have placed few demands on the large pool of

---

1. This same point is made by Fearnside (1984) p 47.
2. This is the site of Paranapanema's Pitinga mine – the largest open cast tin mine in the world.

unskilled labour assembled in nearby colonization projects.[3] But, as we have seen, these dreams were fulfilled in only a handful of large-scale mining projects, the jewels of which were the Carajás and Pitinga developments. For the most part the state failed dismally in its attempts to entice corporate-sector investment into the regional mining economy, leaving many areas of recognized geological potential open to informal-sector development. As gold and cassiterite *garimpos* started to spring up, colonist farmers who had been settled along the adjacent highways turned to mining to supplement their agricultural incomes.

As the 1980s progressed, one of the few observations common to researchers working in different parts of the Amazon, was the widespread involvement of smallholders in the informal-mining economy.[4] By the end of the decade it was clear that a large proportion of the region's *garimpeiros* came from the agricultural sector. Three surveys, the results of which are presented in Table 3.1, confirm this. In these studies social scientists asked a total of 334 *garimpeiros* working in three different Amazonian states what they did before mining.

Half the *garimpeiros* interviewed in each survey had previous experience in agriculture, and two thirds (72 per cent) of the aggregated sample (334 people) had agricultural backgrounds.[5] Extrapolating from this sample, even a conservative estimate suggests that at least half the workforce employed in the Amazon's *garimpos* is drawn from the agricultural sector and it is quite likely that the proportion is sustantially higher.

Even so, this gives no indication of the considerable seasonal movement between mining and agriculture. Only one of the studies mentioned above collected information on this topic. A third (32 per cent) of the 168 *garimpeiros* interviewed by Pereira said that they returned to agricultural work during the rainy season. Another third (35 per cent) continued mining (usually in other parts of

---

3.  For a detailed analysis of formal-sector mining in the Amazon, see Hall (1989).

4.  This trend has been observed in the Madre de Dios region of Peru by Maennling (1987), in Rondônia by Milliken (1991), in northern Mato Grosso by Coy (1991), in Araguaia by Filho (1984), in southeastern Pará by Butler (1985) and Schmink and Wood (1992), and in the Gurupí of Maranhão by Cleary (1990).

5.  The remaining 28 per cent came predominately from cities, the majority having had employment in the informal sector of the urban economy.

Amazonia or Brazil) all year round and could therefore be considered professional *garimpeiros*, while the remainder tended to gravitate towards the urban economy when not mining.

**Table 3.1** *The agricultural experience of* garimpeiros *in the Brazilian Amazon*[6]

|  | state | sample size | have agricultural experience (%) | no agricultural experience (%) |
|---|---|---|---|---|
| Cleary (1990) | Maranhão | 100 | 53 (53) | 47 (47) |
| Pereira (1990) | Pará | 168 | 135 (80) | 33 (20) |
| MacMillan | Roraima | 66 | 54 (82) | 12 (18) |
| TOTAL |  | 334 | 242 (72) | 92 (28) |

All this evidence makes it quite clear that there is a great deal of movement between smallholdings and *garimpo*s in contemporary Amazonia. But as yet there is no detailed research to explain either why this migration occurs, or how it happens. To shed some light on the situation, a survey was undertaken to assess the involvement of Roraima's smallholders in the gold camps of western Roraima between 1986 and 1990. From February to September 1991, 288 colonist households were interviewed in the government colonization projects of Alto Alegre, Apiaú, PAD Anauá and Caroebe (see Figure 1.3).

These projects were chosen because they are typical of roadside colonization schemes throughout the Amazon. All four of them are situated on old sandy soils (ultisols), which are prevalent in the region, and their layout bears an insignia common to virtually all

---

6. All three studies are based on life history interviews in which *garimpeiros* were asked about their previous forms of employment. My survey was applied in Entre Rios to *garimpeiros* entering the *garimpo* of Jatapú in 1991; respondents were classified as having agricultural experience if they had worked in agriculture for at least one year. To avoid bias in interviewing *garimpeiros* working near a colonization project area, *garimpeiros* who came from within 100 kilometres of Jatapú were excluded from the survey. As those excluded numbered 11 people, it can be estimated that local smallholders represented approximately 15 per cent of the Jatapú *garimpo* during its early days.

Amazonian colonization schemes. Plots of land measuring 50–100 hectares lie in a grid pattern along a network of feeder roads emanating from the principal access route. Most of the households settled on these plots of land have come from northeast Brazil (roughly 60–70 per cent), with the largest fraction of the remainder originating in the centre-south (about 15–20 per cent). They, like their counterparts throughout the Amazon, practise subsistence slash-and-burn agriculture. Most smallholders concentrate on the production of a handful of annual crops (rice, manioc, maize and beans), of which rice is by far the most important, typically accounting for half the cultivated area. Even though many farmers plant bananas and sometimes coffee (particularly in Rondônia), perennials are far less significant, both in terms of income and cultivated area, than annual crops.

Of the 288 households interviewed in this survey, 199 (66 per cent) had come from the northeast, 42 (15 per cent) from the centre-south and 55 (19 per cent) from other parts of Brazil. They were asked to recount their life histories and migratory experiences and were questioned about any type of non-agricultural work they had engaged in over the previous five years.[7] For households with no involvement in the regional mining economy, this was as far as the interviews went. But all the other households were questioned further about their mining experiences. Information was gathered on the *garimpo*s they had visited, the time spent on each trip, gold earnings recovered, diseases contracted and subsequent investments (or disinvestments) made. Mining expeditions to other parts of Amazonia (including Guyana and Venezuela) were discounted, along with any incomplete or unreliable interviews. The statements of 94 colonist farmers remained, providing detailed accounts of 184 journeys made by them to the gold mines in the Yanomami Reserve between 1987 and 1990.

## SMALLHOLDER FARMING AND MIGRATION TO THE *GARIMPO*S

A strong emphasis on annual crops ensures that smallholder agriculture is highly seasonal. This observation is important because it bears direct relevance to smallholder participation in the *garimpo*s. A quick look at the agricultural cycle shows that farmers are free to

---

7. For the specific details of the sampling procedures used in this survey, see MacMillan (1993a) pp 75–80.

engage in other activities, like mining, at certain times of the year.

In the dry season Roraima's smallholders typically clear a patch of between two and four hectares of either forest or regrowth. Once it is sufficiently dry (which may take some weeks), the clearing is burnt and is planted at the onset of the first rains. The rice, maize and beans are tended for about five to six months until the end of the wet season when they are harvested. Up until this point the household has been kept busy with the planting, tending and harvesting of these crops. But once the dry season comes round again, smallholders may find they have time on their hands. Even though efforts are often concentrated on the production of manioc flour at this time of the year (as manioc takes 15–18 months to grow, it can be harvested all year round), household labour may well be underemployed. Thus, it is quite common for men to seek alternative jobs during the summer months. Often they set about clearing the area for the following year's crops immediately after the rice harvest. Then, while the cleared vegetation is drying out they go off for two to three months to make some money. They usually leave instructions with a member of the family or a trusted neighbour to fire the clearing when it is dry, so that they can stay away from the smallholding until the onset of the first rains.

The seasonal demand for labour in the *garimpos* is exactly the opposite. During the wet season, the streams, rivers and pits the miners work in invariably flood and the airstrips they depend upon become even more dangerous than usual. Although *garimpeiros* can mine all year round, most stop during the wet season when the economics of the exercise become less favourable. Large quantities of very expensive fuel have to be consumed each day to pump out the water that has accumulated in the prospect overnight. Thus, production and employment in the *garimpos* tend to contract greatly during the wet season.

Once the rains stop, the mines begin to hum with activity. It becomes increasingly easy to recover gold when the high water levels recede. This stimulates investment in the *garimpos*, which in turn generates many more employment opportunities. The timing could not be better for colonist farmers. To them gold mining provides an excellent means of earning some extra money. The survey of Roraima's smallholders shows that they were quick to seize the opportunities arising from the gold rush. Among the 288 households interviewed, about half (49 per cent) contained an individual previously employed on the smallholding who worked in the gold camps of the Yanomami Reserve between 1987 and 1990 (see Table

3.2). In virtually all cases, it was the male head of household who had left the smallholding to go mining (86 per cent). In a smaller number of homesteads younger men (usually the eldest son) went mining (15 per cent), and in only two instances did father and son travel to the mines together.[8]

Migration from the smallholdings to the gold mines is undertaken almost exclusively by men. Indeed, from the whole survey of 288 households, only two women had entered the gold camps. In both cases they went to work as cooks. One of them was single and went on the invitation of a friend who was a *dono de máquina*. The other was a widowed head of household who entered the *garimpo* with her two sons.

**Table 3.2** *Rates at which Roraima's colonist households participated in the 1987–1990 gold rush. Households are classified by origin; northeast (NE), centre-south (CS), and Others*

| Coloni-zation Project | Res-pon-dents | No. of households who participated in the gold rush * | | | No. of households who did not go to the gold rush | | | TOTAL rates of participation | |
|---|---|---|---|---|---|---|---|---|---|
| | | NE | CS | Others | NE | CS | Others | Went | Did not go |
| Alto | | | | | | | | | |
| Alegre | 98 | 44 | 3 | 4 | 31 | 14 | 2 | 51 | 47 |
| Apiaú | 92 | 32 | 4 | 2 | 32 | 9 | 13 | 38 | 54 |
| PAD | | | | | | | | | |
| Anauá | 59 | 26 | – | 8 | 19 | 5 | 1 | 34 | 25 |
| Caroebe | 39 | 4 | 2 | 11 | 3 | 5 | 14 | 17 | 22 |
| Total | 288 | 106 | 9 | 25 | 85 | 33 | 30 | 140 | 148 |
| % | 100 | | | | | | | 49 | 51 |

\* If any member of the household left agricultural employment to go and work in the gold *garimpo*s of western Roraima between 1987 and 1990, then that household was recorded as participating in the gold rush.

Table 3.2 shows that the degree of smallholder participation in *garimpagem* is closely related to an individual's state of origin. Northeasterners are more likely to go mining than migrants from

---

8. The apparently small percentage of sons registered by the survey as working in the *garimpo* reflects a tendency for young men to leave the landholding at an early age.

the Brazilian centre-south.[9] The colonists themselves use cultural distinctions to explain this disparity, arguing that *garimpagem* is in the blood of the northeasterner. Certainly the Brazilian northeast does have a much longer history of mineral extraction than the centre-south, but these culturally-defined assertions are questionable. The proportion of centre-southerners who did participate is clearly not insignificant and there is evidence from other parts of Amazonia (notably Mato Grosso and Rondônia) that they are very enthusiastic miners in different circumstances. Thus, we need to look a little deeper to understand why farmers from the centre-south were not involved to the same extent as their northeastern colleagues in the Yanomami gold rush.

A more likely explanation is to be found in the different agricultural practices of migrants from the northeast and centre-south.[10] Migrant farmers arriving in the Amazon from central and southern Brazil tend to make higher capital investments in their landholdings than their northeastern colleagues. In many cases they arrive with more money at their disposal, having sold land in the south. A detailed analysis of land tenure in the Alto Alegre and PAD Anauá projects confirms this: 95 per cent of the centre-southerners had actually bought their landholdings in these projects, whereas the majority (63 per cent) of migrants from other states, including the northeast, had acquired their land free (mostly from the government's initial distribution of holdings). Furthermore, half the centre-southerners also had alternative sources of off-farm income, suggesting that they were wealthier than many of the northeastern farmers. Clearly, a trip to the gold mines with all the risks it entails may not be an attractive option to farmers who are already on a secure financial footing. Thus, to use an economic phrase, it is quite likely that in these circumstances the opportunity costs of *garimpagem* are higher for centre-southerners than for northeasterners.

The disparity in wealth between migrants from the northeast and centre-south is not restricted to Roraima, nor is it confined to the agricultural economy. Indeed, it is frequently observed in *garimpo*s throughout the Amazon. For, although fewer centre-southerners

---

9. Of the 191 northeastern households interviewed, 55 per cent had a member who went to the *garimpo*s, compared with 21 per cent of those from the centre-south (n=42), and 46 per cent of those originating in other states (n=55).

10. See Fearnside (1980) p 117.

tend to go mining, those that do are more often capitalized professional miners. While there has been no comprehensive survey of this phenomenon, the situation in Roraima tallies with reports from Maranhão, Rondônia and Pará that a disproportionate number of capitalized miners (*donos de máquinas*), pilots, and mine owners (*donos de garimpo*) are from the Brazilian centre-south.[11]

The survey of Roraima's colonist farmers also raises an interesting question about the geography of smallholder migration to the *garimpos*. As Figure 1.2 shows, the colonization projects of Apiaú and Alto Alegre are situated closest to the *garimpos*. But surprisingly, rates of smallholder migration from these areas were actually lower than from the more distant projects of PAD Anauá and Caroebe.[12] It seems strange that a higher percentage of farmers left the remoter projects to go mining, but, interestingly enough, exactly the same observation has been made of colonist behaviour on the other side of the Brazilian Amazon:[13]

> With the discovery of *garimpos* in Rondônia numerous colonists have abandoned at least temporarily their agricultural plots within settlement areas. ... According to local informants many of those that rapidly migrated to the *garimpo* [at Rio Massagana] were members of colonist households from distant settlement areas.

This suggests that rates of smallholder participation in the *garimpos* do not decline sharply with distance. Certainly, members of the Amazonian peasantry are prepared to travel huge distances to go mining. News of gold strikes on the Rio Jatapú, which subsequently proved to be grossly inflated, brought at least two smallholders from the interior of Maranhão to Roraima (a journey of about 2000 kilometres) in the space of a few weeks.[14] Even so, while this points to the *garimpo*'s potency in luring people from their landholdings, it does not adequately explain why, in the case of Roraima, this force appears to operate more powerfully in the remoter colonization project areas.

---

11. Data on Rondônia and Maranhão are from personal communication with Cleary (1992); and on Pará from personal communication with Feijão (1991).
12. Of smallholders in Caroebe and PAD Anauá, 52 per cent went to the *garimpos*, compared with 48 per cent from Alto Alegre and Apiaú.
13. Milliken (1991) p 124.
14. These events, which were mentioned in Chapter 2, are discussed in greater detail in Chapter 6.

To understand why this might be so, it is worth considering the *garimpo*'s impact on the structure of local markets. Mining is one of very few activities that concentrate large numbers of people and capital in rural Amazonia. The sudden demand for food created by a gold strike, buoys up agricultural prices in its immediate hinterland, thereby giving a considerable boost to local smallholders. This might explain why smallholders who live right next to *garimpos* and therefore enjoy an improved market for their produce, do not enter the mines as rapidly as those who live further away. Rather than sacrifice these favourable economic circumstances by going mining, local farmers might find it more profitable to meet this new demand for food and services (notably accommodation and entertainment) *in situ*. Clearly, the same option is not available to smallholders situated in more distant colonization projects. For them migration to the *garimpos* is probably the most obvious strategy for increasing income in the short term.

Informal-sector mining therefore creates the rare conditions that place producers in direct contact with a buoyant rural market, denying rural–urban traders their traditionally privileged position in local commerce. The nature and extent of this local market is closely related to events in the *garimpo* and is highly dependent upon lines of access to it. For example, the main road into the Apiaú colonization project was also the principal access route to all of the *garimpos* in the Yanomani Reserve during the early stages of the rush. At that time, many of the smallholders residing there were able to sell produce (notably rice, beans, poultry, beef and manioc flour) on their doorsteps at favourable prices to *garimpeiros*. But with the subsequent construction of airstrips in the gold camps, most of the transport to and from the *garimpos* was by air. Even though a new airstrip had been built at the end of the Apiaú road to service the mines, most pilots preferred to operate from either Boa Vista or Alto Alegre. In this way Apiaú's interaction with the mining economy began to wane. By the same event, the colonization project of Alto Alegre, which had not previously been an important through route to the mines, benefited greatly from the shift towards air traffic. The rapid proliferation of bars, restaurants and grocery stalls testify that local smallholders were quick to cater for the demands of gold miners who used the town as a staging post on their journeys in and out of the *garimpos*.

The rush to the Yanomami Reserve drew virtually the whole casual workforce (mainly formed by sharecroppers) from Roraima's colonization projects in a short period of time. This sharp contraction in agricultural labour was subsequently compounded by an unusually wet summer in 1988/9. Heavy rainfall prevented many smallholders from successfully burning their clearings, which encouraged them to turn to mining instead. Thus, while the initial wave of migration was largely composed of sharecroppers who did not own land, their ranks were quickly swelled by landowners, many of whom had clear title to their holdings.

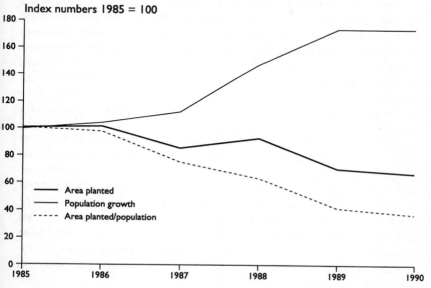

**Figure 3.1** *Area planted under principal food crops, and population growth in Roraima (1985=100)*

Indeed, one of the most interesting observations made by this research is that farmers with land titles (*titulos definitivos*) registered in their names migrated to the *garimpos* at exactly the same rate as smallholders who did not have them.[15] Although it is frequently argued that providing smallholders with secure title to their holdings is the most effective means of 'fixing people to the land', the evidence here suggests that this is not the case. Security of land tenure appears to have no effect on rates of out-migration from

---

15. This analysis was made on the project of Alto Alegre, where an unusually high proportion (44 per cent) of colonists held *titulos definitivos* to their plots of land.

colonization projects to the *garimpo*s. If anything, those with security of tenure are better placed to leave their homesteads for the *garimpo*s because they do not run the risk of returning from the mines to find their land has been taken.

All these indicators point to informal-sector mining having a very significant influence on agriculture throughout the Amazon. In Roraima alone, the sudden movement of labour from agriculture into mining led to a dramatic decline in the amount of land devoted to food production. Figure 3.1 shows that the area planted with the four principal crops (bananas, rice, maize and manioc) fell by 34 per cent between 1985 and 1990. Yet, over the same period, the state's population expanded by 73 per cent, so that the ratio of cultivated land per head of population diminished by 63 per cent during the gold rush.

Hence, even though the mines generated a huge demand for foodstuffs, only a small proportion of this was met by Roraima's smallholders. Most *garimpeiro*s found it more convenient and reliable to supply their mining operations with provisions purchased from supermarkets in Boa Vista. These retailing houses were themselves stocked with goods that had been freighted directly from the south of Brazil by air and road. Poor local transport prevented smallholders from competing effectively against these corporate retailers for a share of the booming urban economy. Thus, with depressing irony, Roraima's most dynamic phase of economic expansion was matched by a growing dependence on imported agricultural produce.

## GOLD MINING AND SMALLHOLDER ECONOMICS

Smallholders planned their trips to the *garimpo*s with care and usually restricted their absences from their homesteads to periods of about three months. On the whole, a proposed trip to the *garimpo*s would be formulated initially by groups of male farmers who knew one another. Their suggestions were aired only subsequently to other members of their households. The outcome was that bands of farmers co-ordinated their migration to the *garimpo*s and entered the mines together. Within such groups novices were introduced to mining by their more experienced colleagues and wealthier farmers often advanced money to impecunious members of the group for the costs of the journey.

It is difficult to know the extent of women's participation in the decision to go mining. Although women were seldom the first to be consulted over a proposed mining venture it is wrong to assume that they accepted the situation passively. Women who recognized what benefits such a trip could bring to the household, often encouraged their partners to enter the *garimpos*. Many homesteads were dominated by matriarchal figures who would certainly not have allowed significant migratory decisions to have been made without voicing their concerns.

A trip to the mines is not cheap. Although costs vary according to the transport used, an excursion may demand a substantial outlay relative to the income of most smallholders. Before 1987, access was either on foot or, in fewer cases, by boat. Smallholders had to provide all the necessary food, medicine and equipment (including fishing tackle, hunting gear and prospecting materials) for the fortnight-long trip. Farmers interviewed in Entre Rios (near Caroebe) typically spent between US $50 and $100 to equip themselves for a walk of similar length into the *garimpo* at Jatapú. Following the construction of the first airstrips, most people entered by light aircraft. While obviously being much quicker, this doubled the expenses faced by smallholders on their mining trips. Typically a return flight cost 15 grams of gold (approximately US $225), although usually only ten grams were paid in advance and five on exit from the mines. In some cases the flights were paid for by *donos de garimpo* or *donos de máquinas* on condition the colonists agreed to work for them on arrival in the mines. In the majority of cases though, the smallholders paid for their own air fare, often by selling livestock, grain, bicycles or, occasionally, land. As the value of a cow was roughly equivalent to ten grams of gold or the cost of a flight into the *garimpos*, smallholders with livestock often sold a cow to finance a mining trip with the objective of purchasing more on their return.

These outlays can only be understood when considered in relation to the amounts of money smallholders usually earn in the mines. Figure 3.2 shows the quantities of gold brought back to the household by 94 colonist farmers who made a total of 184 trips to the gold *garimpos* in the Yanomami Reserve between 1986 and 1990. It is important to realize that these calculations do not represent true *garimpeiro* incomes because they include net costs to the colonist, such as air flights and other expenses (like food and medicine) within the *garimpo*. Real *garimpeiro* earnings are at least five grams per month higher, given that a return flight costs 15 grams and a three-month stay is the average length of time spent between flights. Even so, because different individuals may spend varying amounts of gold on entertainment in the gold fields, real wages cannot be directly extrapolated from the gold earnings brought back to the colonists' household. Travelling salesmen, prostitutes, drug dealers, bar owners and photographers are all kept in employment within the mining camps. It is difficult to make general rules about an individual's expenditure, but it is probably fair to say that colonists tend to be more conservative than professional *garimpeiros* in their spending habits, particularly as many of them enter the *garimpo* with the specific intention of bringing cash back to the household.

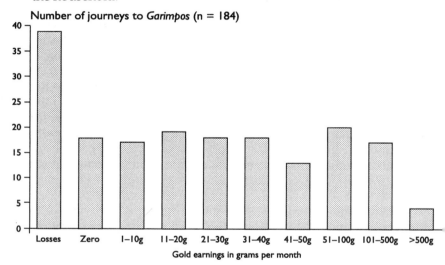

Note: The data are from 94 colonists who made a total of 184 trips into the *garimpos* of western Roraima from 1987 to 1990

***Figure 3.2*** *Quantities of gold brought back to colonist lots*

The data presented in Figure 3.2 show the amounts of gold smallholders brought home from their trips to the *garimpo*. Before starting to interpret these findings, however, two points need to be noted. First, a distinction is drawn between journeys that did not produce sufficient gold to cover the initial outlay of the venture (termed 'losses') and trips in which gold earnings were sufficient to break even but resulted in no net gains to the colonist (termed 'zero'). Secondly, land sales in the colonization projects are likely to overemphasize the proportion of smallholders who earned higher levels of income in the *garimpo*. This is because some colonists who ended up broke (*blefado*) in the *garimpo*s sold their lots to wealthier *garimpeiro*s and often moved to unclaimed land (*terras devolutas*) on the fringes of the colonization projects, where they cleared new holdings. Conversely, colonists who recovered substantial amounts of gold in the *garimpo*s rarely sold their holdings, even if they did invest a proportion of their wealth elsewhere.[16]

A closer look at Figure 3.2 shows that *garimpagem* is a very risky business. In 31 per cent of the journeys made, smallholders failed to bring any gold back to their homesteads. Of these unsuccessful ventures only one third (32 per cent) yielded sufficient gold to cover the overheads of the trip, the remainder (68 per cent) resulted in a net loss to the smallholder. Even so, these unsuccessful trips must be evaluated against the large number of lucrative journeys made. Half the trips made by smallholders yielded earnings of over 20 grams a month. Furthermore, for a very small number of the total journeys made, incomes were considerable. Of the mining ventures recorded here, 3 per cent produced over half a kilogram of gold per month. Thus, while mining is undoubtedly a risky activity, the majority of trips yield a respectable income and the potential gains may be very high.

All the smallholders who were interviewed initially went to the mines either to work manually or as machine hands for *donos*. Six of them later became wealthy enough to purchase their own sets of mining equipment, thus becoming *donos de máquinas*. Usually, only colonists prepared to reinvest their gold earnings in the *garimpo* become *donos*. One of the most common ways of reinvesting earnings is to finance prospecting trips, as Daniel and his partners did in the previous chapter. Even so, this is probably the riskiest activity in the mining economy and few people are prepared to go prospecting unless either they or a partner have previous experience.

Having said that, pure luck is always destined to play a prominent role in this equation. Many experienced prospectors failed to discover new deposits, while some of the most significant finds were uncovered by virtual novices. This risk factor was amplified in western Roraima where, according to the *garimpeiro*s, gold had been laid down among the sediments in a highly random fashion. In other parts of the Amazon, notably in the deposits of southeastern Pará, the metal was believed to have a much more uniform distri-

---

16. Throughout the whole survey (288 respondents) only one incident was recorded of a colonist selling his lot having struck it rich.

bution. Regardless of the vagaries of local geology, it is the luck factor that makes prospecting such an exciting activity. Consequently *garimpo* lore is replete with anecdotes that rationalize freak discoveries. One of the commonest explanations is that the gold shifts around under the ground and only makes itself available to those who deserve it. Hence a site explored unsuccessfully by one prospector may at a later date yield a fortune to another less experienced, but more deserving, individual.[17]

As virtually all incomes in the *garimpo* are based on a percentage of gold production, workers can do little to insulate themselves against the inherent risks of the activity. Only a small fraction of total employment is remunerated by fixed wages and most of these jobs demand certain skills. These include cooking, constructing rafts (*balsas*) on which to mount equipment, piloting aircraft, carrying out mechanical repairs and building airstrips. Most colonists therefore accept that *garimpo* incomes are highly variable and perceive this as an inherent part of the activity. They rationalize loss-making trips by placing them in a wider picture, in much the same way as a gambler would do. Although the odds may not be favourable, it only takes one lucky strike to recover all previous losses.

The opportunity cost of any one excursion relates to the profitability of an individual's agricultural enterprise as well as the timing of their absence in relation to the agricultural calendar. We have already seen that most smallholders go mining during the summer months and they usually transfer their reduced workload at this time of the year onto other members of the household. The important point to note is that although farm income may diminish, it is rarely altogether lost. Rough calculations made during the relatively productive year of 1991 suggest that a smallholder tending two hectares of rice, maize and manioc, with one further hectare of bananas, could expect a monthly cash income equivalent to 29 grams of gold (CR $134,800 or US $337).[18] This is taken to be the

---

17. To qualify as 'deserving' in this instance, *garimpeiros* have to be poor, generous and fairly reckless. Above all, people who shun accumulated wealth are thought to enjoy particularly good fortune when prospecting. There is no better way to fulfill these characteristics than to blow one's earnings on massive binges for fellow *garimpeiros*.

18. This is cash income only from sold produce, and does not include the considerable value of familial consumption. In fact, it is rare for colonists to plant as much as a hectare with bananas, which explains the relatively high income that this farmer earned. The calculations here are made at a rate of US $12 = 1 gram of gold, which applied during 1991.

best case situation for smallholders in Roraima, who are neither capitalized horticultural producers nor small ranchers. The higher value of gold on world markets during the principal years of the gold rush (1987–89), coupled with the very bleak outlook for Roraima's agriculture at that time, suggest that any excursion to the *garimpo* that yielded 20 grams a month or more was probably recompensatory.

By the same standards Figure 3.2 indicates that exactly half the trips generated favourable returns. This all seems good news for smallholders, but these calculations do not consider the highly significant financial implications of contracting a disease. Ill health is rife in the *garimpo*s. Half (49 per cent) the smallholders who went mining contracted an illness (predominantly malaria) on at least one of their journeys and 29 per cent of all mining trips made by smallholders resulted in some kind of sickness.

Being ill in the gold camps is an expensive pastime. For while a bout of malaria can be easy to cure if the strain of plasmodium is rapidly identified by microscope, the necessary equipment and trained personnel are rarely present in the *garimpo*. Here treatment is not only inadequate but it often leads to the development of resistant malarial strains. Most prospectors take a limited pharmacy with them, but its efficacy is compromised by their inability to identify the specific type of malaria contracted. A *garimpeiro* with malaria is faced with three main options: to treat it in the *garimpo* (which normally costs over 30 grams of gold);[19] to fly out for treatment at the nearest hospital (which costs between 5 and 10 grams and will obviously put a stop to their mining income); or to leave it untreated and continue working at a lower rate of productivity. Whatever the case, it is quite clear that a dose of malaria incurs significant costs and colonists often spend a large percentage of their mining incomes on treating the disease.

Unfortunately, malaria does not simply stay in the mining areas, but frequently causes hardship back in the colonization projects. A number of smallholders mentioned that, on returning from the *garimpo*s with malaria, they were too weak to prepare a sizeable area for cultivation the following year. Notwithstanding the costs to the individual concerned, this movement between the gold camps and colonization projects does much to increase rates of disease transmission. Women and children who have often been sustaining

---

19. Within the *garimpo*, a daily dose of quinine costs one gram of gold and each intravenous serum pack is four to five grams.

themselves on poor diets in the absence of their menfolk, may well suffer. A gradual decline in the incidence of malaria in Roraima since 1983 was temporarily reversed during the gold rush years. In 1989, the incidence of malaria in Roraima rose to 79.7 positive cases per 1000 population.[20] Gold mining is certainly the culprit, because the expansion of land for agricultural production, which is the other main contender for increases in malaria, was negligible at this time.

Providing basic health care in the mining camps could have done much to reduce the spread of malaria and other diseases in the state. But while this would have been beneficial to both the *garimpeiro*s and the Yanomami, it was a politically unacceptable option. Drafting government health workers to the gold fields would not only serve to legitimize the illegal invasion of the Yanomami Reserve, but would also make mining an even more attractive option to smallholders by removing one of their most significant budgetary expenses.

## SMALLHOLDER DECISION-MAKING AND RISK EVALUATION

In view of these findings, it might seem surprising that so many colonists go mining. Half the journeys they make are not profitable and many of them actually incur expenses, which need to be met from very limited incomes. Add debilitating diseases and extortionate hospital bills to the equation and it seems that mining may not be such an attractive option after all. So why do large numbers of smallholders migrate to the *garimpo*s, especially when it is widely believed that risk aversion strategies lie at the heart of peasant economics?

Some of the answers lie in the way smallholders make decisions. First, since the consequences of their economic strategies are unequally shared within the household, a gender bias is incorporated into the decision-making process. There are clearly exceptions to this observation, but in general women and children tend not to dominate the formulation of decisions, even though they are usually obliged to undertake an increased workload if the men from their household leave to go mining. In the absence of their menfolk some women continue to work in agriculture, while others move to the towns and engage in petty trading to take advantage of the booming urban economy. In both cases women become respon-

---

20. SUCAM (1991).

sible for the provision of household income, fulfilling a crucial role, which permits the temporary exodus of male labour from the small-holding. For the men, a trip to the *garimpo* is undoubtedly hard work, but it is nevertheless an adventure and it does represent a welcome break from the monotony of agricultural work. Besides, during these trips away, farmers enjoy a level of financial and social independence rarely experienced on the smallholding. It is there-fore not surprising that in a few cases their responsibility towards family welfare wanes on entering the predominantly male working environment of the gold fields.

*Migrant farmers flocked to the gold camps in search of wealth. Here, Pedro displays his monthly earnings: about 20 grams.*

Secondly, colonists seldom appraise either *garimpo* incomes or the health risks of mining in a realistic fashion. In part, this stems from ignorance, as the majority of farmers interviewed had no previous mining experience prior to the rush. But even smallholders who mine regularly tend not to evaluate these points accurately. Contrary to the findings of the malarial agency, SUCAM (Superintendência de Combate a Malária), smallholders argue that there is an equal chance of contracting malaria in both mining and agriculture. In this way disease is effectively discounted as a relevant factor in weighing up the two options. Similarly, the possibility of making a big strike is often exaggerated by smallholders, who are drawn to the *garimpo* not only by the modest wages they are likely to receive, but by the faint possibility that they might hit the jackpot (*bamburrar*). Every colonization project contains a smallholder who has hit the big time in the *garimpos*. Their large house and sizeable herd of cows stand as a continual reminder to other colonists that mining can deliver the goods to whoever is prepared to take the risk. Clearly, this is a possibility that simply does not exist in agriculture. For, although farming provides greater security, is less disease ridden and generates a subsistence living, it offers absolutely no prospects for getting seriously rich.

Smallholder migration to the *garimpos* can only be interpreted with accuracy if it is considered in its context as a livelihood strategy. Through the eyes of the colonist farmer, mining is one of various activities they can turn to in order to supplement their low agricultural incomes. In their quest for off-farm wages, Roraima's farmers have previously engaged in brazil-nut collecting, the informal urban economy (often in the construction trade), and the public sector (typically on the local council payroll). During the early 1980s large numbers of colonists settled in the south of Roraima migrated to Rondônia each summer to work as labourers in the rice harvest – a round trip of over 3000 kilometres.[21] This gives some indication of the important role seasonal income formation plays in homestead economics. Indeed, of the 157 colonist households from the colonization projects of Alto Alegre and PAD Anauá who were interviewed for this survey, only 15 per cent depended on the small-

---

21. This seasonal migration to Rondônia is reported in SUDAM (1984), as is brazil-nut collecting. Abers and Pereira (1992) give details on employment in the informal urban economy.

holding for their sole source of income.[22] This suggests that although farming does offer a subsistence livelihood, most small-holders regard agriculture on its own as a rather unsatisfactory means of making a living.

This, more than anything else, explains why colonists are very reluctant to reinvest the limited capital they gain from other sources back into farming. Of the 94 smallholder–miners interviewed, only 19 (20 per cent) said that they had invested a proportion of their gold earnings in their landholdings.[23] For the most part, they saw their *garimpo* incomes as a windfall profit, permitting the purchase of substantial items they seldom had the resources to buy. So, while a proportion was spent on entertainment (particularly by single men), a considerable amount was invested in consumer durables (refrigerators, radios, gas stoves, beds, TVs), as well as being used to pay off outstanding debts, buy means of transport, or finance specialized hospital treatment for ill members of the family. Thus, even though lack of financial resources is commonly regarded as a principal constraint on colonist agriculture,[24] smallholders are frequently more interested in investing the limited capital available to them elsewhere.

Furthermore, colonists were given no advice on how their gold could be invested so as to increase their meagre agricultural incomes over the longer term. In this respect extension workers missed a rare opportunity to encourage smallholders to adopt perennial cropping systems that were more closely tuned to local ecology. Thus, most of the smallholders who invested gold in their landholdings (15 out of 19) purchased cows, some of which were sold shortly afterwards. Livestock tends to increase in value relative to inflation, is easily transported and is readily sold at any time of the year. But above all, because cattle raising places minimal demands on household labour, it does not prevent smallholders

---

22. These data are based on the economic activities of colonists over the period 1986–1990. The 85 per cent who engaged in off-farm activities tended to do so on a seasonal basis. Of these 31 per cent had non-agricultural incomes but did not go mining, 16 per cent had non-agricultural incomes and also went mining, while 38 per cent had no source of off-farm income other than *garimpagem*.

23. This may be conservative, for smallholders tended to note only tangible items when discussing the expenditure of their *garimpo* earnings. They seldom assessed the often considerable outlays made in employing casual labour, until prompted.

24. See Fearnside (1980).

pursuing alternative economic strategies. Quite the opposite. Owning livestock may actually enhance their ability to take risks. Buying and selling cows relative to high-risk ventures like mining is an effective way of riding out the large fluctuations in income that characterize such gambles. The latter point receives greater consideration in the next chapter, but at this stage it is worth noting that smallholder agricultural management is often shaped by a desire to keep alternative options open. This offers an insight into why colonists are often reluctant to adopt longer-term cropping systems.

## CAN *GARIMPO* MIGRATION BE MANAGED THROUGH APPROPRIATE AGRICULTURAL POLICY?

These findings suggest that informal sector mining makes good economic sense to smallholders throughout the Amazon. As long as this remains the case pressure on mineral-rich Indian lands, like the Yanomami Reserve, will continue. And so we come to the crunch. In attempting to police such areas, the government is battling to restrain hoards of rural and urban poor people from pursuing one of the very few economically viable options open to them. Currently it does this by trying to restrict access to Indian reserves. While this in itself is a difficult task, the efficacy of a policy clearly directed towards combatting the effects and not the root causes of the problem must be questioned. Surely in the longer term greater efforts must be made to address the socioeconomic forces that currently fuel the invasion of Indian lands.

Having examined the motives behind smallholder participation in the gold rush, and having recognized that farmers account for over half the Amazon's *garimpeiros*, it is worth considering whether *garimpo* migration can be regulated through changes in agricultural policy. Perhaps the key question here concerns the relationship between landlessness and migration to the gold camps. It is well known that an increasingly inequitable distribution of land in the Brazilian northeast has been primarily responsible for fuelling migration into the Amazon and many of these landless migrants have subsequently joined the *garimpo* workforce. But while this is certainly true, it is wrong to infer from this, as some people have done,[25] that *garimpeiros* are for the most part landless rural workers.

---

25. See, for example, de Silva et al (1986) p 25 and Butler (1990) p 5.

Table 3.3 presents data on the land tenure status of 234 *garimpeiros* interviewed in Pará and Roraima.

**Table 3.3** *The land tenure status of garimpeiros in the Brazilian Amazon*

|  | state | n= | are land-owners (%) | parents have land (%) | completely landless (%) |
|---|---|---|---|---|---|
| Pereira (1990) | Pará | 168 | 81 (48) | 54 (32) | 33 (20) |
| Macmillan | Roraima | 66 | 20 (30) | 15 (23) | 31 (47) |
| Total |  | 234 | 101 (43) | 69 (29) | 64 (27) |

In both studies *garimpeiros* were classified either as landowners (irrespective of whether or not they had land titles), the offspring of landed parents (but not owning land in their own right), or completely landless (neither respondent nor parent possessing land). The key observation is that over half the *garimpeiros* interviewed in both surveys either had their own land, or had access to land via their parents' holdings. If the data from both studies are aggregated, then 43 per cent of respondents are landed, and only 27 per cent can be considered truly landless.

Many migrants who flooded into the Amazon after being squeezed off their holdings in the northeast may well have subsequently acquired land while moving around the basin during the gold rush of the 1980s. Although, with the strong pressures on land in southeastern Pará and Rondônia, landless *garimpeiros* would have had few opportunities to acquire holdings in those areas, there is an abundance of relatively accessible land around other mining centres, such as the Tapajós and Roraima. Indeed, the *garimpeiros'* union in the Tapajós actually co-ordinates the distribution of agricultural land to landless miners in the area.[26]

But there is more to this story. We have already seen that for every person working in the *garimpo* itself even more people are employed in related activities in urban areas. Abers's research in Boa Vista (which is discussed in greater depth in Chapter 5) shows that many of the people currently employed in this informal urban economy were originally rural producers from the northeast.[27] They moved to the cities, having been pushed off the land, either

26. Personal communication with Alberto E C da Paixão of SEICOM, January 1992.
27. Abers (1992).

violently or by unfavourable economics, and now form part of a transient labour force, which moves from city to city as new opportunities arise. Thus, the largest proportion of landless migrants who moved into the Amazon during the last two decades probably ended up, not in the *garimpo*s themselves, but, in the informal sector of the gold-boom cities. This explains why the concentration of land in the northeast, which clearly fuels migration into the Amazon, is not reflected in a higher proportion of landless *garimpeiro*s.

Before proceeding, it must be understood that the following discussion is based on the results of only 234 interviews. While this does allow for some new interpretations of the migratory processes related to mining in the Amazon, it is clearly an insufficient basis on which to formulate policy. Though these findings are analysed, it is important to recognize that more data need to be collected on this subject.

Ironically, while many of the people currently involved in the Amazonian informal-mining economy have at some stage been pushed off land in the northeast, it is questionable whether land reform will do much to slow down migration to the *garimpo*s. The real issue here is not that people have no land, but that they are not using the land they have as their only form of employment. Evidence from Roraima suggests that, while agriculture provides a subsistence livelihood, if favourable opportunities arise, farmers will seize on any opportunity to invest their labour and (albeit limited) capital outside the agricultural economy. That large numbers of landed farmers, including those with land titles, are going to the *garimpo*s is a clear indication that Amazonian agriculture, as it is currently practised, does little to 'fix people to the land'.

The crux is whether appropriate agricultural policy can prevent those farmers who already own land from migrating to the *garimpo*s. Certainly, the desperately low agricultural incomes and lack of infrastructural support for Amazonian smallholders suggest that there is scope to make the agricultural option more favourable. Furthermore, providing smallholders with accurate information on average *garimpo* incomes, and encouraging them to consider the true costs of malaria when appraising the economics of mining, might somewhat reduce their enthusiasm for *garimpagem*. But none of this will have much impact in slowing rates of *garimpo* migration unless an agricultural system is developed that absorbs more labour in the dry season. Reducing the seasonality of agriculture in the Amazon is one of the first steps required to make it a viable livelihood that need not be supported by other forms of income.

Such measures are aimed at reducing the need for impoverished farmers to survive by exploiting mineral resources illegally. But, even so, it is by no means clear that policies aimed at addressing rural poverty will necessarily slow down rates of migration to the *garimpos*. The Dantesque image of *garimpeiros* toiling away in pits of mud gives the false impression that they mine because they are desperate and this is the only livelihood available to them. As we have seen, only a relatively small fraction of professional *garimpeiros* depend entirely upon that form of employment for a living. Everybody else in the pit is there to supplement their other forms of income, whether they are farmers, builders, street sellers, rubber-tappers or even ranchers. The point is that deterministic forces may play less of a role here than is often believed, and for this reason reducing poverty will not necessarily be reflected in smaller numbers of *garimpeiros*. Even if fewer people need to go mining to survive, it can equally well be argued that more of them will chance their luck in the gold mines once their alternative incomes become more secure. No doubt migration to the *garimpos* will continue as long as gold mining offers the slim possibility of striking it rich.

## CONCLUSIONS

First, contrary to some conceptions, *garimpeiros* are not necessarily landless peasants. Indeed, a high proportion are either landowners or have access to land and see the *garimpo* as an opportunity to supplement their income. Thus, it is misguided to assume either that landownership prevents migration, or that a redistribution of land is the key to reducing Amazonian *garimpo* populations.

Second, *garimpo* earnings represent an important source of off-farm income for Amazonian smallholders. Their land management strategies often reflect the wider socioeconomic context in which they operate.[28]

Third, *garimpo* earnings are highly variable. Even so, half the trips made by Roraima's smallholders into the *garimpos* of the Yanomami Reserve exceeded normal agricultural incomes.

Fourth, making small farmers aware of the reality of *garimpo* life, health risks and the true nature of gold earnings would allow them to assess their migration to Amazonia's *garimpos* on a well-informed basis. Documentary film work and radio programmes made

---

28. For a more detailed discussion of this see Hecht (1987).

accessible to small farmers in the northeast and Amazonia could do much to enhance their understanding of the realities of *garimpo* life.[29]

Fifth, a stronger emphasis on planting and marketing perennial crops could enhance smallholder security by preventing the drastic falls in income associated with unusually heavy rains during the 'dry season'. Such climatic events have swollen *garimpeiro* populations, not only in Roraima, but also in Araguaia, Pará.[30]

Sixth, through a lack of imaginative agricultural extension work colonists were denied the opportunity to invest their gold earnings in longer-term silvicultural or agroforestry projects. Not only are such techniques more closely tuned to natural nutrient cycling systems, but they might also help reduce risk. The small percentage of *garimpo* earnings that were invested in the land were banked via the purchase of cattle.

And, finally, providing health care in the *garimpos* would increase gold earnings brought back to the lot by small farmers, as well as reduce the transmission of malaria further afield. Although the government may be reluctant to set up health posts within the *garimpos*, malaria could be reduced by distributing mosquito nets to embarking *garimpeiros* and using radio broadcasts to outline preventive health care.

---

29. Personal communication with B Forsberg, May 1991.
30. See Filho (1984).

*Chapter 4*

# The Golden Cow?
# Ranching and Mining

Having examined the migration provoked by the gold rush, I now turn to the exchanges of capital associated with it. Here the focus shifts onto the relationship between ranching and *garimpagem* in Amazonia, a theme which will be explored in the context of Roraima. Essentially, I look at how cattle producers became involved in the Yanomami gold rush and at the impact this had on ranching, both in the state and further afield. Since the 1960s, ranching in the Amazon has been shifting from its traditional domain of the region's natural grasslands into new areas of forest. Even though this trend is directly related to recent highway developments, the gold rush has done much to accelerate it. Before proceeding, therefore, it is worth taking a quick look at the different social, economic and environmental contexts of ranching as practised in both the savannah and forest. Taking this as our starting point we can then begin to appreciate the true significance of the transition noted above.

## CATTLE RAISING ON THE SAVANNAH AND IN THE FOREST

In the brief history of ranching outlined in Chapter 1, I show that savannahs were the first areas to be occupied by cattle breeders. These enterprises have grown over the course of the last century, and the descendants of pioneer ranchers have risen to positions of influence on the local political stage. Traditional ranching families own large swathes of the natural grasslands that extend across southeastern Pará, Maranhão, Amapá, and Roraima. For example, four politically influential families (Martins, Souza-Cruz, Brasil, and Mota) dominate the ownership of Roraima's savannahs. Most ranches on the savannahs have at least 1500 hectares of land, but may even exceed 10,000 (making them large, but not huge by Amazonian standards). Having said that, most of these families have multiple holdings, so may own in excess of 100,000 hectares. In spite of holding title to large tracts of land, Roraima's traditional ranching elite invests very little of its capital in its ranches, and uses outdated and inefficient management practices. Nutrient-poor soils and seasonal drought ensure that stocking rates remain extremely low, with seven to ten hectares of savannah devoted to each head of cattle. As a result, productivity is abysmal, with an average of six kilograms of beef being produced per hectare per year.[1] Nor have there been any major attempts to adopt more progressive management practices like selective breeding, artificial insemination (the standard herd reproduction rate is still only 40 per cent) and pasture improvement.[2]

Ranching in the forested areas is altogether different. To start with, the holdings tend to be much smaller than those of the savannah, usually between 500 and 2000 hectares. Only a proportion of the total area owned is actually grazed, and artificial pastures are usually stocked at rates of one animal unit per hectare. Thus, cattle raising in forest areas is more intensive than on the savannah and it is not constrained by the same nutrient and water deficiencies. Even so, the considerably higher rates of productivity of forest ranches (60–90 kg of beef per hectare per year) have to be weighed against the much higher investments per hectare that this type of ranching demands. Forest clearing alone costs approximately US $250 per hectare,[3] to which the price of grass seed and fertiliser must also be added. The higher capital investment in these ranches is, however, partly offset by the sale of timber to local sawmills, and by the gradual increase in the value of these roadside properties over the long term.

The social composition of ranchers in the forested area differs markedly from that of the savannah. As reported from other parts of the Amazon, these roadside ranchers comprise a new class of urban professionals, entrepreneurs and retailers, which dates from the late 1970s. They are all people who have found a niche in the Amazon's rapidly expanding cities, often working as government employees.[4] On becoming richer, they channel their profits from

---

1. Gianluppi (1991) p 1.
2. Of 178 ranches studied in a recent survey, only 26 per cent had planted pasture and 33 per cent had no type of enclosure in which the livestock could be herded (CIR 1992).
3. Cf Hecht's (1982) data from Pará, p 164.
4. This concurs with research findings from Rondônia. Of 100 public employees interviewed by Torres (1988) in the urban area of Machadinho,

the urban economy into medium-sized ranches (500–2000 hectares) along the newly-constructed highway network. These are generally progressive market-oriented ranching enterprises, into which more is invested than their larger traditional counterparts on the savannah.

While urban professionals probably own most of the roadside properties, another social group has emerged in recent years to form a second group of ranchers in the forested zone. These are capitalized smallholders, who constitute what appears to be an increasingly significant kulak class in Amazonia.[5] Clearly, most colonists have very limited access to capital. But, as the previous chapter illustrates, the small percentage who do manage to accumulate some money, either from salaried work (often in the municipal government) or through the *garimpo*, frequently invest it in ranching. Usually, these capitalized smallholders graze 30 to 100 head of cattle on one to five amalgamated lots (100–500 hectares) and tend to sell beef locally through informal outlets in colonization project towns.

As both the social and natural environment of the savannah is quite different to that of the forest, the shift in ranching from the former to the latter is not without its social and ecological impacts. On the savannah, seasonal burning aimed at stimulating the production of new shoots from the native bunch grasses favours their development over that of other tree and shrub species. Although many of the savannah trees are resistant to sporadic outbreaks of fire, they cannot tolerate repeated burnings, which tend to hinder their regeneration over the long term. This same problem is exacerbated by grazing, for livestock eat the shoots of germinating trees.[6] Hence savannahs, which originally may have contained quite a few scattered trees and shrubs, are transformed into open grasslands with virtually no trees. While this does reduce the species richness of what has been shown to be a highly diverse ecosystem, ranching

---

only one respondent did not own land or demonstrate interest in purchasing a holding. Noted in Milliken (1991) p 134.

5. For a more detailed discussion of this process in Rondônia, see Martine (1990).

6. This may be of concern to local, particularly indigenous groups, who depend upon the tree species of the savannah for economic purposes. The Macuxi of northern Roraima make great use of the Buriti palm (*Mauritania Felexuosa*) for construction and as a source of food, but after years of ranching in the area, the regeneration of this species appears to be hindered.

on the savannah still makes more sense from an ecological perspective than ranching in the forest. Here, biodiverse mature tropical forests, replete with intricate nutrient cycling mechanisms, are being destroyed and replaced by artificial pastures. Aside from the biodiversity issue, this process is known to reduce soil fertility and accelerate erosion even on gentle slopes. The degradation accompanying forest clearance for grazing is so severe that a large proportion, if not the majority, of pastures are abandoned within a decade. Ranchers are obliged to clear new swathes of forest each year just to ensure sufficient grazing for their herds. Nor are the consequences of this activity confined to the Amazon. Forest destruction on this scale is affecting climate in a way that is not clearly understood, both by altering exchanges of heat and moisture to the atmosphere and through its contribution to the greenhouse effect.

Ranching may also generate social tensions in both forest and savannah regions. Throughout the Amazon, groups of Indians, rubber tappers and smallholders find themselves competing with cows for particular areas of land. On the savannahs, groups like the Nambiquara in Rondônia, the Xavante in Mato Grosso, and the Kayapó in Pará, have come into conflict with ranchers over land rights. Nor is the situation any different in northern Roraima, where the Macuxi and Wapixana contest the ownership of natural grasslands with a well-established ranching elite. This longstanding conflict has sparked violent incidents in recent years as the Indians struggle to have two large areas of the savannah set aside as Indian reserves. The first, São Marcos, covering 707,459 hectares originally set aside as an 'Indian Colony', is due to be legally reclassified as a fully-fledged Indian reserve. The demarcation of the proposed Raposa/Serra do Sol Indian Reserve, which at 1,347,810 hectares is virtually twice the size, is much more contentious. There are 178 ranches situated within this area and even though many of them are over 50 years old, their owners would be evicted should the demarcation proceed. Just as significantly, the boundaries of the proposed reserve encompass all the states' productive diamond *garimpos*, with the unique exception of Tepequém. Because this area has been the traditional heartland of ranching and mining, the two bastions of the state economy, there is considerable local resistance to the proposed reserve. As I show in Chapter 6, those with most to lose from its demarcation, namely local politicians, ranchers and *garimpeiros*, are the reserve's most vociferous opponents.

While social conflicts on Roraima's savannahs mirror events in other grasslands throughout the Amazon, the same cannot be said of contemporary developments in the forested parts of the state. The expansion of ranching into the forests of southern Roraima is exceptional by Amazonian standards because it is not accompanied by rural violence. There are two main reasons for this. First, the ranching sector has been expanding less rapidly in Roraima than elsewhere and, therefore, does not represent such an aggressive agent of change. Secondly, unlike many other parts of the Amazon, there is very little competition for land in the forests of southern Roraima, and huge areas still remain unoccupied. Hence, if ranchers wish to establish large properties in this area, they are not obliged to appropriate the land from others. Therefore, while the rubber-tappers of Acre, the smallholders of Pará and Maranhão, and the Indians of Rondônia and Mato Grosso challenge ranchers over the use of forest lands, none of the same conflicts are currently apparent in the woods of southern Roraima.

# RANCHER BEHAVIOUR AND CAPITAL FLOWS

Notwithstanding the considerable differences in ranching on the savannah and in the forest, certain observations can be made about ranchers and their behaviour irrespective of the ecosystem in which they operate. Perhaps the most obvious concerns the prestige that land ownership still commands throughout Brazil. Owning land frequently underlies political authority, particularly in rural areas. A large proportion of Amazonian politicians are landowners. The ranchers' union, UDR (União Democrática Ruralista), claimed to have 75 deputies and 12 senators among its membership for the northern region.[7] In Amazonia, a rancher is also considered a frontier pioneer, furthering a national goal by bringing new areas into production. For these, among other reasons, Amazonian ranching continues to receive government subsidies in spite of the social and environmental costs of the activity.

The corporate tax incentives administered by SUDAM, giving tax credits of up to 75 per cent of investment to approved projects, have been the most contentious source of subsidized capital for Amazonian ranching since the 1970s. They were eventually withdrawn in 1989, but cheap loans, typically at 5–8 per cent above the rate of inflation, are still available to private ranchers from alternative

---

7. *Folha de Boa Vista*, 30 August 1987. In national terms, the 'northern region' covers all the states whose land surface falls entirely within Amazonia.

sources of rural credit. The most notable of these is a regional development fund called the FNO (Fundo Constitutional da Região Norte), which is administered by the Amazonian bank, BASA (Banco da Amazônia SA). In Roraima only six ranching projects were approved by SUDAM (which had a total of 631 projects in the Brazilian Amazon by 1985), and credit lines like the FNO represent a much more significant source of capital for the state's ranchers. Although agricultural and urban development also fall within the mandate of the FNO, the ranching sector receives the lion's share of the available budget. In 1991/2, 75 per cent of the FNO was allocated to the beef ranching sector.[8]

Rural credit is an important item in balancing the books of some ranches, but it is seldom the only source of capital available to ranchers. Many of Roraima's cattle producers have alternative business interests, often in the urban economy or the *garimpos*. Just over half (53 per cent) the 137 ranchers with properties in the proposed Raposa/Serra do Sol Indian Reserve have sources of income other than ranching.[9] Indeed, in many instances the ranch represents little more than a mechanism for banking the capital derived from these other ventures, as well as a device with which to capture cheap loans from rural credit programmes such as the FNO. Even though personal connections are an important influence on the distribution of rural credit, the agencies that provide this capital rarely check to see how it is being utilized. Thus it is easy for ranchers to divert these funds to other faster growing sectors of the local economy.[10]

So, just as smallholders transfer their labour into other activities when agriculture is in decline, ranchers tend to shift capital into alternative ventures as new investment opportunities arise. This is clearly illustrated in the behaviour of Roraima's ranchers during the gold rush. Throughout the 1980s, the local price of beef rose

---

8. Personal communication with BASA employee, 1991.
9. Of the 70 ranchers who had other business interests, 28 (40 per cent) had investments in the *garimpo*, 15 (22 per cent) were in commerce, ten (14 per cent) held jobs as civil servants, three (4 per cent) were doctors, three (4 per cent) served in the armed forces and two (3 per cent) were politicians. The remaining nine included two restauranteurs, two garage owners, a lawyer, a businessman, a tourist agent and an independent freight merchant.
10. Personal communication with agriculture secretariat, 1991. Exactly the same process has also been observed by Wesche and Bruneau (1990) p 51 in Itacoatiara, Amazonas.

considerably due to demand from the rapidly increasing migrant population. In such circumstances, one might expect ranchers to meet this demand and respond to the favourable market for beef by reinvesting a large proportion of the newly-raised capital in live-stock production. But, while the first half of the equation holds true, most ranchers preferred to reinvest the capital they had raised from carcass sales in other rapidly expanding sectors of the economy, most notably the *garimpo* or the urban retail and service sectors. In fact, some ranchers were so eager to take advantage of this favour-able economic climate that they embarked upon an indiscriminate slaughter of their herds, killing productive heifers along with infer-tile beasts, in order to raise capital at short notice.[11] The net result was a 40 per cent decline in Roraima's beef herd (from 360,000 to 220,000 between 1980 and 1989), accompanied by impaired produc-tivity in the aftermath of poor management practices.[12] Within a decade, the state had changed from being a net exporter of livestock to an importer of beef.

It is likely that the growing pressure to demarcate the indigenous reserves for the Macuxi exacerbated this trend, as the uncertainty of landownership on the savannah discouraged the reinvestment of capital in the area's ranches. By 1990, ranchers with holdings inside the proposed São Marcos and Raposa/Serra do Sol reserves were barred from receiving rural credit, and a number of them wanted to sell livestock and invest the proceeds elsewhere. Even so, some of those ranchers who had properties outside the proposed Indian reserves were slaughtering their herds at unprecedented rates. This suggests that the rapid growth of alternative economic oppor-tunities, offering considerable returns on short-term investment, was the overriding factor in drawing capital out of the state's ranch-ing sector. Whatever the dominant process, the economic changes associated with the gold rush led to a rapid contraction of the state's beef herd.

---

11. Gianluppi (1991). The percentage of clandestine slaughters also rose dramatically during the gold rush. Articles in the *Folha de Boa Vista* esti-mate that 40 per cent of all livestock was illegally slaughtered in the state (29 July 1987), which then rose to 70 per cent (18 July 1987). On 17 June 1988 it was reported that the government abattoir had not butchered a single beast for 30 days due to the lack of supply caused by unofficial slaughterings.
12. SUDAM/OEA/PROVAM (1991) p 38. However, even this estimate is probably conservative; records held by the state secretariat for agriculture suggest that the total herd was already less than 180,000 strong by 1986.

# THE RELATIONSHIP BETWEEN THE *GARIMPO* AND THE RANCH

While the mining boom presented new investment opportunities for the ranchers, some of the more powerful *garimpeiros* sought to transfer capital into ranching. Purchasing land is an attractive proposition to wealthy *garimpeiros* because they are able to use ranches to complement their mining activities. First, as was briefly mentioned in the previous chapter, *garimpeiros* can ride out the large fluctuations in mining incomes by buying and selling live-stock relative to their *garimpo* operations. In effect, they are able to reduce risk across their total portfolio by transferring capital from high-risk investments, like mining, into the more secure ranching economy.

Second, *garimpeiros* may purchase land with the specific intention of getting access to mineral deposits. Even though landownership does not give title to subsoil wealth under Brazilian law, such claims are normally respected in the informal-mining sector. This means that the landowner is usually recognized as the owner of any *garimpo* established on his or her property. Consequently, *garim-peiros* may try to buy land that they believe contains minerals. Where this does occur, such as in the Tapajós and southeastern Pará,[13] land prices may come to reflect the mineral, not the agricultural, potential of the soil.

Finally, as is illustrated below, a roadside landholding represents an ideal base from which to co-ordinate mining operations. Food, mining equipment and bulky minerals like cassiterite can all be stockpiled on the ranch and may be transported by light plane directly from the ranch's airstrip into the *garimpo*s. In the latter stages of the Roraima gold rush, the federal police tried to restrict air traffic to the *garimpo*s by monitoring flights from Boa Vista airport. One consequence of this was to push up the value of ranches in the urban periphery. Landholdings within a 50 kilometre radius of Boa Vista became strategically important airstrips, as they allowed traffic to continue flowing between the *garimpo*s and the city in spite of the ban.[14]

---

13. Butler (1985).
14. José Altino's invasion of Surucucús in 1985 provides probably the best illustration of this. Altino coordinated this operation, which involved over 30 *garimpeiros*, from a ranch located 30 kilometres east of Boa Vista. He continued to make use of the same ranch, which belonged to a prominent

The following account presents a more detailed analysis of the relationship between ranching and the *garimpo* and gives a clear indication of how *garimpeiro*s manage their ranches in relation to their mining activities.[15]

Robertino is a pilot who left his home state of Minas Gerais in 1978 to work in Pará. Following a year's employment flying light aircraft for ranchers, he became increasingly attracted by the opportunities available in the *garimpo*s. For one year he worked as a pilot servicing the mining camps around Redenção and Itaituba, before moving to Roraima in 1981. Impressed by the state's mineral potential, Robertino was one of the key figures to provide capital in the early stages of the gold rush and was responsible, together with his partner Alexandre, for constructing the first airstrip at Cambalacho in December 1986.

Unlike many less experienced ranchers, Robertino directly supervised his ventures in the *garimpo*s, and estimates that his air-taxi company and mining operations earned him approximately 120 kilograms of gold from 1986 to 1990 (US $1.8 million @ US $15 per gram). He reploughed about 65 per cent of this revenue into the state's *garimpo*s. The remaining 42 kilograms were principally invested in buying a new light aircraft for his air taxi company, and purchasing two ranches that had already been established: one of 1000 hectares near Apiaú and a second of 1800 hectares near Mucajaí (the latter was sold with 120 head of cattle on it and cost him approximately six kilograms of gold in 1988).

During the gold rush, Robertino used the Mucajaí property, which is located 50 kilometres south of Boa Vista along the state's only paved road, as a support base for his *garimpo* operations. He installed workshops to service both his aircraft and mining equipment and supplied his *garimpo* work-force with beef slaughtered on the property. As his returns increased, he improved the ranch infrastructure and expanded the size of his beef herd, which reached a peak of 250 head in early 1990.

---

local politician, Lourdes Pinheiro, throughout the gold rush as a support base for cassiterite extraction.
15. This account is distilled from an interview recorded on 7 February 1992 in Boa Vista.

Robertino channelled considerable investments into the three *'garimpeiro* reserves', which were briefly established within the intended Yanomami Indian area (see Chapter 2). To him, these legalized mining zones appeared to offer a secure future for his ventures. He commissioned another airstrip, sponsored further prospecting missions, and expanded both the capital and labour that were employed in the extractive process itself. As gold had been borrowed from friends to finance these investments, the subsequent closure of the *garimpos* left him heavily indebted. Obliged to repay his creditors at short notice, Robertino sold off mining equipment, lorries, a car, his ranch at Apiaú with 200 cows, and all bar 15 head of his beef herd at Mucajaí.

The example clearly illustrates that land-management practices on the ranch may be closely related to the co-ordination of mining operations. Stocking rates and investment decisions on Robertino's property all varied in response to changing external economic and political factors. Clearly, the land management practices he employed were totally divorced from the economics of long-term livestock production. This is a point worth noting because, if Robertino is only one of numerous people in the same situation, then the processes noted here have widespread ramifications for land use throughout the region.

Robertino himself was one of a select few (probably less than ten individuals), who recovered more than 100 kilograms of gold from the Roraima's *garimpos*. And, although a modest Amazonian ranch (something in the region of 1000 hectares) could probably be purchased for four or kilograms of gold (US $50,000–75,000), only a small percentage of *garimpeiros* accumulate enough capital to do this. We now enter the very uncertain world of pinning numbers to the informal-mining sector and it should be appreciated that the following estimates represent little more than informed guesses. Within the *garimpo* economy it is really only those people who are either *donos de garimpo*, *donos de máquinas* (including *balsas* and *dragas*), owners of light aircraft, owners of airstrips, or partners in gold trading companies who are in a position to accumulate, if lucky, five kilograms of gold (the price of a ranch). A very rough estimate suggests that in the Roraima gold rush there were possibly 100 *garimpos*, between 300 and 500 *máquinas* (including *balsas* and *dragas*), 25 registered gold dealers (though about the same number were operating illegally), approximately 300 light planes, and about

80 airstrips (many of which were jointly owned). These calculations suggest that at the very maximum, possibly 1000 individuals, or 2.5 per cent of the total workforce, would have had the potential to accumulate five kilograms of gold or more. But this number can probably be cut by half or even further reduced if it is considered: first, that many of the *garimpos*, airstrips, planes, *máquinas* and gold-trading shops belonged to the same people; and secondly, that the risks of mining, coupled with police intervention, prevented a large proportion of these entrepreneurs from obtaining five kilograms of gold. Even if we accept that about 400 individuals, representing 1 per cent of the total workforce, obtained five kilograms or more, a sizeable proportion of them will have chosen not to invest their gold earnings in ranching.

*Deforestation. Cattle and trees do not coexist.*

Nonetheless, these rough calculations make the crucial point that, because the gold-mining economy employs so many people, even the very small percentage of Roraima's *garimpeiros* who bought ranches with their gold earnings number in the hundreds. Besides, this process is not restricted to Roraima alone. USAGAL estimates that, even during the peak years of the late 1980s, Roraima's *garimpos* were responsible for only 10 per cent of Amazonian informal-sector gold production and employed the same percentage of the total Amazonian *garimpeiro* workforce.[16] There is plenty of evidence that successful *garimpeiros* in other parts of Amazonia invest their gold in ranching.[17] So, on a regional level, the scale of investments from mining into ranching may be ten times higher than in Roraima. This then provides a broad understanding of the size of capital flows into the ranching economy from gold mining. But, as we are interested in the extent to which ranching management practices are influenced by the mining sector, we must not neglect from our calculations those ranchers who invested in mining. It should be recalled that a large number of ranchers who had already established their properties with other sources of capital subsequently transferred resources into the mining sector. Once again this is extremely difficult to quantify, but even so, it does point to a significant relationship between ranching and informal-sector mining, which may have a widespread impact on land use and land management throughout Amazonia.

## GOLD, RANCHING AND DEFORESTATION

Four of Boa Vista's most influential *garimpeiros* were interviewed in February 1992 about transfers of gold made by them and their colleagues into ranching.[18] Two maps (Figures 4.1 and 4.2) were drawn up from these discussions. They plot 60 instances of *garimpeiros* working in the gold camps of the Yanomami Reserve buying ranches with gold. All these properties were estimated to be

---

16. Feijão and Pinto (1990)
17. See for example Uhl et al (1991).
18. The four respondents were: one owner of an air taxi company who also traded in cassiterite, one *dono de garimpo* who also owned an airstrip, one mineral dealer; and one owner of an air taxi company who was also *dono de garimpo* and owner of two airstrips. All the respondents, except the mineral dealer, were also *donos de máquinas* and all of them were land-owners. For more details of the interview procedure and verification of the data given, see MacMillan (1993a).

between 800 and 2000 hectares in size, with 27 of them in Roraima (Figure 4.1) and the remainder in other Amazonian states (Figure 4.2).

Figure 4.1 illustrates that only a small number of the ranches purhased by *garimpeiros* in Roraima are situated on the savannah. As I have noted, savannah properties tend to be much larger than foresed holdings, probably making them less appealing to potential *garimpeiro* purchasers. Even so, pressure to demarcate the Macuxi reserve on these grasslands was certainly an important factor in disuading potential investors from buying land in this area. Thus, most of the gold channelled into holdings was invested in properties located in the forested part of the state. And while ranching in this context does not necessarily exacerbate land conflict, it certainly does fuel deforestation. The key question here concerns the extent to which *garimpagem* accelerates forest clearance in its hinterland via the investment of gold earnings into ranching.

Deforestation is a complex subject. Contrary to popular images, over 85 per cent of the forest cover in the Brazilian Amazon is still standing. Over the past two decades, most of the clearing has occured in the southern part of the basin, notably in Rondônia, northern Mato Grosso, and southeastern Pará, which have been the foci of regional economic development. To date, development has proceeded at a much slower pace in the northern Brazilian Amazon (the states of Roraima, Amapá and Amazonas), where over 95 per cent of the forest cover is still standing. The case of Roraima is illustrative. By 1990 only 2 per cent (3800 km$^2$) of its natural forest cover (totalling 180,000 km$^2$) had been cleared.[19]

The real issue is not that the Amazon has been destroyed, but that it is in the process of being so. And for this reason it is the rate of deforestation, not the total area cleared, that demands closest attention. Here the picture looks less rosy, for deforestation rates have accelerated sharply in recent years. In the decade preceding the gold rush (January 1978 to April 1988) 2600 km$^2$ of Roraima's forests were removed, giving an average annual deforestation rate of 260 km$^2$ per annum. In comparison, 1100 km$^2$ of Roraima's forests were cleared over the 16-month period spanning the height of the gold rush (April 1988–August 1990).[20] The point is that, during the gold rush, the average rate of deforestation in Roraima

---

19. Fearnside (1991a).
20. Fearnside (1991a).

**Figure 4.1** *Map of Roraima showing the distribution of ranches purchased by garimpeiros with gold from the 1987–1990 gold rush*

*Garimpeiro*s with ranches marked on Figure 4.1

| | | |
|---|---|---|
| 01 Chico Malária | 07 Alcides  Figueiredo | 12 Manuelzinho |
| 02 Quincas Bonfim | (now dead) | 13 Oricado Branco |
| 03 Antonio Gomes | 08 Moraes | 14 Jeremias |
| 04 Kão | 09 FUNAI | 15 João Pau Preto |
| 05 Vando Acreano | 10 Paulo & Gonzago | 16 Luizão |
| 06 Vando Preto | 11 Robertino | 17 Geraldo |

| | | |
|---|---|---|
| 18 Boca Rica | 22 Daniel Souza | 26 Domingo Preto |
| 19 Manuel Martins | 23 Lourino | 27 Zezão |
| 20 Botinha | 24 Lazo Perninho | |
| 21 João Neto | 25 Chimarão | |

increased markedly (by 184 per cent) over that of the previous decade. The opposite is true of states in the southern Amazon (Pará, Rondônia, and Acre), where the average rate of forest clearance between 1988 and 1990 actually slowed relative to that of the previous decade. Indeed, since the same calculations made for Mato Grosso and Amazonas indicate that their average rate of deforestation in 1988–90 remained more or less the same as in 1978–88, it is only in Amapá and Roraima that a marked increase is observed. Interestingly enough, informal sector mining was the principal agent of development in both states during the late 1980s.

To understand exactly how *garimpagem* affects deforestation, it is necessary to take a detailed look at where the main areas of forest clearance are located in relation to the mining. By using satellite images it is possible to compare the spatial distribution of deforestation in Roraima at the end of the gold rush (in 1991) with that recorded three years before the rush had started.[21] The study confirmed that in the *garimpos* themselves only relatively small areas had been cleared for airstrips and mining. Outside the *garimpos*, in the rest of the state, most of the increase in deforestation was concentrated in and around agricultural colonization projects and along pre-existing roadsides. The only new front of forest clearance to emerge in Roraima during the gold rush is to the west of Alto Alegre, near the edge of the Yanomami Reserve. Here, some ranches had been established along the Apiaú and Mucajaí rivers, and squatters (*posseiros*) had simultaneously opened up an area along a forest trail between the same two rivers. Interviews (in 1991) with the *posseiros* revealed that many of them had been involved in the gold rush before they laid claim to agricultural land in this area. This suggests that the movements of labour and capital between the *garimpo* and its hinterland may be responsible for

21. Five LANDSAT TM images held by the IBGE in Rio de Janeiro, were studied: 31 July 1989 233x058, 31 December 1989 232x059, 22 September 1990 231x059, 22 September 1990 231x060, 15 October 1990 232x058. These were compared with a map of vegetation disturbance dating from 1984 (IBDF 1984).

opening up new areas of the forest for agriculture and ranching. Having said that, it is important to add a proviso. As most of the newly-cleared land (observed in this study) was along the pre-existing road networks, it appears that unless the *garimpo* actually stimulates the development of new roads there may be little change in the overall pattern of deforestation. Therefore, while certainly fuelling deforestation, *garimpagem* seldom generates totally new fronts of rain-forest clearance. This is because (as Figure 4.1 illustrates) much of the gold invested in ranching (and to a lesser extent smallholder agriculture) is not channelled into creating new pastures in remote areas, but is directed into further expanding roadside properties that already exist.

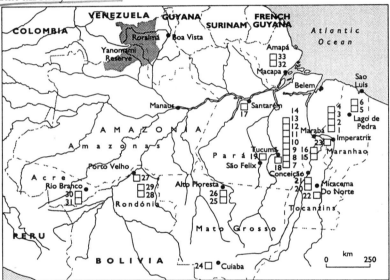

Source: Map compiled with interview data collected from *garimpeiros* in Boa Vista 1991–92

**Figure 4.2** *Map of ranches purchased in Amazonia Legal by garimpeiros working in the Yanomami Indigenous Reserve 1987–90*

*Garimpeiros* with ranches marked on Figure 4.2

| | | |
|---|---|---|
| 01 Zé Amaral | 07 Amadeus | 12 Rolando Kohl |
| 02 Minerinho | 08 Tarzã | Freitag |
| 03 Raimundo Nenêm | 09 Antonio Louro | 13 Gelicio |
| 04 Quincas Bonfim | 10 Zé Garopa | 14 Zé Anofre Robeiro |
| 05 Rubens | 11 Angelo Nadai | 15 Pé na Cova |
| 06 Baiano Formiga | | |

| | | |
|---|---|---|
| 16 José Martins de Fonseca | 22 Roberto Carlos | 27 Rubens |
| 17 Antonio Picão Neto | 23 Miguel & Cristovão Moleto | 28 Klaus Schultz |
| 18 Luiz Vilarinho | 24 Lauro Texeira | 29 Pedrinho |
| 19 Zé Flavio | 25 Jovair | 30 Adaiar Ruiz |
| 20 Zé Bigode | 26 Arnaldo José de Oliveira | 31 Santos Dumont |
| 21 Alouizo | | 32 José de Macapá |
| | | 33 João Neto |

Even though land values in Roraima are still the cheapest in Amazonia, the *garimpeiros* invested even greater sums in ranches situated outside the state, where the ranching economy showed more potential. Figure 4.2 maps just some of the properties that Roraima's *garimpeiros* purchased in other Amazonian states, making no mention of holdings that were also bought with *garimpo* incomes further afield in areas like the northeast.[22] The distribution of these ranches curves like an arc from Maranhão in the east to Acre in the west, mirroring the 'Amazonian frontier' of agricultural and ranching development introduced in Chapter 1. Throughout the 1970s and 1980s the most rapid rates of deforestation have been concentrated within this zone,[23] and the data presented in Figure 4.2 suggest that gold from the informal-mining sector may exacerbate this.

# INFORMAL SECTOR MINING AND LAND CONFLICT

Altering the pre-existing pattern of land tenure is perhaps the most significant impact that the mining sector can have on the rural economy over the long term. Changing landownership not only affects the management of any given piece of land, but, more importantly, it may alter the size of the productive units.

---

22. An example of this is provided by the *garimpeiro*, Luizinho da Agropécuaria, who had been mining in Roraima and Venezuela since 1973. By the late 1980s, he had become one of Roraima's wealthiest *garimpeiros*, owning ranches both in the state and in his native Ceará, where he farmed 5000 head of cattle on his 7500 hectare ranch at Inhamuns. He was a particularly influential figure in the early stages of the gold rush, owning one helicopter, two light aircraft, and 14 *balsas* on the Rio Uraricoera, and employing 200 people in the *garimpos* (Correio do Garimpo, November 1988).
23. Fearnside (1989) p 14.

In Roraima, the land market accelerated during the late 1980s, as both the supply and demand for land expanded simultaneously.[24] Landholdings came onto the market at an increased rate, both from large landowners who wanted to capitalize on the rising land values, and from other owners who were obliged to sell land for economic reasons, often to pay off debts incurred in the *garimpos*. Meanwhile, the demand for land increased as successful *garimpeiros* looked to invest newly accumulated capital in property, inflating the local land market. As Figure 4.1 illustrates, *garimpeiros* were particularly interested in properties on the outskirts of Boa Vista, where ranches fulfilled a strategic role in maintaining the flow of air traffic between the city and the gold fields. Land values also rose to the south and west of Boa Vista, notably in the municipalities of Alto Alegre and Mucajaí, because these areas offered relatively cheap land serviced by comparatively good roads. However, as the mining boom had buoyed up the value of rural property, land prices in certain areas reflected the strategic value of a site more closely than its agricultural potential. It is therefore not surprising that the bottom fell out of this artificial market following the closure of the *garimpos*.[25]

Although the rush only brought a temporary change to the state's land market, it nonetheless had a considerable impact on land tenure in this short space of time. This was due both to the accelerated pace at which land changed hands and to changes in the hierarchy of buyers and sellers in the local land market. Prior to the mining boom, public-sector employees and urban entrepreneurs (mainly retailers) were virtually the only members of society with sufficient income to purchase land, and so landholdings that came up for sale often passed into their hands. The *garimpos* effectively broke this oligarchy because mining incomes offered previously impecunious *garimpeiros* the chance to enter the land market as buyers. The ranches mapped in Figure 4.1 represent only the most spectacular examples of this process. At the other end of the scale were numerous *garimpeiros* who bought smallholdings with their gold earnings.

---

24. This discussion is based on an interview with a rural estate agent in Boa Vista in September 1991.
25. At the average value of US $21 per hectare, land in Roraima is still considerably cheaper than in any other Amazonian state. Funatura (1992) p 17.

This is an important point, for it indicates that *garimpo* incomes were financing land purchases at all levels of the rural property market. It therefore becomes difficult to assert that the *garimpo* necessarily exacerbates the amalgamation of landholdings in its immediate hinterland. Roraima is illustrative. A glance at Figure 4.1 indicates that some successful *garimpeiros* were purchasing large blocks of land along roadside locations. Indeed, many of these ranches were bought in the very colonization projects in which land was being set aside for smallholder agriculture. But, on the strength of these observations, it is wrong to argue that capital from the *garimpo* necessarily leads to the amalgamation of colonist plots into larger properties. For, although some large holdings were undoubtedly created in this way, many of the ranches the *garimpeiros* purchased had probably been established by other landowners in the years preceding the gold rush. While a proportion of these were no doubt large holdings from the start, others would have resulted from the gradual amalgamation of smallholdings, financed by alternative sources of capital. As we have already observed, Roraima's colonization projects have been steadily depopulated since their inception. Therefore, in the years preceding the gold rush, more capitalized landowners had been taking advantage of this out-migration to buy colonist holdings and merge them into small ranches. The overriding impression is that this process of land concentration was already well developed before gold mining appeared on the scene. Many of the ranches that passed into the hands of wealthy *garimpeiros* had already been established by the time the gold rush started.

This is supported by evidence collected from the colonization projects of Alto Alegre and PAD Anauá as part of the field survey described in the previous chapter. Colonist farmers with two or more plots of land were interviewed about how they came to own their holdings. Of 38 multiple-plot owners interviewed, only 17 (44 per cent) had been to the *garimpos*, and most of them (9 out of 17) had in fact expanded their landholdings prior to the rush with other sources of off-farm income. Less than a third (21 per cent) of those interviewed had actually expanded their landholdings with proceeds from the *garimpos*.

Here it should be recalled that capital from the *garimpos* was not only providing some landless *garimpeiros* with enough money to buy their own landholdings, but it was also enabling numerous other smallholders to resist the economic pressures that traditionally lead to the abandonment of homesteads. Thus, it may well be that the dominant processes driving the accumulation of land-holdings in settlement areas up to 1985 were actually reversed during the gold rush. It is therefore wrong to assume that the *garimpo* necessarily leads to a *de facto* increase in the concentration of landholdings in its hinterland.

This does not mean that people are not displaced from their land-holdings as a result of the *garimpo* economy. Indeed, we have already noted that a number of landowners, particularly the less capitalized smallholders, were forced to sell their properties to pay off mining debts. Furthermore, while it may not be as strong a process as certain authors have argued,[26] it is nonetheless true that some landholders do use *garimpo* earnings to expand the total size of their properties. In Roraima, there are still large areas of unclaimed lands (*terras devolutas*) allowing landless people the option of moving into the forest to stake out a claim to a new patch. Although there are no official records, the rate of spontaneous settlement in Roraima appeared to be gathering momentum during the late 1980s. Initially, these *posseiros* were displaced farmers and incoming migrants, but following the closure of the gold camps in 1990, large numbers of expelled *garimpeiros* swelled their ranks.[27]

The *posseiros* laid claim to land on the periphery of official colon-ization projects and established their homesteads at regular inter-vals along trails they had cut through the forest. In replicating the geometric layout of the official settlement schemes, the squatters believed that the eventual titling of their lands would be facilitated. By the early 1990s the *posseiros* were responsible for bringing sig-nificant areas of new land into cultivation and the government agencies were following in their wake, issuing land titles (INCRA), constructing feeder roads (DNER) and spraying the homesteads with insecticide to reduce malaria (SUCAM). In this way, the colonization projects of Apiaú and Confiança expanded rapidly. It was during this time that the land area between the Mucajaí and Apiaú rivers (which was noted in the study of deforestation above) was also being settled by *posseiros*.

The availability of land and the government's support for the *pos-seiros* probably helped defuse any social tensions that may have

---

26. See Filho (1984).
27. This return to agricultural production was encouraged by the state government, which made large areas of land available in colonization projects in the immediate aftermath of the rush. The reasons for this are discussed in greater depth in Chapter 6.

arisen from processes of land concentration and from the closure of the *garimpos*. Apart from the direct clashes between the *garimpeiros* and the Indian populations on whose land they were mining, there was virtually no evidence of the gold rush causing land conflicts in the state. As other Amazonian states typically have higher pressures on rural land, the lack of violence witnessed in Roraima is perhaps the exception rather than the rule for Amazonia as a whole. Throughout the 1980s, land tenure changes in Rondônia, northern Mato Grosso and especially southeastern Pará, generated vicious agrarian conflicts as smallholders defended their land claims from more powerful interests.[28] Furthermore, because these areas of rural violence are all in close proximity to *garimpos*, a connection has sometimes been drawn between the informal-sector mining economy and agrarian conflict. Even though it has been argued above that the links between the *garimpo* and land concentration are sufficiently complex to defy such a general assertion, the subject does merit closer attention.

Figure 4.2 illustrates that many of the ranches bought by Roraima's *garimpeiros* are clustered in southeastern Pará and along the state's eastern border with Maranhão and Tocantins – an area renowned for its rural violence. Here social conflict stems from the eviction of a rural peasantry by more capitalized ranchers, a process which had been fuelled by government incentives to the ranching economy since the 1970s.[29] However, even though SUDAM-administered tax concessions for corporate ranches were withdrawn in 1990, there is little sign that rural violence in the area has diminished. Indeed, data collected by the CPT (Comissão Pastoral da Terra) note that Pará hosted more rural violence than any other Brazilian state in 1991, two years after the SUDAM incentives to the ranching sector had been withdrawn. Thus, the pressure on land is as strong as ever, suggesting that, despite diminished access to public-sector capital, ranches continue to expand to the detriment of smallholders.

The data presented in Figure 4.2 show that gold from the *garimpos* of Roraima was one source of capital being channelled into ranching in this area during the late 1980s. Roraima's *garimpeiros* presumably saw the ranching economy of Pará and Maranhão as an attractive option due to its integrated road network and proximity to the major urban markets of Belém and Brasília. But their desire to

---

28. Schmink and Wood (1992); Hine (1991).
29. Hine (1991).

purchase land in these states was probably amplified by their previous knowledge of this area. It was noted in Chapter 2 that many of the *garimpeiros* who worked in Roraima originated from Maranhão and a large proportion had spent time in southeastern Pará during the early 1980s. Given that people usually buy land in areas with which they are already familiar, the geography of gold investments in ranching is undoubtedly related to the migratory patterns of the Amazonian *garimpo* workforce. Incomes generated from resource exploitation in northern Amazonia are being repatriated to the fringes of the eastern Amazon, from which many of the migrants originated.

On the strength of the data presented in Figure 4.2, it is virtually impossible to assess the real scale, let alone the consequences, of capital flows from Amazonia's *garimpos* into the ranching economy of Maranhão and southeastern Pará. A couple of relevant points can nonetheless be made concerning the nature of this process.

First, it has to be recalled that Roraima represents only 10 per cent of the Amazonian mining economy. If *garimpo* revenues from the other mining areas throughout Amazonia are also being channelled into the ranching economy of the southeastern Amazon, then the capital flows under study are clearly not insignificant.

Secondly, attention should be given to the size of ranch *garimpeiros* are likely to own. It is probable that their holdings are much smaller than the large corporate ranches that received the lion's share of SUDAM investments during the 1980s. So, although beef ranching in the area may still be expanding, the macro picture probably masks a shift in capital from larger to smaller ranchers. Clearly, further research is required before the true extent of this link between the mineral and ranching sectors of the Amazonian economy can be understood.

## DISCUSSION AND CONCLUSIONS

Capital is a prerequisite for economic development, yet although public-sector funds are often closely monitored in Amazonia, scant attention is currently paid to the sources and flows of private capital in the regional economy. This is nonetheless a relevant focus for contemporary research. As public investment in development decreases, private capital is likely to attain an increasingly important role in shaping regional development processes. Most of this capital is generated within the informal sector, not only from the *garimpo*, but increasingly in the Brazilian Amazon from the cocaine trade. Furthermore, as this money is often banked in rural and urban properties, rather than in financial institutions, a large proportion of it never passes into the formal sector of the economy. In these circumstances, the government's ability to define the pattern of regional development is severely compromised.

If we are to obtain a realistic understanding of the forces shaping land use, greater attention must be paid to the geography of capital flows between the *garimpo* and other activities in the rural economy. In this chapter we have seen that this relationship may have a profound effect on the management practices of rural producers. However, even though this is an important process, which shapes the extent of the *garimpo*'s impact on the region's rural economy, it is rarely considered in contemporary evaluations of Amazonian development. A need exists for planners to expand the remit of current environmental and social impact assessments so that the consequences of capital flows from one activity to another are no longer ignored. For example, if the financial returns from mining ventures (or logging operations) are invested directly into ill-managed ranching, this information should be incorporated into any analysis of the total non-economic costs associated with the initial development.

Finally, here we see ranchers tailoring their management practices more closely to external economic and political changes than to the internal productive economics of cattle raising. This observation is of particular concern to agronomists working towards a more widespread adoption of long-term land-use strategies in the region. Agroforestry and silvicultural systems are being developed on the basis of their sustained yields and are promoted in accordance with the income they generate over the long term. But, while such initiatives represent laudable attempts to reduce the environmental degradation that accompanies current Amazonian farming practices, they are poorly suited to the priorities expressed by many of the region's landowners. In crude terms, these concerns relate to protecting savings from erosion by inflation and to the flexibility with which capital can be either injected or withdrawn from the system at short notice. Perhaps the largest challenge for those concerned with the environmental impacts of current Amazonian land uses is to find an appropriate alternative to cattle raising that fulfils these objectives.

## Summary

First, there is evidence from all over the Amazon that ranches are often used as vehicles for banking capital.

Second, there were clear links between the mining and ranching economies of Roraima during the gold rush. Ranchers invested in the *garimpo*s and *garimpeiro*s purchased ranches. This relationship is not exclusive to the state in which the mining occurred.

Third, the Roraima rush therefore came to influence the management practices of ranchers throughout Amazonia, which were often more closely related to external socioeconomic changes than to the longer-term productive economics of cattle raising.

Fourth, capital flows between the mining and ranching economies have ramifications for the structure of land tenure, and the rate of deforestation throughout rural Amazonia. The extent and strength of these processes is related to the precise geography of these capital flows.

And finally, if the current trend of diminished public-sector investment in Amazonia is sustained, the *garimpo* and other sources of private capital are likely to become increasingly important determinants of regional development processes.

# Chapter 5

# Local Prospects: Riverine Dwellers, Indians and Mining

*Adapting to change. Raimundo, a fisherman from the Xeriuni, confronts urban life in Caracaraí.*

In the previous two chapters we saw how smallholders and ranchers were drawn into the gold rush for predominantly economic reasons. Other groups were slower to get involved and we now examine why this was the case. In other words, we look at how the riverine (*caboclo*) population of the lower Rio Branco and the Macuxi Indians of the savannah reacted to the Roraima gold rush. Even though they behaved in quite different ways, it becomes apparent that some common elements shaped their responses to the various opportunities arising from the rush.

## RIVERINE DWELLERS AND THE *GARIMPO*

Government directives throughout the 1980s have considerably altered the lifestyles of the *caboclos* who inhabit the lower Rio Branco and its tributaries. At the start of the decade, an agricultural model, similar to the one developed for colonization projects along the federal highways, was applied in these riverine areas. Traditionally, the *caboclos* resided in houses dispersed along the river banks — a settlement pattern adapted to the demands of extractavism. However, in the early 1980s the state government (notably the Secretary of Agriculture) encouraged them to move into planned communities, on the grounds that this would facilitate the provision of health care and education in these remote areas. Typically, communities were established on sites on which there was already a cluster of houses, although in two cases totally uninhabited areas were settled. The *caboclos* were given materials with which to construct new houses in a grid pattern and were allocated a plot of land nearby (usually 100 hectares) to cultivate. In the largest of these communities, Santa Maria de Boiaçu, migrant families from the northeast were also settled and the small town became an agricultural colony. It was anticipated that a 130-kilometre road would link Santa Maria de Boiaçu to the BR 174, but although this connection had been planned in 1980, it was still incomplete in 1991. Diesel-powered electricity generators and tractors were provided for each of the new settlements, but by the end of the decade few of them still worked. Extension workers from the agricultural secretariat encouraged the *caboclos* to devote less time to fishing and hunting and to concentrate on agricultural production.

Riverbank settlement projects like this reflect many of the same values that were enshrined in the highway-building programme of the 1970s; in this respect they were certainly not restricted to Roraima.[1] But, as with the roadside colonization projects, government support for these river-bank settlements waned rapidly

---

1. See for example, Schmink and Wood (1992: 276–340) for an excellent discussion of events in São Felix do Xingu, Pará.

once they had been established. By the mid-1980s the assistance Roraima's *caboclo*s had been promised for the production and transport of agricultural goods had evaporated. Left to fend for themselves, they switched back to extractavism and continued as before. Well, not entirely, because new legislation introduced by the environmental protection agency, IBAMA (Instituto Brasileira de Meio Ambiente e Recursos Naturais), served to classify many of their traditional hunting and fishing practices as illegal. The sale of turtles and bush meat, which represents an important source of income to *caboclo*s, was prohibited. By the end of the 1980s IBAMA was enforcing these laws, as well as more rigid fishing regulations, with alarming vigour.

The economic problems confronted by the Amazon's *caboclo* population were exacerbated by a simultaneous decline in the value of extracted products. Rubber, the very bastion of the region's extractive economy, is a case in point. In the mid-1980s, the Brazilian government stepped in to subsidize rubber production to protect tappers from a steady decline in the value of their product. This subsidy certainly benefited the small number of Roraima's *caboclo*s who travel to Amazonas on a seasonal basis to cut rubber. But it offered little respite to the economic hardship faced by the majority of the state's *caboclo*s who depend on fishing, brazil-nut gathering and sorva tapping for most of their income. As true rubber *(Hevea brasiliensis)* is scarce in Roraima, sorva (*Couma* sp.) is historically the most important non-timber vegetable product extracted in the state. At the start of the 1980s, its production measured in tons was typically tenfold that of brazil nuts, the second main product.[2] However, by 1988 the price of sorva latex had dropped to such a low that the traders would no longer venture off the main channel to purchase it. This meant that the unique link between some of the more remote communities and the urban market was effectively severed.

These combined pressures encouraged *caboclo*s to look for alternative sources of income and a large number of families moved away from the lower Rio Branco to seek urban employment. This reflects a pattern that has been observed throughout rural Amazonia since the 1970s.[3] In the case of Roraima, the rates of out-migration from *caboclo* communities during the 1980s peaked between 1987 and 1990. Settlements that had existed on the banks

---

2. IBGE (1980—84).
3. See Ayres (1992); Torres and Martine (1991).

of the Rio Branco in 1980 were abandoned by the end of the decade. Accounts from residents suggest that the riverine population of the lower Rio Branco and its tributaries declined by at least 60 per cent from 1980 to 1991.

Families that remain along the river banks (approximately 100 households in 1991) continue to live off the production of manioc flour (*farinha*), hunting and fishing. To avoid being fined by IBAMA, the *caboclo*s have developed more subtle techniques for catching turtles, which, along with dried fish, still provide an income of sorts in the summer months. Although river traders are increasingly reluctant to purchase turtles (on account of IBAMA's legislation), *caboclo*s are able to continue selling them, albeit in reduced numbers, to the crews of barges which regularly ply the Rio Branco transporting fuel and construction materials between Manaus and Boa Vista. As mentioned above, a few young men from the lower Rio Branco also migrate seasonally to the rivers Jaú and Uniní (both tributaries of the Rio Negro in Amazonas) to extract rubber in the rainy season. Otherwise most households received a cash income from the annual brazil-nut harvest and the occasional sale of manioc flour and dried fish. Apart from this, a handful of people are employed as nurses, teachers, radio operators and, in one case, an agricultural technician, and so receive government salaries.

It is remarkable that hardly any of the *caboclo*s sought work in the *garimpo*s when they were faced with an increasingly difficult economic situation on the river bank. Only one person from a total of 71 *caboclo* households interviewed along the lower Rio Branco and its tributaries, went to the *garimpo*s during the gold rush. Other than this, only four people from the riverine agricultural community of Santa Maria de Boiaçu (estimated population of 280) were known to have gone mining. Two of them were northeastern colonist farmers settled there at the start of the 1980s. Thus, less than 2 per cent of all the residents inhabiting the banks of the Rio Branco and its tributaries in 1991 participated in the 1987–90 gold rush.

This is all the more surprising because reports from other parts of Amazonia note riverine people behaving in a totally different way. During the 1960s, *caboclo*s provided much of the initial labour in the original placer mines of the Tapajós.[4] Similarly, contemporary studies note that members of *caboclo* households near Altamira on

---

4. For an account of events in the Tapajós, see Gaspar (1990). For the Xingu around Altimira see Clara da Silva (1991).

the Rio Xingú work in local *garimpo*s. Clearly, there is nothing intrinsic about the lifestyle of Amazonian *caboclo*s to make them averse to mining. The situation in Roraima is therefore unusual, particularly when the geography of the situation is considered. For, although the principal mining areas were not very close to the *caboclo*s' houses (as they are along the Rio Madeira in Rondônia, where *caboclo*s work in the *garimpo*s), they were not that far from the areas in which the *caboclo*s worked. One centre of *garimpo* activity was in the headwaters of the Rio Catrimani, which is one of the main sorva-producing rivers (although it is now permanently inhabited only by the Yanomami). Furthermore, in the course of the gold rush, *garimpeiro*s had also ventured up other tributaries to go prospecting, which were populated by *caboclo*s like the Xeriuini.

It is therefore surprising that more *caboclo*s did not turn to the *garimpo*s to solve their economic difficulties. They mentioned that the violence and disease associated with mining dissuaded them from entering the *garimpo*s. Unlike the colonists, who tended to justify their decision not to go mining on economic terms, the *caboclo*s were quite prepared to admit that they were scared. Others mentioned being reluctant to leave their families, and pointed out that a long absence would jeopardize other activities, such as producing manioc flour or gathering brazil nuts. A lack of experience in mining, the expense of entering the *garimpo*s, the inherent risks, the illegality of the practice and the threat of Indian attack were among the more pragmatic responses given.

However, while the *caboclo*s often justified their minimal participation in the gold rush on ethical grounds (inferring that it was wrong to interfere with the Indians, leave the family, or indulge in a violent and illegal practice), it is misleading to assume that their (perhaps inflated) morality was the only obstacle standing between them and the mines. Notwithstanding their geographic proximity to the *garimpo*s, other factors actually served to constrain their entry into the mines. In the manual phase of the *garimpo*s, mining is restricted to the dry season. As this coincides with the brazil-nut harvest and the peak fishing season, the *caboclo*s of the lower Rio Branco are unlikely to have left for the *garimpo*s during what is their most productive time of year. Even if some of them had wanted to go mining at this early stage, they would probably have needed outside help to discover the correct access routes to the gold fields. As the post-1986 gold rush developed, air transport from Boa Vista eroded the seasonality and inaccessibility of mining. But flights into the *garimpo*s were not only very expensive, they were also dominated by urban merchants, whom the *caboclo*s did not know. Unlike smallholders, the *caboclo*s rarely possess anything as valuable as cows, which they could sell at short notice to pay for the flight. In order to enter the mines, therefore, most of them would be obliged to accept an air fare into the *garimpo*s on credit (ten grams of gold), and subsequently repay the owner of the air taxi company out of their mining incomes.

Under such an arrangement, the *caboclo*s are immediately disadvantaged on two counts. First, with their minimal involvement in both the *garimpo*s and the urban economy of Boa Vista, they know very few people who would be prepared to advance them an air fare. *Garimpo* entrepreneurs/patrons who do offer passages in this way usually distribute them only to people they know or to individuals recommended to them by friends. Secondly, the characteristic trading relations of the riverine economy make *caboclo*s reluctant to become indebted to strangers. The economic influence of patrons and river merchants typically extends along lines of kinship, and fictive kinship, so that virtually all transactions along the river bank are underpinned by personal bonds. In many ways, the disadvantageous economic terms that *caboclo*s usually accept under debt bondage (*aviamento*) are offset by the security inherent in establishing a social tie through trade with an influential patron.[5] However, a *caboclo* entering the *garimpo* is obliged to accept a debt that is not underwritten by any social relationship with the creditor and is, in this way, denied some degree of insurance against the contract. Even though the large number of gold dealers ensure that *garimpeiro*s are never exposed to the same monopolistic prices characteristic of the riverine economy, the *caboclo* is nonetheless making a commitment to the unknown on what appear to be highly unfavourable terms.

It is illustrative that the only resident who left the Rio Xeriuini (one of the Rio Branco's most populated tributaries) to go mining was personally invited to do so by a local politician who had befriended him. He was advanced the air fare and repaid it from the income he gained constructing timber rafts (*balsa*s) in the *garimpo*s on the Rio Uraricoera. In this way, he generated sufficient capital to purchase a fishing boat and outboard motor and became a fisherman in the port of Caracaraí. His success in the *garimpo*s encouraged others to try and enter, but they were effectively

---

5. For a more detailed discussion of barter and trading relationships in rural Amazonia, see Hugh-Jones (1992).

thwarted because they did not have similar contacts among suitably influential people. His cousin, Domingo, also went to Boa Vista in a vain attempt to secure an air fare to the *garimpos*. He neither knew, nor obtained an introduction to, any of the *garimpo* gatekeepers. As Domingo himself explained:[6]

> I reckon that there are a lot of people who are interested [in going to the *garimpos*], but the difficulty comes when you arrive in Boa Vista ... it's really hard. You've got to know a *garimpeiro* patron and I just don't know anybody like that, so I never got anywhere.

Thus, *caboclos* are no less attracted to the material benefits of gold mining than any other rural producers. And, although they may have reservations about the dangers or ethics of mining (which many of them stress), their low rate of participation in the activity is also a reflection of the geographical, economic and social constraints that stand between them and *garimpagem*.

Indeed, the absence of a social relationship between the extractive and *garimpo* economies was probably the key factor in preventing larger-scale *caboclo* involvement in Roraima's *garimpos*. This is a marked change from early developments in the Tapajós gold fields, when traders such as Nelson Pinheiro formed powerful links between the two sectors of the rural economy. He recruited many of the original *garimpeiros* from the rubber estates along the tributaries of the Tapajós, and their work relations remained similar to those existing in the extractive economy.[7] A study of the Itaituba elites reveals that, following Nelson Pinheiro's lead, a number of rubber patrons from the Tapajós subsequently diversified into *garimpagem*, which presumably facilitated the transfer of labour from extractive to mining activities in the area.[8]

Despite living nearby, Roraima's *caboclos* could not easily reach the *garimpos* on their own (as they could on the Rio Madeira), nor were the relevant social bridges available to facilitate access (as there were among the Tapajós). Consequently, they turned to the other options available through their familial and social networks and migrated to urban areas. The movement of Manuel Candido, the most influential patron in the Rio Branco's extractive economy, to the fishing port of Caracaraí in 1987 was particularly significant

---

6. Interview recorded on 7 November 1991 in Santa Maria de Xeriuini.
7. Gaspar (1990) pp 42–3.
8. Miller (1985).

in opening new opportunities to *caboclos* at this time. Responding to the falling price of extracted products (notably sorva), Manuel Candido stopped trading along the Rio Branco and instead purchased an ice-making plant and a small fleet of fishing boats in Caracaraí. He was capitalizing on a rapidly-expanding market, precipitated by growing urban demand for fish (principally in Boa Vista) during the gold rush years. Although many of the *caboclo* families along the lower Rio Branco already had strong ties with Caracaraí, Manuel Candido's new investment greatly accelerated their migration to the town and, in his new fishing enterprise, he came to employ many of the people with whom he had previously traded. The *caboclos* might equally well have been drawn into the *garimpos* had he instead chosen to invest his capital in the mining economy.

# URBAN GROWTH AND RURAL–URBAN MIGRATION

As a result of these events, Roraima's *caboclos* did not leave the river bank for the *garimpos*, but instead moved to the city. Here they joined the ranks with millions of new arrivals in the Amazon's already swollen urban centres. The gold rush itself has done much to stimulate the explosive growth of cities in northern Brazil. Marabá, Itaituba, Redenção, Imperatriz and Alto Floresta all mushroomed in the 1980s on the back of the informal-mining economy. Roraima is no exception, rates of urbanization have increased from 43 per cent in 1970, to 64.6 per cent in 1990.[9] Alternative data, extrapolated from the number of residences, estimate that in the first half of 1991, 72 per cent of the state's inhabitants were residing in urban areas.[10] The real figure probably lies somewhere between the two, but the important point is that, in Roraima, as in Amazonia as a whole, the trend towards urbanization was so strong that, by the end of the decade, more people were living in cities than in rural areas.

Boa Vista, the nucleus of the gold rush, absorbed the greater part of these changes. By 1991 it was 23 times the size of either Caracaraí or Mucajaí, which both vied for the title of the state's second largest

9.  IBGE (1992).
10.  SUCAM (1991). For a broader analysis of demographic trends in the Amazon, see Bogue and Butts (1989).

city (each has a population of about 5100). Business boomed.

*A new housing scheme on the edge of Boa Vista.*

SEICOM, the state secretariat for industry and commerce (Secretária da Econômia, Industria e Comerçio) registered 3779 new enterprises in the formal economy alone between 1987 and 1989; these were principally in the service sector and retail trade. This compares with a total of only 602 commercial establishments in Roraima as a whole in 1980.[11] It is revealing that the larger proportion of migrants were not employed directly in the gold-mining economy itself, but in other informal-sector activities. A survey of 410 households in Boa Vista conducted in February 1991 by Abers and Pereira notes that 46 per cent of the 852 workers they

---

11. IBGE (1983), quoted in Abers and Pereira (1992).

interviewed were employed in the informal sector. Only 13 per cent of the total sample were directly associated with the *garimpo*. From this Abers and Pereira draw the important conclusion that, 'While the *garimpo* is significant for urban growth, activities related only indirectly to the gold rush are responsible for most of the urban economy's dynamism.'[12]

Abers's own work suggests that although the majority of people who came to Boa Vista during the gold-boom years had migrated from other urban areas, many of them were originally rural dwellers. Having migrated from the countryside to the city, they then formed part of a large urban workforce, which tends to move from city to city as new economic opportunities arise:[13]

> While about half of the migrant household heads [interviewed in Boa Vista in 1991] were born in rural areas, the majority had significant experiences living in cities before moving to Boa Vista. While rural to urban migration plays an important role in their migration patterns, rural out-migration represents only the first step in a long history of otherwise largely urban migration experience.

Given that the initial transition from countryside to city may initiate a lifetime on the road, it is worth having a closer look at the rural–urban migration generated by the gold rush. Such a perspective reveals that even though rural–urban migration has significant repercussions on people's subsequent migratory behaviour, it is seldom a clearly-defined process. The experience of Roraima's *caboclos* illustrates that people may move between the rural and urban economies for many years without necessarily becoming permanently incorporated into the urban labour force.

To understand the forces behind rural–urban migration in contemporary Amazonia we will look at the experiences of 19 households that moved to Caracaraí from the Rio Xeriuini in the late 1980s.[14] The *caboclos* themselves estimate that there was a total of 58 households living on the Xeriuini in 1985; therefore in a period

---

12. Abers and Pereira (1992). This also points to the considerable multiplier effect associated with *garimpagem*.
13. Abers (1992) p 49.
14. Of these 19 households, 15 (79 per cent) had migrated from the Xeriuini to Caracaraí between 1988 and 1991, three had moved since 1986, and only one had resided in the city for over five years. This discussion is based on interviews with *caboclos* on the Xeriuini and in Caracaraí between November 1991 and January 1992.

of five years, one third of the river's population had migrated to Caracaraí. This not only brought considerable changes to the three small communities the migrants moved away from (Santa Maria de Xeriuini, Terra Preta, and Lago Grande), but also altered the urban morphology of Caracaraí. These households are linked by strong kinship ties,[15] and they built their houses close together, thus creating a new suburb known locally as the Bairro de Xeriuini.

A simple comparison of household economics on the river bank and in the city is revealing. The main sources of employment for the 19 *caboclo* families in Caracaraí are commercial fishing (ten of the households contain somebody employed as a fisherman) and manual docking work – unloading the barges that bring fuel, construction materials and some foodstuffs up from Manaus to Boa Vista. There is only one head of household employed exclusively as a docker because it is common for individuals to substitute fishing for docking on a seasonal basis. The barges can only get to the port when the river is full, which is also the period of maximum fishing restrictions (April–September). Principal sources of income for the remaining families include public sector salaries (five), petty commerce (one), boat building (one) and construction (one), though it should be understood that most families have members employed in a variety of informal-sector activities simultaneously.

A *caboclo* household in Caracaraí (two adults and six children) calculates that monthly groceries cost US $150 (this excludes transport, rent, bills and entertainment), which is roughly double that of their rural counterparts. But these greater outlays are offset by urban wages, which are considerably higher. During the five-month fishing season, a fisherman possessing his own boat and motor may receive a maximum revenue of US $640 a month, although a proportion of this has to cover boat maintenance and the overheads of the trip.[16] Fishermen permanently employed on other people's boats can earn between US $270 and $400 a month over the same period, depending on their position of responsibility within the crew.[17] Dockers estimate that they earn US $250 a month for the five months of the busy wet season, but this is reduced to US $30

---

15. For example, one respondent had a blood relative in all bar one of the other 18 households that had moved to Caracaraí.

16. Only one head of household interviewed possessed his own boat and he was the one mentioned earlier who had been to the *garimpo*. He had obtained it with the money he earned in the mines.

17. These data are underpinned by an expanding market for fish, resulting from the considerable demand generated by Boa Vista's rapid growth.

per month or less during the dry season. Government employees, such as gardeners, primary-school teachers and nurses, typically receive US $50–70 a month, but during the early 1990s their income began to decrease in real terms as public sector wages failed to keep pace with inflation.

It is, however, virtually impossible to calculate total family income from these data. Most households seek to maximize revenue by spreading available labour across different sectors of the urban economy in response to seasonal and political fluctuations. Again, the extent of an individual's social networks is of key importance in determining the ease of movement between jobs. The salient point is that, during the gold rush, urban wages were considerably higher than incomes from the riverine economy. The following example of a *caboclo* household's balance sheet on the Rio Xeriuini is intended to illustrate the disparity between urban and rural incomes. The data presented in this example were derived from one particular household and fit within the broad limits of production recognized both by the *caboclo*s themselves and by other studies of the Amazonian extractive economy.[18]

A household of two adults and four children on the Rio Xeriuini estimates that it can produce up to 100 sacks of manioc flour (one sack is 50 kilograms or 77 litres) and 100 barrels (*barricas*) of brazil nuts in a good year (one barrel weighs between 72 and 78 kilograms when fresh, and 60 kilograms when dry). Normal production is estimated at 60 sacks of manioc flour and 50–80 barrels of brazil nuts, of which 30 sacks and 50–80 barrels are typically sold. At 1992 prices paid by traders on the river bank (US $7 per *barrica* of brazil nuts, and US $15 per sack of manioc flour), this yields an average monthly income of US $66–84 (although it should be recalled that income is not evenly distributed throughout the year). This may be supplemented by the sale of salted fish and turtles during the dry season, but the market for these products is quite limited. On the Xeriuini, commodity prices are typically 20–50 per cent higher than in Caracaraí, but the riverine household consumes much less marketed produce than the urban one. The household under study estimates that its monthly grocery bill is in the region of US $50 and includes salt, sugar, matches, biscuits, powdered milk, coffee, cooking oil, soap and radio batteries.

---

18. Even so, there are problems with collecting this sort of data from verbal accounts. For other studies of *caboclo* household economics see Ayres (1992); Wagley (1953); and Sizer (1991).

These calculations suggest that the household generates a monthly surplus income of US $16–34, most of which is spent on items like fuel, tools, alcohol, tobacco, shooting and fishing equipment, as well as some medicines. However, it is quite likely that in many cases riverine producers will not hold any of this modest income in their hands. Direct barter still accounts for a large proportion of river-bank transactions, and traders often reduce payment by 15 per cent if the producers demand cash payment for the sale of their goods. Besides, as many *caboclo*s still purchase goods on credit from river traders, their incomes are significantly eroded by usurious rates of interest, which in some cases exceed 40 per cent per month. Therefore, even though this comparison illustrates that annual household incomes in Caracaraí are about four to six times those of the Rio Xeriuini, rural dwellers are unlikely to see a fraction of the cash income that their urban counterparts receive.

This gives some insight into why the *caboclo*s were so keen to move to Caracaraí during the gold rush. But the key question in all this is whether they are likely to stay in the city and become part of the transient urban labour force identified by Abers. Or will they move back to the predominantly subsistence livelihood of the Rio Xeriuini when the urban economy contracts? It might be more appropriate to ask *if* they can go back. The crux here lies in whether their subsistence option has been foreclosed by their initial migration to the city, or, to use Marxist terms, whether rural–urban migration is synonymous with proletarianization. In certain parts of Brazil the pressure on land is so great that, once the peasantry is either forced off or moves off the land, that is it; they cannot return. Migrants caught in such a situation have little alternative but to embrace an urban livelihood. Smallholders in the northeast and south of Brazil, squatters (*posseiro*s) in southeastern Pará, and some rubber tappers in Acre, are all appropriate examples.

But in other areas, particularly in northern and western Amazon, the struggle for land is less intense. Riverine peoples around Belém and along the middle reaches of the Solimões are know to move frequently between urban and rural economies.[19] Thus, there is certainly nothing extraordinary about the antics of Roraima's *caboclo*s, who regard cities as integral to their economic domain as river banks. Recognizing that *caboclo*s often move freely between urban and rural areas is significant, because it suggests that many

---

19. For Belém, see Nugent (1991). For the middle Solimões, see Ayres (1992).

of them will leave Caracaraí for the river bank if the urban economy starts to falter. As their relatives defend their (usufruct) claim to the land on the Xeriuini in their absence, they are free to return at any moment. Indeed, three *caboclo* migrants employed as badly-paid public-sector workers in Caracaraí intended to return to the Xeriuini for the 1992 brazil-nut harvest. Clearly, rural–urban migration in this context is synonymous with movement between the subsistence and exchange spheres, which is so characteristic of peasant economics.

The point to be drawn from all this is that only some of the households that moved into the cities during the gold rush actually made the crucial first step noted above. It is therefore wrong to assume that the sudden growth of the urban population directly reflects the process of proletarianization. Without a doubt, some do undergo this transformation and it would be interesting to return to Caracaraí in ten years' time and find out what proportion that is. But whatever the figure, the gold rush itself can only be held partly responsible. The forces that serve to push peasants off the land are probably far more significant in this game than those that draw them to the city. Here, a highly inequitable distribution of land, agrarian violence, drought and declining agricultural prices have been eroding the rural peasantry for over 20 years (most notably in the northeast).

## INVOLVEMENT OF THE MACUXI INDIANS IN THE *GARIMPOS*

Comparing the behaviour of the Macuxi Indians with that of the *caboclo*s offers an insight into how two different social groups react to similar socioeconomic changes. Like the *caboclo*s, the Macuxi produce for both subsistence and exchange. They participate in a local economy dominated by extensive kinship and fictive kinship ties, and engage in a whole range of economic activities. These include hunting, fishing, agriculture, diamond mining, urban employment and working as cowhands on the savannah ranches. Hunting and fishing are for domestic use only, as is the largest share of agricultural production. Therefore, apart from the limited sale of manioc flour, it is the diamond *garimpo*s, ranches and urban employment that provide the Macuxi with virtually all their cash income.

Unlike the *caboclo*s, the Macuxi have a long history of informal-sector mining. For over 70 years they have provided much of the labour for the diamond *garimpo*s of the savannah. They have been involved in all stages of the mines' development from the early workings in the 1920s, through the introduction of rudimentary diving equipment in the 1950s, to the more recent period of semi-mechanized mining in the 1980s. Notwithstanding a dramatic influx of non-Indian *garimpeiros* to this area following their expulsion from the Yanomami Reserve, the Macuxi still accounted for 20 per cent of the total workforce of the savannah diamond *garimpo*s in 1991.[20] The mining camps are literally on their doorstep, often less than an hour's walk from their villages. Indeed, most Macuxi villages contain residents who work periodically in the diamond mines, and at least five villages manage and run sets of their own mining equipment (*máquinas*) in the *garimpo*s.[21]

Despite this long involvement in the local mining economy, the Macuxi did not flock to the gold fields of western Roraima during the 1987–90 rush.[22] To understand why this is so, it is worth considering the differences between the diamond *garimpo*s of the savannahs and the gold camps in the Yanomami Reserve. The two types of mining differ most obviously in accessibility. The Macuxi can walk or ride (either by horse or more commonly by bicycle) to the diamond mines and face none of the expenses or difficulties that a trip to the gold *garimpo*s would incur. This ease of access also facilitates the policing of the diamond *garimpo*s, which are considerably less violent than the more isolated gold-mining areas. Comparatively stable communities with permanent houses have been established in the diamond *garimpo*s, and there are many more women and children in these areas than are ever encountered in the gold mines. Overall, the tension and aggression of the gold mines is generally absent in the diamond *garimpo*s and, as a result, mining on the savannah tends to be a much more relaxed affair.

But this also reflects considerable economic differences in the two types of mining. The diamond *garimpo*s are much older than the

---

20. Porantins (1991) p 7.
21. These data come from a survey of 53 Macuxi villages conducted in 1991. Of the 53 village leaders interviewed, 64 per cent had worked in the *garimpo*s at some stage in their lives, and villagers from 64 per cent of the communities surveyed had mined periodically over the previous three years. For more details about sampling procedure, see MacMillan (1993a).
22. Residents from only three of the 53 Macuxi villages surveyed had been to the gold fields of the Yanomami Reserve. Even so, these data do not consider the large numbers of Macuxi who reside in Boa Vista (Ferri 1990), a larger percentage of whom were probably involved in the gold rush.

gold fields and are usually much less productive. Therefore, even though the overheads associated with diamond mining are minimal and the same work relations apply in both types of *garimpo*, the earnings from diamond mining are on the whole substantially lower than gold incomes. Even so, with the modest income gained from a fortnight's manual work in the diamond *garimpo*s, the Macuxi can acquire the goods they would otherwise have difficulty obtaining. They usually spend their mining incomes on basic household items like salt, soap, oil, coffee, aluminium pots, hammocks, clothes, or even bicycles. It is rare for the Macuxi to invest income from the *garimpo* in either livestock or consumer goods (other than radio/cassette recorders). In short, *garimpo* earnings represent a small cash income to complement their predominantly subsistence agriculture.

The Macuxi are in contact with politically influential ranchers and *donos de garimpo* who could provide them with access to the gold fields of western Roraima. But even so, they use the same arguments as the *caboclos* to explain their lack of involvement in the gold rush – the difficulties and expense of entering the gold camps and the risks of disease and violence. The costs and distances involved would necessitate a longer stay in the gold *garimpo*s than many are prepared to tolerate from the point of view of both family life and agriculture. A few people mentioned their reluctance to participate in an illegal activity that was detrimental to the welfare of their perceived relatives, the Yanomami. Therefore, in spite of having the contacts that could give them access to the gold fields, most of the Macuxi did not regard gold mining as attractive employment.

There is probably more to this story, however. And here it is worth recognizing the strong social relationships that characterize *garimpagem* on the savannah. For, while an excursion to the diamond mines provides the Macuxi with a break from village life, it also offers them an opportunity to visit relatives and friends in more distant areas. Typically, a small group of men (usually four to six people) will leave their village and mine autonomously (*por conta própria*) for a two or three-week period in the summer. It is not uncommon for them to work alongside friends and relatives from other settlements. Social events planned in nearby villages may even influence the timing and location of their mining venture. This suggests that, to the Macuxi, social objectives may be just as important as economic considerations when planning a trip to the diamond *garimpo*s.

Perhaps more significantly, the diamond *garimpo*s offer the Macuxi a chance to extend their social network beyond their own community.[23] Mining diamonds and working on the local ranches brings them into contact with locally powerful people. This may be particularly important to adolescent Macuxi who often look for waged employment outside their villages. For them, a spell mining diamonds is frequently the first step towards economic independence. *Dono*s who spot diligent young men in the *garimpo*s may subsequently offer them employment, either on their ranches or in Boa Vista. In short, gaining recognition in the diamond *garimpo*s may prove to be an adolescent Macuxi's most valuable passport to life outside the village.

On the savannah the Macuxi seem to mine with a considerable degree of autonomy in a very familiar social and physical landscape. Although the economic returns from gold mining are undoubtedly higher, it does involve working in a totally different social context. A trip to the gold fields does not involve the same interaction with familiar people and places, which the Macuxi value. Thus, from their perspective, the economic benefits of gold mining probably do not compensate for the sacrifices it entails. Consequently, they find it surprising that other people are prepared to commit themselves to the gold rush in a way that few of them would. To one Macuxi this indicated a fundamental difference between Indian and non-Indian values:[24]

> People come from Maranhão, getting hungry, without any money, hitch-hiking to get to the *garimpo*s. If, for example, they opened a *garimpo* in Maranhão no Indian is going to leave here getting hungry, hitch-hiking without money to get there, as they come from there to here. I do not think that the Indian has such a strong desire for the *garimpo*.

Perhaps it is this outlook that enables the Macuxi to balance mining against their other activities. They seldom allow their excursions into the diamond mines to prejudice agricultural production. Individuals tend to go mining only when they are satisfied that everything is under control in their manioc gardens. Furthermore, their trips to the *garimpo*s are brief and so rarely generate a shortage of

---

23. Personal communication in 1991 with Paulo Santilli, an anthropologist who has worked extensively with the Macuxi.
24. Both this and the succeeding quotation came from interviews recorded in the Maloca of Boqueirão in April 1991.

labour in the village.[25] Although a number of village heads claimed to have the authority to restrict migration to the *garimpo*, these powers were rarely exercised in practice. In fact, it is usually social pressure exerted by other members of the village that prevents an exodus of labour during critical periods. However, this is not only difficult to apply, but may also create tensions within the community, as the following quotation illustrates. Here one Macuxi is speaking about his colleagues who leave the village to go mining:

> Their attitude differs from ours, they are practically divorced from communal activities, and when they go to the *garimpo*s they have a different way of thinking ... they reckon that if they go mining they will make something, but they are not producing [agriculturally] here, and there [in the *garimpo*s] they obtain nothing.

While it might be difficult for villagers to regulate outmigration, it is an important factor in preventing Macuxi villages from becoming too dependent on the mining economy. This allows them to strike a balance between agriculture and mining that often eludes migrant society. They are certainly not the only Indian group to achieve this equilibrium between mining and other activities. The Amarakaeri in the Madre de Dios region of Peru are an example of a different indigenous society behaving in a similar way.[26] Having said that, the rapid expansion of diamond mining on the savannahs of northern Roraima has exacerbated local social tensions to such a degree that the balance noted above is threatened.

## MINING AND THE INVASION OF INDIAN LANDS

Thousands of *garimpeiro*s have moved onto the Macuxi's lands (both in Brazil and Guyana) following the closure of the gold camps in the Yanomami Reserve. Regrettably this is a common problem. Economically valuable mineral deposits exist on Indian lands throughout Amazonia. A detailed survey of archives held by the government's mining department (DNPM) notes that 2245 mineral claims have been registered, covering 33.5 per cent of the total

25. Of the 53 village leaders interviewed in the above mentioned survey, 23 (68 per cent) stated that migration to the *garimpo*s did not cause a shortage of labour in the community. Nine (26 per cent) noted a small shortage, and only two said that people's involvement in *garimpagem* gave rise to a shortage of labour that hindered the completion of communal jobs.
26. Gray (1986) p 39.

*Yanomami Indians look into the back of a transport plane at the Surucucus air base. This base was central to the military operation Free Forest, which sought to expel miners from the Yanomami Reserve.*

Indian land area in the region.[27] Even though these claims are made by mining companies, they rarely obtain the necessary permission to exploit them, and so many of these areas are mined illegally by *garimpeiros*. During the 1980s, all the indigenous groups in Roraima had their lands invaded by miners. Although strict laws exist to prevent such trespassing, they are rarely enforced. The expulsion of *garimpeiros* from the Yanomami Reserve was quite

---

27.  This figure refers to 'Amazonia Legal'. It includes 560 mineral research permits (*alvaras de autorização de pesquisa*), and 1685 claims (*requerimentos incidentes*). CEDI/CONAGE (1988) p 4.

exceptional in this respect. But far from offering a long-term solution to the issue of mineral extraction on Indian land, it simply transferred the related problems from one Indian group to another.

As the miners were squeezed out of the Yanomami Reserve, many of them moved eastwards to the diamond *garimpo*s of the savannah. With the unique exception of Tepequém, all these diamond camps are situated on the proposed Macuxi reserve called Raposa/Serra do Sol. In 1991, the Indigenous Council of Roraima (CIR) claimed that as many as 13,000 people had invaded this area.[28]

Mining is never without its costs. Traditionally the Macuxi have accepted them as being the inevitable consequences of a generally useful activity. But in this instance their tolerance was surpassed. The influx of *garimpeiros* was accompanied by a malarial epidemic, which killed 21 Macuxi and affected over 400 others between 1990 and 1991.[29] The rivers that provided them with drinking water and fish became increasingly polluted.[30] Not surprisingly, tensions between *garimpeiros* and Indians rose, most notably in the villages closest to the principal mining areas. At least four Macuxi were killed in fights with *garimpeiros* between 1990 and 1991.[31] Conflict was heightened by the uncertain nature of the Macuxi's legal rights to the land and the unwillingness of the federal police to intervene. As the proposed Raposa/Serra do Sol Reserve had not been officially demarcated, the *garimpeiros* did not regard their presence in the area as being illegal. Indeed they presumed that the lack of a police presence actually legitimized their occupation of the area. In addition, local politicians were defending the invasion to ensure the continued growth of the state's mining economy. Thus, even though it contravened both the Brazilian constitution and Guyanese immigration laws, only derisory attempts were ever made to regulate this illegal occupation of Indian land.

Although the authorities would not intervene decisively, the Macuxi themselves vigorously resisted the invasion. The CIR stepped up its campaign for the expulsion of the intruders and the

---

28. Porantins (1991) p 7. While a proportion of these tresspassers were ranchers (as mentioned in the previous chapter), the overwhelming majority were *garimpeiros*.
29. Ibid.
30. Although mercury is used in the *garimpo*s of the savannah to separate the small quantities of gold from other sediments, it is not used as extensively in these diamond mining areas as it is in the gold fields.
31. CIR (1992).

demarcation of the Raposa/Serra do Sol Reserve. In May 1992, the Macuxi established roadblocks on the access routes to the *garimpos* along the Rio Maú. Their objective was not so much to close down the mining on their lands as to gain control over the activity. Like the Yanomami, Mundurukú and Amarakaeri, the Macuxi appreciate the benefits of mineral extraction when it is practised on their terms.[32] But in spite of having a powerful ally in the form of the Roman Catholic Church, they face many difficulties in achieving this goal. To assess their prospects, it is worth taking a brief look at how other Indian groups have confronted the same issue.

The Kayapó are probably the most successful of Brazil's Indians in controlling gold mining on their lands. Between 1981 and 1985, different Kayapó leaders made a series of arrangements with *garimpeiros* who were working in different parts of their homelands. In all cases, the Kayapó policed the mining areas and kept the *garimpos* open in exchange for a negotiated fee of between 1 and 10 per cent of total gold production. One such agreement struck over the *garimpo* of Maria Bonita merits attention, for it became the vehicle through which the Kayapó achieved the demarcation of their lands.[33] They closed down Maria Bonita in 1985, after the expiry of a contract that had provided them with 1 per cent of the mining tax. Together with the Brazilian air force, they expelled 5000 *garimpeiros* from the site. By insisting that Maria Bonita would only be reopened if FUNAI agreed to demarcate their reserve, the Kayapó waged a successful campaign for the preservation of their land rights. In May of the same year, chief Paiakan, the group's main negotiator, signed an agreement establishing a three million hectare reserve for them. He subsequently agreed to reopen Maria Bonita on condition the Kayapó received 5 per cent of the mining royalties.

This is exceptional and few other Indian groups have been able to manage *garimpagem* on their lands so successfully. The Yanomami, for example, consistently failed to strike any kind of deal with the gold miners of western Roraima. So what is it that determines the balance of power between Indians and *garimpeiros* in such circumstances? The history and social organization of the indigenous group itself are perhaps as relevant as anything else. Here the Kayapó, who are well versed in dealing with Brazilian society, have

---

32. For the Yanomami, see Ramos et al (1985). For the Mundurukú, refer to Burkhalter and Murphy (1989) and for the Amarakaeri, see Gray (1986).
33. For a more detailed analysis of these events, see Schmink and Wood (1992).

an obvious advantage over the Yanomami. Nevertheless, even the most acculturated Indian groups will still find it difficult to handle *garimpeiros* if they are unable to present and defend a united policy over mining on their lands. The groups' internal social and political organization therefore become crucial in the struggle over mineral deposits. The real strength of the Kayapó lay in masking internal conflicts, so that all five of their villages presented a united bargaining front to the *garimpeiros*. This was bolstered by spectacular demonstrations of power and skilful use of the media. It would be difficult to find a greater contrast with the highly dispersed settlements of the Yanomami.

If these two groups represent the extremes of a spectrum, then the Macuxi probably sit somewhere between the two. They, like the Kayapó, are experienced in dealing with outsiders and do have regular village meetings to formulate appropriate strategies. But while the Kayapó have enough difficulties reaching a consensus among a population of 1500 people dispersed throughout five villages, the Macuxi have to play the same diplomatic game with ten times as many people and settlements. It is therefore hardly surprising that considerable internal rifts have emerged in their campaign. The majority of villages (particularly those nearest the mining areas) still defend CIR's proposal to expel all the ranchers and *garimpeiros* from the reserve. But a number of settlements (particularly those that receive government investment) argue against this, claiming that a contraction in the savannah economy will be detrimental. These conflicts are exploited fully by the politically influential ranchers and *garimpeiros* who are threatened with eviction. So, even though the Macuxi have learnt from the Kayapó and are using the *garimpeiro* invasion to focus attention on their land claims, one can only speculate whether they will be as successful.

# Chapter 6

# The Politics of Gold Mining

*The Amazonian electorate is predominantly urban. Health, education and employment are in short supply.*

As land-use changes in Amazonia are highly sensitive to alterations in the political climate, state policy has been one of the principal factors behind the occupation and settlement of the region since colonial times. In recent years road building, colonization programmes, the *Calha Norte* project and rural credit schemes all provide clear examples of government directives influencing the nature of Amazonian development. This chapter illustrates how the rapid exploitation of mineral resources during the 1980s has shaped the region's political climate and how this in turn has affected policy. On a local scale, consideration will be given to the effect of gold mining on the sociopolitical composition of state governments. The wider consequences of these local changes are then assessed by analysing the dynamic relationship between the state and federal governments. As we shall see, the nature of this relationship not only determines the *garimpeiros'* access to mineral resources, but also shapes other land developments in rural Amazonia over the longer term. Therefore, we start with a brief look at political changes in the Brazilian Amazon since the 1930s and pay particular attention to the roles of the state and federal government within this context.

## THE CHANGING RELATIONSHIP BETWEEN STATE AND FEDERAL GOVERNMENTS

A small number of landowning groups have been disproportionately influential in shaping the development of the Amazonian rural economy. The power of these regional elites rested not so much on the extent of their landholdings, but more significantly on the resources contained therein. The result was that local oligarchies dominated the extraction of rubber in Acre, the collection of brazil nuts in the southeast of Pará and the rearing of livestock on the grasslands of the Ilha de Marajó, Amapá and Roraima. Historically, these rural elites have been important players on the local political stage, commanding influence through clientelistic networks associated with the economic activities they dominate.

Even though Amazonian occupation has been a national goal since colonial days, the current drive for regional growth is rooted in the expansionist philosophy of the Vargas administration (1930–45). The development ideology articulated at that time viewed public infrastructure as a vehicle for the settlement and economic development of peripheral areas. Over the past 50 years, successive governments have sought to extend their influence in Amazonia with these objectives in mind. In broad terms they have achieved this by subdividing the regional political structure so that more administrative units are created, stepping up the presence of the armed services in the region, investing heavily in the transport and energy infrastructure and placing large swathes of land under the administration of central government organizations.

The federal government initially asserted its authority in the Amazon by implementing administrative reforms. One key piece of legislation was the 1937 constitution, which, for reasons of national security, permitted the union to establish federal territories in frontier areas. At that date Acre, which had been annexed from Bolivia in 1903, was the only existing federal territory in Amazonia, but in 1943 it was joined by the newly-created Rondônia, Amapá and Roraima. Even though the federal territories were to be developed by channelling capital through government agencies, they received only a small proportion of the funds disbursed by the regional development organization, Superintendência da Valorização da Amazônia (SPVEA) and its successor, SUDAM. Indeed, by 1985, less than 10 per cent of the total funds administered by SUDAM had been allocated to the territories.[1] The net effect was that these early reforms were predominantly bureaucratic and did little to alter the structure of the rural economies on which the influence of local elites rested. Hence a potential cause for conflict between powerful landowners and the federal government was effectively pre-empted and Vargas's *Estado Novo*, as it came to be known, did not impinge on the local elites' control of land, which remained their principal vehicle for the political control of rural areas. Thus, agrarian oligarchies continued to dominate local politics, either as appointed administrators of the federal territories, or as elected politicians in the democratically governed states (Amazonas, Pará, Maranhão, Mato Grosso).

However, this picture changed noticably in the 1960s and, since then, there has been growing animosity between the local and federal governments. The military dictatorship (established in 1964) centralized power even further and wrested greater control over the administration of land from local government, although not without some considerable trade-offs with the larger landowning class.[2] Administration of the federal territories was delegated to the navy for Amapá, the army for Rondônia and the air force for Roraima. More significantly, a series of laws, which were justified on the grounds of national security, annexed huge tracts of land and placed them under the administration of federal agencies in the early 1970s. INCRA was by far the most significant of these

---

1. Up to January 1985 Acre had received 1.6 per cent of total SUDAM funding, Amapá 2.25 per cent, Rondônia 4 per cent, and Roraima only 0.65 per cent. Freitas (1991) p 55.
2. Personal communication with J Hine, 1992.

agencies, which, under decree law 1164 of 1971, was made responsible for the management of a 100-kilometre swathe of land along all federal highways. This legislation (which was subsequently revoked in 1988) enabled the federal government to extend its control over the development of Amazonian resources through the construction of new highways.

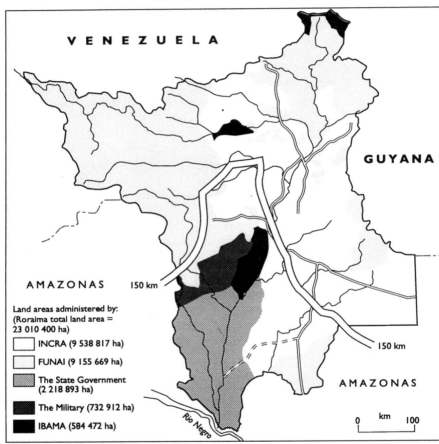

Source: Government of Roraima 1992

*Figure 6.1* The public administration of land in Roraima

Being a frontier state of strategic interest, Roraima was a prominent target for this transfer of land from state to federal government. Figure 6.1 illustrates that 62.5 per cent of Roraima's lands were under federal government administration in 1992.[3] INCRA exerts control over the largest area of 9,538,817 hectares (41.5 per cent), situated within 150 kilometres of the frontier, and a wide band along federal highways, while FUNAI, IBAMA and the army administer a further 4,917,360 hectares (21.4 per cent).

In fact, only 37 per cent of the state's total land surface lies outside federal government administration and, more significantly, the state government exerts complete control over only 9.6 per cent (2,218,893 hectares) of Roraima. Most of this land is concentrated in the inaccessible lower reaches of the Rio Branco basin.[4] Thus, on an administrative level at least, the local government has only a limited say in the exploitation of state resources. This is especially true of minerals, as virtually all Roraima's *garimpos*, with the unique exception of Tepequém, lie on land administered by FUNAI. The efficacy with which the federal government polices these areas is therefore a crucial factor in regulating state mineral production.

The new roads posed a considerable threat to the interests of the local agrarian elites. This was not simply because they led to a transfer of land away from state government administration, but also because they precipitated a restructuring of the rural economy that marginalized the productive activities controlled by the elites. The difficulties facing Amazonia's agrarian oligarchies at this time were further compounded by the migration the road-building programme generated. This was certainly the case for the Mutran family of southeastern Pará, whose domination of the local brazil-nut trade was undermined by the activities of squatters following the completion of the PA 150 in the early 1970s. The squatters challenged the Mutran's ownership of the land and also began to erode their economic base by clearing the brazil-nut forests on the family's estate for agriculture.[5] In short, the pre-existing social and economic landscape on which the authority of local oligarchies rested, underwent a rapid transformation following the road constructions of the 1970s. As a result, the landed families were increasingly challenged over their domination of the local political stage by actors associated with the newly-expanding sectors of the Amazonian

---

3. Roraima 1992.
4. Pará provides a similar example of how these laws placed large areas of Amazonia under federal government administration. See Schmink and Wood (1992) p 108.
5. For a detailed account of these events see Hine (1991).

economy. These were most notably land speculators, timber merchants, urban retailers, government administrators and, as we shall see below, *garimpeiros*.

These internal dynamics of state politics did little to reconcile the continuing struggle between local and federal governments over the control of Amazonian resources. Surprisingly, the outcome of this contest has been increasingly shaped by economic and not political factors. This is because, throughout the 1980s, the federal government experienced growing difficulties in maintaining the physical and administrative infrastructure it had so vigorously assembled in Amazonia during the previous decade. To use a sporting metaphor:[6]

> On the one hand, in constructing the highway network and directly encouraging external investment in Amazonia, it [the state] marked out the playing field for the region's future development. On the other, the state proved to be so incapable of controlling the consequences that it now has difficulties in putting a team on the pitch.

While the inability to control regional development processes is most obviously a manifestation of the Brazilian economic crisis of the 1980s, it also reflects the impotence of the bureaucratic federal agencies in applying government policy.[7] Their chances of fulfilling such directives are now further compromised by tax reforms incorporated within the 1988 constitution, which bestowed greater financial autonomy on municipal and state governments, augmenting their share of tax revenues from 50 to 66 per cent.[8] As the influence of federal government wanes, therefore, local interests once again assume an increasingly important role in Amazonian resource exploitation.

Even so, it is wrong to believe that the fragmentation of federal government control is the unique cause of this emerging local political force. Factors intrinsic to Amazonia have done much to enhance this transition. Indeed, by examining the political dynamics associated with the *garimpo*, it can be argued that the region's mineral boom actually strengthened the hand of Amazonian state governments over that of the union. In purely economic terms, the rapid growth of the Amazonian mineral sector gave the region and

---

6. Cleary (1993) p 334.
7. See Bunker (1985).
8. Amparo (forthcoming).

its politicians a new significance in domestic and even international politics. But an equally important point is that the growth of the gold-mining sector presented local interests with an opportunity to extend their political and economic influence in a sphere that could not be penetrated by federal government intervention. By its very definition, informal-sector mining occurs outside the domain of government authority and, being denied direct control, Brasília can only influence the Amazonian mineral sector through clumsy external interventions. Thus, in complete contrast to the history of Amazonian land administration over the previous two decades, the federal government was unable to wrest control of the regional mining economy from local interests during the 1980s.

But what exactly were the political opportunities that arose from the 1980s' Amazonian mineral boom? And how successfully were they exploited? Answering these questions is fundamental if we are to understand how the Amazonian mining lobby emerged as such a powerful force on both the regional and national stage. To address this we look at the principal channels through which *garimpeiros* gained power in Amazonia during the 1980s. Having done so, the local situation is once again placed in its national political context to evaluate the significance of these events for the exploitation of Amazonian mineral resources.

## RORAIMA, SERRA PELADA AND THE *GARIMPEIRO* VOTE

The intense migration that accompanies gold mining often leads to a rapid transformation of the local electoral base. In Roraima this was unusually significant, as it occurred on the eve of the state's first democratic elections in 1990, which marked the transition from federal territory to statehood. Four distinct groups of voters existed before the rush: colonist farmers, Indians, urban professional classes (principally public-sector employees) and urban working classes (mainly employed in the informal sector). The arrival of 40,000 *garimpeiros*, and an even greater number of urban immigrants linked to the mining economy, created a new clearly-defined segment of the electorate, which was numerically superior to any of the four groups noted above. Whoever succeeded in harnessing this vote would be guaranteed considerable political influence in both state and national affairs.

There was a rapid proliferation of the local media in the form of three radio stations, six newspapers, and one state television channel, all mouthpieces for an array of political parties competing for the *garimpeiro* vote. Even though virtually all the candidates promised to support the interests of the miners, two principal figures championed their cause. The first was Romero Jucá, ex-president of FUNAI (1986–88), who, having been dismissed from that office, was subsequently appointed governor of Roraima. Although not directly involved in mining, Jucá had overtly sanctioned the *garimpeiros'* invasion of the Yanomami lands during his governorship (1988–90), and had campaigned vigorously for the reduction of the single indigenous area into the 19 separate islands, which were briefly established by inter-ministerial decree 250/88. While Jucá contested the seat of governor, José Altino Machado, head of the union for Amazonian *garimpeiros*, USAGAL, ran for senator. José Altino is one of Roraima's most influential *garimpeiros* and had been fighting for the extraction of mineral resources within the Yanomami Reserve since the early 1980s. This was manifested, not only in the unsuccessful invasion of Surucucús in 1985, which he coordinated (see Chapter 2), but also in his skilled lobbying for the creation of three *garimpeiro* reserves within the Yanomami park, which were established under the presidential decree of 25 January 1990 and 16 February 1990, before being revoked later in the same year (see Figure 2.1).

On polling day, however, the *garimpeiro* lobby failed to vote either candidate into office. Jucá was ousted by Brigadier Ottomar de Souza Pinto, a previous governor, whose marginal victory rested on considerable support from smallholders. José Altino was similarly unsuccessful. Two of the three government posts he contested were won by established local landowners and the third by Marluce Pinto, Ottomar's wife. Thus, in spite of a considerable electoral base and substantial financial resources, the two principal figures of the mining lobby failed to secure key positions in the elections.

There are a number of reasons for this unexpected result, one being the contraction of the local mining economy in the run-up to the elections. But, while outmigration might have somewhat diminished the electoral support of Jucá and Altino, there were still sufficiently large numbers of *garimpeiros* within Roraima to have swept them into office had their campaigns been more effective. The electoral results therefore reflect their inability to translate the large number of potential supporters into a sufficiently powerful vote. Here the odds were stacked against them, and against anybody else seeking to use gold mining as an electoral platform, on two counts.

First, even though voting is compulsory, it is likely that a substantial proportion of the potential *garimpeiro* vote is never expressed. The transience of miners may discourage them from registering in states they are only passing through, especially if they are working in inaccessible areas far from any ballot box. Electoral registration is no doubt further impeded by the *garimpeiros'* aversion to official documentation, particularly in areas like western Roraima, where mining is practised illegally.

A second, and perhaps more fundamental, obstacle is the limited extent to which *garimpeiros* identify themselves as a professional class with common political objectives. Any one *garimpo* contains smallholders, ranchers, tradesmen and merchants who are united not so much in their mutual love of mining, but in their displacement from other sectors of the economy. Since the flexible nature of work relations in the *garimpos* serves to erode notions of a common professional identity among the workforce, a large section of the *garimpo* workforce will give its political and economic support to activities outside the *garimpo*. This is especially true if a trade-off is perceived between the two. It is perhaps only the smaller group of professional *garimpeiros* who place the future of informal-sector mining at the centre of their political agendas.

The Roraima result differs markedly from the outcome of the Marabá municipal election in 1982 (the *garimpo* of Serra Pelada lies within the municipality of Marabá), even though both campaigns were fought in similar circumstances. *Garimpeiros* whose access to mineral deposits was under threat accounted for the majority of the electorate in both cases. However, this is probably the limit of any valid comparison, for Serra Pelada was unique in having mining densely concentrated in a very confined area, which facilitated state intervention in the organization of the *garimpo*. Indeed, the federal government troubleshooter who implemented the state directives, Major Curió, succeeded in harnessing the *garimpeiro* vote. Having dramatically improved the working conditions at Serra Pelada, Curió capitalized on the popularity this engendered by making electoral registration a necessary precondition for access to the *garimpo*. The plan worked and, on polling day, a wave of populist support swept him into office as a congressman.

Curió's successful exploitation of the *garimpeiro* vote was exceptional. Even so, it provides a good illustration of the *garimpo's* potential to influence politics up to the level of central government and, furthermore, it challenges the suggestion that *garimpeiros* lack political cohesion. In searching for the root of Curió's success, it is worth recognizing that his victory rested as much on the help he received from the federal government as it did on the *garimpeiro* vote. Without the former it is doubtful whether he would have obtained the latter. Indeed, by placing him in Serra Pelada and providing the funds to reform the *garimpo*, the military government was actively seeking to empower Curió as a political ally. They saw in him an opportunity to displace the dominant Mutran family from office and to bolster support for the ruling party in congress. The concentration of mining activity in Serra Pelada and the threatened takeover of the *garimpo* by the Companhia Vale do Rio Doce (CVRD) were two key factors that played in Curió's favour. He was particularly adept at cultivating the opportunities they presented and, through charismatic addresses to the workforce, he carved out a powerful electoral platform.

In contrast, the dispersed clandestine mining of Roraima did not allow *garimpeiro* leaders such as Jucá and Altino to consolidate political support. The different responses of the two work forces, when faced with the prospect of expulsion, illustrates the extent to which they acted as politically cohesive units. Serra Pelada's *garimpeiros* formed a formidable social force. In October 1983, a contingent of them went to Brasília to lobby for their right to continue working at the site. This was only one element in an efficient and ultimately successful campaign to keep the mine in the informal sector. By June 1984, protests were less restrained: several thousand *garimpeiros* blocked the Belém–Brasília highway and other more minor roads, disarmed the police, and burnt down the CVRD buildings at Parauapebas. In contrast, Roraima's *garimpeiros* displayed little coordinated political activism. Other than a handful of demonstrations in the central square of Boa Vista between July and September 1990, one of which culminated in an attack on the Bishop's residence, the workforce dispersed with remarkable passivity. Unlike the Serra Pelada workforce, which had been transformed into a politically influential mass by Curió, Roraima's *garimpeiros* appeared to be little more than a disorganized rabble.

The rapid influx of *garimpeiros* into a particular area does alter the electoral base, but this is not necessarily mirrored by sudden alterations in the local political climate. Indeed, while the demographic changes that accompany mineral rushes undoubtedly present new political opportunities, these are seldom realized by candidates who do not already enjoy considerable support in governmental circles. This is precisely because electoral success in Brazil, as in many other democracies, is still largely a function of the resources a candidate has at his or her disposal. The backing that Curió received to improve conditions in Serra Pelada provided the foundation on which both his support and subsequent victory rested. As a result, aspiring politicians must extend their access to resources through alliances if they are to turn an electoral base into a campaign success. For this reason, numerical superiority alone is rarely sufficient to equip *garimpeiros* with a clear voice in Brazilian politics.

*A gold trader in Boa Vista. The gold rush brought a new political elite to Amazonia.*

# THE *GARIMPO* AND THE FORMATION OF AN ELITE CLASS

The specific nature of the Roraima rush, coupled with the inability of institutions and individuals to exploit the situation effectively, ensured that the *garimpeiro* lobby gained only limited power through direct elections. Nonetheless, the explosive growth of the informal-mining sector still influenced the tone of state politics in two distinct ways. First, members of the already established local elite invested in mining and came to defend those interests on the political stage. Secondly, the opportunities for social advancement presented by the rush enabled recently arrived *garimpeiros* to enter the local elite and gain political influence. Certainly in Roraima, it was through the personal involvement of powerful individuals in *garimpagem*, and not via the formal mechanics of the democratic system, that the *garimpo* lobby acquired greatest influence in state politics.

Local politicians are well placed to make investments in the *garimpos*, not simply because they have access to the necessary sums of capital, but also because they are linked into extensive social networks, both in urban and rural areas. Furthermore, as the mineral resources on Indian lands are widely perceived to be common property, few politicians regard investing in the *garimpos* as incompatible with their public responsibilities. In addition, involvement in the gold rush actually offers them an opportunity to strengthen their electoral position. Contacts may be forged with economically powerful *donos*, who might provide financial backing for future election campaigns, and support can be engendered among the electorally significant *garimpeiro* workforce. More specifically, politicians who invest in mining demonstrate a personal commitment to the progress and development of Amazonia, which the electorate often perceives to be threatened by external political pressures.

A number of public figures therefore seized the opportunity to invest in gold mining in the Yanomami Reserve. In the 1991 Ottomar administration, at least four state deputies, one senator and one federal deputy had financed mining operations in this area between 1987 and 1990.[9] A number of senior civil servants also invested in the gold rush. These included the chief of the state police force, the

---

9. These data are collected from newspaper reports and interviews with local politicians.

transport secretary and, ironically, the secretary of state for the environment, interior and justice. When interviewed, one of these politicians presented a candid explanation of why he and his colleagues decided to invest in the *garimpos*:[10]

GJM: Why did you decide to invest in the *garimpos* when you had both a public position and rural property. What was it that attracted you to the *garimpo*?

P: Right, listen closely. The *garimpo* arrived here like a fever that passed through the heads of everybody who lived here. At that time it was almost impossible to meet anybody who was not affected by that wave of *garimpo* wealth, which spread across the whole city [Boa Vista]. Look then at what happened to me as a politician. My political colleagues began to invest in the *garimpo* and they invited me to enter as a partner. That was how it was. Anybody who had a little bit of money on the side took it and invested in the *garimpo* in that illusion of El Dorado.

GJM: So how did you manage your investment there? Did you contract an overseer ?

P: Yes we had a manager, a person of confidence whom we knew. Do you understand? Our investment was like this. … I bought the equipment in partnership with another friend of mine who was also a politician. We calculated all of the costs and split them 50-50 for everything we needed; a set of machinery, food, fuel, the transport flights; and then we put the work team in to start production.

This quotation illustrates the ease with which investments can be made in the *garimpo*, providing local entrepreneurs with an opportunity to diversify their economic base into mining. This is particularly important when assessing processes of elite formation, for it ensures that people who already carry some economic and political weight are not excluded from this rapidly expanding sector of the regional economy.

The pre-gold rush elite in Roraima consisted of the well-established ranching families of the savannah, as well as an urban professional class. The latter was dominated by civil servants, but also included a small group of retailers and a handful of diamond

---

10. Interview recorded 27 December 1991.

traders. Other than this, a few officers in the air force, such as Brigadier Ottomar de Souza Pinto, remained influential, having come into power while the state was a federal territory. Most state and municipal politicians had interests in at least one of these fields, and virtually all of them owned land. The structure of their portfolios at the start of the gold rush typically shaped their response to the various opportunities it presented. For example, those who already had investments in urban commerce were well placed to expand into the booming retail and entertainments sectors. Similarly, diamond traders expanded into gold purchasing, whilst anybody in possession of a light aircraft employed it in servicing the *garimpos*. Others, particularly those whose only concern was ranching or diamond mining, were less able to penetrate the lucrative and stable urban-based service sector and often chose to invest in the gold extraction process itself. The case of the extended families who traditionally dominated the savannah ranching economy is illustrative. As we saw in Chapter 4, they were keen to transfer capital from ranching into mining because the FUNAI proposal to establish the Raposa/Serra do Sol Reserve threatened to displace them from the savannahs.

In effect, these ranchers took a gamble and backed the wrong horse. For, although mineral extraction may be a lucrative venture, it tends to be a much more risky investment than the service sector of the *garimpo* economy. Furthermore, it demands a level of supervision few ranchers were prepared to give; consequently, a number of them were swindled by untrustworthy managers whom they had employed to oversee their mining operations. In spite of all these problems, it was probably the sudden closure of the *garimpos* that dealt the hardest financial blow to these ranchers, particularly those who had over-committed themselves to mining because of the uncertain future of savannah ranching. They, like other investors, suffered considerable financial losses when, in 1991, the federal police began to destroy all the mining equipment they encountered within the Yanomami Reserve.

While these alterations in the financial affairs of Roraima's elite provide some understanding of subsequent political changes in the state, the relationship between economic power and political influence is slightly more complex. For, although secure financial backing is undoubtedly a prerequisite for any successful campaign, strong electoral support is an equally important ingredient; marrying the two is, as Curió demonstrated, the skill of the politician. Thus, under rapidly changing socioeconomic circumstances, Amazonian politicians have been forced to rearticulate both their electoral platform and their economic interests in order to maintain their hegemony. The speed and flexibility with which they respond to such a challenge is beginning to emerge as one of the most striking characteristics of Amazonian elites. The ability of the Mutran family to reclaim the mayorship of Marabá in the 1989 elections, only seven years after Curió ousted them from office, is the most spectacular, but by no means the only, example. Miller provides further evidence of this resilience by demonstrating that some of the figureheads who traditionally dominated the extractive economy around Santarém (in Pará), were able to maintain their local influence by diversifying into informal-sector mining from the 1960s onwards.[11]

As we have seen, Roraima follows a similar pattern. Rather than experiencing the total replacement of an old elite with a new class of miners, there was a merging of the two groups into a new political class. First, members of the pre-gold rush elite were quick to invest in mining and to extend their political appeal to the electorally significant *garimpo* workforce. The failed campaigns of Altino and Jucá testify the skill with which old hands, like Ottomar, adapted to changing circumstances and maintained their grip on power. Even so, the rush was not without its political victims, the most obvious of whom were the savannah ranchers. By investing in the gold extraction process itself and not the more secure service economy, their economic weight was eclipsed by the urban-based professional and commercial classes. Of course there are exceptions to this rule. Some ranchers, like Zélio Mota, were able to make this transition. Zélio's success lay in extending his previous diamond-trading concern into the new gold trade. But the experience of others, like José Augusto Macaggi, head of the Roraima's land-owners' union, the UDR (Rural Democratic Union), is more representative. Despite personally managing his own *balsa* on the Rio Uraricoera over a 16-month period, José generated about the same income he had earned previously as an agricultural consultant and ranch owner. Less astute members of the savannah ranching fraternity, like Junior Magalhães and Petita Brasil, lost considerable sums of money by investing the proceeds of land and livestock sales in the *garimpo*. In general terms therefore, the savannah ranchers were economically and politically marginalized by events at the end of the 1980s. They suffered both the financial impact of

---

11. Miller (1985).

their unprofitable experiences in the *garimpo* and declining political authority as their control of the savannah economy was gradually undermined by FUNAI policy.

Secondly, as members of the old elite were moving into mining, the new class of *garimpeiro* entrepreneurs was penetrating the economic domain of Roraima's establishment. We have already seen that members of the local elite whose interests were confined exclusively to the rural sector tended to lose ground to an increasingly powerful urban class, but the composition of this urban fraction also changed as *garimpeiros* entered. These new arrivals were typically entrepreneurs who came to Boa Vista to ride out the mineral boom. The retailing of *garimpo* equipment, mineral extraction, gold trading and the provision of air transport were often at the centre of their portfolios, but they also invested in rented accommodation, car sales, taxi companies and the ubiquitous entertainments sector. Even so, the speed with which these entrepreneurs entered Roraima was in many cases matched only by the swiftness of their return to Porto Velho, Marabá, Santarém or other towns from which they originated. In the aftermath of the rush therefore only a small proportion of this rich *garimpeiro* class remained to form part of the local sociopolitical fabric.

These newcomers were able to use their considerable economic wealth to gain political influence. Making an investment in ranching is perhaps the first step for entrepreneurs seeking an entry into local politics (see Chapter 4). Having gained a social position in this way, they are well placed to extend their influence further by using their accumulated wealth as a tool for political negotiation on the local stage. The 1990 elections, which marked Roraima's transition to statehood, were particularly significant in this respect, as numerous candidates were searching for campaign funds. Competition was heightened because the transition would bestow a greater degree of political autonomy than ever before upon the elected government. In its first year of office it would be charged with the formulation of a state constitution. The federal government's inconsistent approach towards the Yanomami question in the run-up to the elections suggested that channels like this would provide local politicians with greater influence over the exploitation of local mineral deposits than eventually proved to be the case.

The resultant clamour for power gave politically inexperienced *garimpeiros* an opportunity to gain influential positions in state government by backing election campaigns. This represents a direct channel through which the mining lobby can acquire a political voice. Indeed, Roraima's *garimpeiros* were more effective in articulating their interests in this way than by their unsuccessful attempts to gain office through the formal electoral system. It is important to understand the exact mechanics through which the newcomers entered local politics without getting elected themselves. The following detailed case study presents a clear illustration of how powerful *garimpeiros* can acquire positions of considerable local influence through backing electoral campaigns.

Originating in the south of Brazil, Elton Ronhelt came into contact with the Amazonian elites through informal-sector mining. In 1983 he established a company, Edgar Ronhelt Mineração Limitada, in partnership with his brother Luz and the Mestrinho brothers, Thomé and Gilberto.[12] The company had mining operations throughout the *garimpos* of Amazonia, but came to concentrate its activities in the region known as the Cabeça do Cachorro in northwest Amazonas. In 1985, FUNAI and the DNPM granted it permission to mine two out of the three mineral concessions the company held on the Alto Rio Negro indigenous reserve.[13] Simultaneously, Paranapanema, the large state mining corporation, was given permission to mine a different site in the same reserve. The two companies worked together under the protection of the police force of the state of Amazonas.[14] Mineral dealers in Boa Vista explained that, having received permission to mine the concession, Edgar Ronhelt Mineração Limitada invited Paranapanema to provide the financial and technical resources to develop the site in return for a percentage of the profits.

The partners restructured their business interests in 1986. Gilberto Mestrinho sold out of the company and dedicated himself to his political career; Thomé Mestrinho established a new mining company called Mineraçaõ Montes Roraima Limitada,[15] and the Ronhelt brothers kept the company operating under the new name of GoldAmazon. Both Monte Roraima and GoldAmazon had operations in the Yanomami Indigenous Reserve during the Roraima

---

12. Gilberto Mestrinho is the longstanding governor of Amazonas state. He has strong political connections with Roraima, where he was elected a federal deputy in the 1970s.
13. The details of these concessions are published in CEDI/CONAGE (1988) pp 21–2, and are illustrated cartographically in Wright (1990) p 40.
14. Wright (1990) p 41.
15. Gama de Silva (1991) p 282. The same text also notes that Thomé Mestrinho owned a further company called Mineração Thomé Medeiros Recursos Naturais Limitada.

gold rush, although neither was spectacularly successful. None-theless, GoldAmazon did attract the attention of the press on two occasions during this period. Elton himself had the misfortune of being caught *in flagrante delicto* at Boa Vista airport in a light plane containing an assortment of machine guns and semi-automatic weapons, but was released without charge.[16] A month later he became the sole owner of the company when his brother Luz died in a plane crash while commuting to the *garimpo*.[17] With two helicopters, a number of light aircraft, and two DC3 transport planes, Elton owned one of the largest airfleets in Roraima. A high proportion of his revenue came from providing prospecting and transport services in the *garimpos*, but this was also supplemented by mining and trading in tin ore, which was sold mainly to Para-napanema.

Elton Ronhelt and Thomé Mestrinho stood as candidates in the 1990 Roraima elections, but neither of them obtained sufficient votes to qualify for the second round of the two-tier electoral system. On receiving the results, Elton placed the GoldAmazon air fleet at the disposal of Brigadier Ottomar de Souza Pinto, who used it successfully to whip up support among colonists in remote rural areas and thus clinch his victory against Romero Jucá. On taking office, Brigadier Ottomar appointed Elton Ronhelt head of the department of mining and hydroelectric projects in the state devel-opment corporation, CODESAIMA. His daughter, Denise Ronhelt, who owns a registered gold-trading company in Boa Vista, was appointed state secretary for tourism. As no DNPM office exists in Roraima, Elton effectively became the most senior government figure concerned with mineral development in the state.

There are many other examples of *garimpeiros* achieving political influence in similar ways throughout Amazonia. Again, in Roraima, Antonio Dias, an entrepreneur who became wealthy retailing *garimpo* equipment during the gold rush, was appointed vice gover-nor by Ottomar. At the time of his appointment, Antonio had resided for no more than five years in the state and had no previous political experience. Similarly, Rubens da Silva, another successful *garimpeiro*, was appointed head of the Roads Department in exchange for the support he lent to Ottomar's campaign. In Pará, Senhor Wilson, the owner of Agropeças in Tucumã, and João Kai-Kai, owner of Pioneiro dos Motores, provide two well-known

---

16. *O Journal de Boa Vista*, 12 August 1988.
17. *Folha de Boa Vista*, 21 September 1988

examples of *garimpo* retailers extending their economic influence into the political sphere by supporting electoral candidates.

The relationship between Ronhelt and Paranapanema illustrates that larger interests may use this same avenue to influence local politics. According to local cassiterite dealers, the mineral company, Companhia Industrial Amazonense (CIA), which is joint owned by Brascan (95 per cent) and Best Metals and Solders (5 per cent)[18] provided José Altino and João Fagundes with vehicles to help canvas the electorate. João Fagundes was elected as a federal deputy, leaving the less fortunate Altino with a political ally who can represent his interests in government; presumably the same privilege is extended to CIA. Similar examples are found in other parts of the Amazon. Evidence presented during the hearings for President Collor de Mello's impeachment showed that Mercedes Benz had made huge financial contributions to Curió's unsuccessful 1990 election campaign in Marabá, Pará.[19]

Because of this, *garimpeiro*s who gain political influence often use it to support the interests of large mining companies over the informal-mining sector. Elton Ronhelt's appointment forged a strong link between Paranapanema and the government of Roraima. This is well illustrated by an interview, which Ottomar, Elton Ronhelt and Lacombe (the director of Paranapanema) gave to the national newspaper, *Folha de São Paulo*, in July 1991. Having appealed to the *garimpeiro* vote during his election campaign, Ottomar's statement on this occasion favoured the participation of formal-sector companies in any future development of the state's mineral resources, representing a distinct change in policy.[20]

Thus, the ease with which economic wealth can be translated into political muscle is relevant to local processes of elite formation. Even so, while this may allow rich upstarts, like *garimpeiro*s, to gain influence rapidly, the new entrepreneurial class, which the *garimpo* empowers, seldom comes to replace a local elite entirely. Rather, the facility with which the established class can diversify into mining and rearticulate its hegemony through dealing with powerful *garimpeiro*s favours a fusion of the old elite group with the new. In

---

18. DNPM (1982a) p 868.
19. See Veja 22 July 1992 pp 18–26. Schmink and Wood (1992) p 128 give details of a similar deal made in Pará in the 1970s, in which a logging contract was awarded to the pension fund CAPEMI in return for its financial support of a political campaign.
20. *Folha de São Paulo*, 11 July 1991.

this way a common interest in the mining economy emerges as previously established politicians invest in *garimpagem* and powerful *garimpeiros* enter local politics. This is precisely why the mining lobby became such an important political force in Amazonia during the 1980s.

# THE EMERGENCE OF A REGIONAL POLITICAL IDENTITY AND THE STRUGGLE OVER MINERAL RESOURCES

Once *garimpeiros* gain office in state governments they can alter the course of local development in three main ways. First, they may come to determine the allocation of regional development funds, such as the FNO, which are an important source of capital to local investors (notably ranchers). Secondly, they can influence state policy, as was the case when Roraima's constitution was being drawn up in 1991. Finally, they may also sway decisions concerning the development of the local infrastructure, such as the construction of roads and hydroelectric projects. As head of the Mining and Energy Department of the state development company, CODESAIMA, Elton Ronhelt overruled previous plans and commissioned the construction of Roraima's first hydroelectric project on the Rio Jatapú at the easternmost tip of the Perimetral Norte highway. By 1992, the initial works were being undertaken by Paranapanema, the very company with which Ronhelt had been most closely associated in the *garimpos*.[21]

However, it is the relationship between the state and federal governments that determines the precise extent to which locally-influential *garimpeiros* can shape the course of Amazonian development. As local interests tend to dominate when the influence of federal government slips, the state's control over land development is directly proportional to the impotence of the union. This was certainly the situation in Roraima during the gold rush itself. For various reasons, neither FUNAI nor the military were able to prevent the *garimpeiros* entering the Yanomami Reserve. Local

---

21. The site for the hydroelectric plant is just downstream from the *garimpo* on the Rio Jatapú discussed in Chapter 7. Elton Ronhelt gave precedence to the Jatapú site over two others that had been favoured by previous state governments. Work had already begun on one of them at Paredão on the Rio Mucajaí, funded by a loan from the Midland Bank. The second site, which had also been surveyed by the time Elton came to office, was on the Rio Cotingó.

interests seized this as an excellent opportunity to pursue their own agenda – the central item of which was, and still remains, the exploitation of the state's subsoil wealth.

They were probably surprised to see the explosive growth of the mining economy being matched in scale by the media coverage and international concern that it generated. Non-governmental organizations (NGOs) such as the CCPY (Comissão Pela Criação do Parque Yanomami), the Environmental Defense Fund (EDF), Cultural Survival (CS), and Survival International (SI), were particularly active in lobbying the Brazilian government to address the fate of the Yanomami. The backbone of their campaign lay in mobilizing western electorates and governments to put pressure on Brasília over the issue. But, although this strategy ultimately proved decisive, their demands were resisted by the Sarney administration while it remained in office. Sarney continued to favour the *garimpeiro* lobby, signing the interministerial decree 250/88 to carve the proposed Yanomami territory into 19 separate islands, thereby permitting *garimpeiro*s to work in the intervening National Forest (see Chapter 2).

It took a change of government before the international pressure applied to Brasília had anything other than a superficial impact on the situation in Roraima. But, when change came it was swift. Within the first month of his presidency, Fernando Collor de Melo had revoked the controversial decree 250/88, had visited the Yanomami Reserve, and had ordered the removal of the *garimpeiro*s. In spite of this dramatic change of policy, it was immediately apparent that the federal government lacked the necessary infrastructure in Roraima to realize these goals. In attempting to address this problem, the federal government set about empowering its agencies in the state. Considerable human and financial resources were channelled into the appropriate agencies through three specific projects. The federal police force was bolstered via Operation Free Forest, the National Health Foundation (FNS) through the Yanomami Health Project, and FUNAI was strengthened subsequently by the demarcation programme.

These measures dealt a severe blow to the aspirations of the now politically-influential mining lobby in Roraima. The local magnates employed every available strategy to disrupt the federal government's programme. But the federal government was not prepared to allow the interests of a peripheral elite to tarnish its international reputation. By this stage, the plight of the Yanomami had become something of a showcase for Brazilian environmental policy on the eve of the United Nations Conference on Environment and Development (UNCED) held in Rio de Janeiro in June 1992. As one Washington-based NGO noted: 'No other single issue is more indicative of the Brazilian government's political will to defend the Amazon and its inhabitants than the fate of the Yanomami territory.'[22]

Brasília was sensitive to such remarks because they had potentially damaging financial repercussions on the domestic economy. The EDF had already demonstrated its ability to hamper Brazil's access to foreign credit, for in 1985 it successfully lobbied the World Bank to suspend funding the POLONOROESTE project until certain social and environmental conditions of the loan were fulfilled. The Yanomami situation was somewhat different in that it was never directly incorporated as a condition for any specific loan. But even though they may not have been formalized in a written contract, the concerns expressed by overseas observers, such as the UN (who wrote to Collor on the subject on 12 February 1991) may nonetheless have affected Brazilian liquidity. Here it is worth recalling that the Collor administration had been involved in protracted loan negotiations with the IMF (International Monetary Fund) since it came into office. After two years of discussion, a deal was eventually clinched in January 1992 providing US $2.7 billion to aid debt repayments and to facilitate domestic economic reforms geared towards reducing inflation. Although this sum is small in relation to the country's external debt, which exceeded US $118 billion at that time, the loan did make Brazil credit worthy in the eyes of the international banking community. This is not to argue that the demarcation of the Yanomami Reserve in November 1991 was a principal factor in securing this loan, merely to note that, among other criteria, Brazil's environmental policies probably had some influence on the final decision taken by the IMF.

Therefore, on the eve of UNCED, Brasília was under considerable political and economic pressure to remove the *garimpeiros* from the Yanomami Reserve. Naturally, there were voices other than those of the indigenous movement lobbying for the same ends, notably that of the ATPC who wanted to restrict the production of Surucucús cassiterite. As the pressure grew, a locally powerful *garimpo* lobby, which had previously withstood the concerns of Brasília, was no longer able to dictate the course of mineral development in Roraima. This was an exceptional situation; nowhere else

---

22. EDF (1992) p 2.

had the federal government intervened so decisively in the informal-mining sector and usurped local interests. This is just as true for the numerous concessions made by the Sarney government to Roraima's *garimpeiros* as it is for the eventual decision to leave Serra Pelada in the hands of the informal-mining sector. Local elites were swift to equate the growing external pressure on the central government with their diminishing control over the exploitation of the subsoil. Responding to these adverse political circumstances, they seized on nationalistic sentiments as a vehicle to reassert their influence over the region and its resources. In Roraima this was clearly articulated by the Movement Against the Internationalization of Amazonia, which united *garimpeiro* leaders like José Altino with influential ranchers like José Augusto Soares Macaggi. They lobbied for reductions in the size of Indian reserves, argued for the continued presence of *garimpeiros* and ranchers within them, and condemned the activities of bodies such as the Roman Catholic Church and CCPY for preventing Brazil from realizing its mineral potential.

Although this movement arose from the specific situation in Roraima, its emergence coincided with a growing debate about Amazonian sovereignty at a regional level. The relevance of this discourse lay in providing a catalyst to consolidate an increasingly cohesive political identity. In effect, it helped bring together local politicians around an Amazonian issue and, in so doing, it furthered the development of a regional political agenda. The inter-parliamentary commission on the internationalization of Amazonia, which united various local politicians to investigate the activities of foreigners in the region during 1992, provides one such example. But the same rhetoric, emphasizing local sovereignty and challenging existing indigenous policy, underlay other expressions of regional political thought. A statement from the governors of western Amazonian states signed in Manaus on 14 November 1992 provides a good example. Having noted that 'the socioeconomic development of the Amazon constitutes a legitimate, unquestionable, non transferable and inviolable right of the region's inhabitants', this text proceeds to argue that 'Indian areas should be adequately demarcated within reasonable limits, which should not exceed 200 hectares per Indian family of whatever ethnic group.'[23] Both this document, and the unsuccessful Código Amazônico, which was signed by all the governors of Amazonian states in 1991,

23.  Roraima (1991) p 5.

sought to place greater authority over the demarcation of Indian reserves and the management of natural resources in the hands of the regional political elite.

The internationalization debate has been aired since the 1960s, and for this reason its origins predate the contemporary developments in the informal-mining sector discussed here. Nonetheless, its resuscitation and, more significantly, the political changes this precipitated, cannot be divorced from more recent socioeconomic changes in the region. By raising questions of Amazonian sovereignty, the local elite was not only able to challenge the actions of the federal government, but also gained a convenient anvil on which a stronger regional political identity could be forged.

There were two principal mechanisms through which informal-sector mining increased regional political cohesion. First, it eroded the influence of local agrarian oligarchies whose interests were diverse. In forcing them to redefine their economic foundations along more common lines, and by partially replacing the old guard with a new entrepreneurial class, the *garimpo* sculpted a regional elite that shared a common political interest in resource development. As noted above, there was an assimilation of divergent economic and political interests as members of the existing establishment invested in the *garimpo*, while at the same time powerful *garimpeiros* acquired local political influence. In this respect, the 1980s gold rush helped smooth out the disparate concerns of rural oligarchies and prepared the way for a new regional elite to seek increasingly united political objectives.

The second point is that the same rush enhanced the subsequent development of this regional political identity by strengthening the intraregional links operating between state governments. The widespread involvement of politicians in the informal-mining economy helped construct an intricate social network among the Amazonian political elite. The case study of Elton Ronhelt provides an insight into how these links develop. Through the *garimpo* he established strong ties with the government of Amazonas. Likewise, Antonio Dias, another member of Ottomar's state cabinet has strong connections with politicians in Pará following his mining experiences in that region. While not negating the importance of other factors in this context, it should be noted that the *garimpo* often provides a common denominator that links politicians in one part of the Amazon to colleagues in neighbouring states, thereby facilitating intraregional political networking.

In conclusion, the recent political and economic history of

Amazonia suggests that local interests are becoming increasingly influential on both the regional and national stages. This has very real implications for the future pattern of resource development and land use in Amazonia, particularly as political changes on a national level have meant that the federal government's already limited control over regional planning appears to be slipping even further. The precarious state blockade of the Yanomami Reserve collapsed in the wake of the UNCED conference and, by the start of 1993, over 12,000 *garimpeiros* had resumed their work inside the area. FUNAI was hardly in a position to act, having had its already meagre budget slashed by over 80 per cent in the financial year 1992/3.[24] At the same time, the newly appointed secretary for the environment, Coutinho Jorge, was laying foundations to decentralize many of IBAMA's responsibilities,[25] thereby giving state governments greater control over local environmental planning. Clearly, if this movement continues (and here it should not be forgotten that Brazilian politics is notoriously unpredictable) then environmental and social policy in Amazonia will be increasingly determined by those who exploit the region's natural and human resources most successfully. As one well-qualified commentator puts it: 'This is not necessarily a positive trend ... decentralization may be disastrous for the environment and vulnerable groups such as Indians and traditional extractors.'[26]

---

24. *Financial Times*, 20 February 1993.
25. Address given by Coutinho Jorge to the University of Glasgow Institute of Latin American Studies, 5 March 1993.
26. Sawyer (1990) p 18

## Chapter 7

# The Destruction of Eden?

So far we have looked at how the mining economy works and have explored its influence on local land uses and politics. But little has been said about what this means for the future of Amazonia and its residents. In this chapter I evaluate the social and environmental impacts of informal-sector mining in the region. To set the context for subsequent discussion, a short account of a *garimpo's* development is related. Not only does this serve as a timely reminder of what mining is all about, but it also provides a clear insight into the ways in which any one *garimpo* can affect its hinterland. In this way we acquire a starting point from which to explore the impacts of mining in greater depth.

## THE JATAPÚ GOLD STRIKE

A close look at Figure 2.1 shows that geological intrusions, similar to those found in the Yanomami Reserve, exist along the Guyanese border in southeastern Roraima. A number of prospecting teams were commissioned by ranchers and influential *garimpeiros* to survey this area following the closure of the gold fields on the Yanomami Reserve. In June 1992 a strike was made in the headwaters of the Rio Jatapú. It provoked an immediate influx of *garimpeiros* to the small agricultural community of Entre Rios (see Figure 1.2). They congregated in the village situated at the eastern end of the Perimetral Norte highway (BR 210) before embarking upon the fortnight long walk into the newly-established mine. Within two months, the strike had attracted over 400 people. The majority of them had come from Boa Vista, but others had travelled directly from Venezuela, Maranhão, Itaituba and the Cabeça do Cachorro, all on the strength of a poorly founded rumour.[1]

The villagers of Entre Rios were quick to take advantage of the opportunities presented by the influx. Residents opened up their homesteads as guesthouses, farmers sold agricultural produce for

---

1. See footnote 7 of Chapter 2 for the states of origin of 66 *garimpeiros* interviewed entering the *garimpo* at Jatapú.

gold and the village lorry driver made a tidy sum charging for rides. The Jatapú strike boosted what was a previously stagnant rural economy by increasing the demand for food, accommodation and transport. From the outset of the rush, *garimpeiros* were the most welcome visitors ever to have set foot in the sleepy village of Entre Rios. However, as the mine evolved, its influence on the local economy changed, and eventually its spin-offs for the area were not as substantial as the locals had initially hoped they would be.

*'Itaituba', from the village of Entre Rios, sporting his prospecting dish as a hat. He was one of the hundreds drawn to Rio Jatapú by rumours of a big strike.*

The original strikes were made along a small depression in which a limited amount of gold was concentrated. But beyond this restricted area the mineral was thinly spread over higher ground, necessitating the use of pumps for its extraction. The problem was that, under manual extraction, the *garimpo* could not generate sufficient quantities of gold to maintain itself. As we have seen, the *dono de garimpo* receives dues of between 40 and 50 per cent of the total gold produced, from which airdrops of food and equipment are commissioned. The goods are then either distributed or sold to the workforce in accordance with the work relationship adhered to.[2] But this system broke down in the early days of the Jatapú rush because the influx was out of all proportion to the size of gold deposit discovered. A desperate food shortage prevailed, which could only be remedied by the immediate construction of an airstrip.[3] This would not only increase gold production by permitting the installation of the appropriate machinery, but would also strengthen communications, thereby facilitating the resupply of the site.

The confused politics of the situation gave an extra impetus to the airstrip's rapid construction. The deposit had actually been discovered by a *garimpeiro* named Goiano, who was prospecting on behalf of Zézé, one of Roraima's few female miners. The standard arrangement is for the prospector and patron to share any profits that accrue from such research, but in this case Goiano failed to inform Zézé of his strike in the Jatapú, attempting to establish himself as the sole *dono de garimpo*. Zézé became aware of Goiano's deception the instant that rumours of his find broke in Boa Vista, and resolved to challenge him. She entered the mining site on foot, accompanied by a handful of gunmen and a large group of *garimpeiros*. After a showdown, which left two dead and a third seriously wounded, Zézé impressed her legitimate authority upon the *garimpo*.[4] Like many other *donos*, she had been left seriously indebted to other miners following their expulsion from the Yanomami Reserve, so her immediate concern was to open an airstrip at Jatapú and invite her creditors to install their mining equipment. As a

---

2. Under the *meia-praça* system, the *garimpeiros* pay 50 per cent of their gold earnings and receive free food; under *conta própria*, they typically pay 40 per cent of their gold produce, but have to pay for their food.

3. Apparently these chaotic events are commonplace during a *fofoca* (rush). Some of the *garimpeiros* leaving the Jatapú *garimpo* compared it to similar circumstances that prevailed during the *fofoca* of Novo Cruzado, which became one of Roraima's most productive mines. In both situations there was a dispute over ownership, which was resolved violently and the considerable food shortages caused by the rushes allegedly claimed a small number of lives in each case.

4. Zézé and Goiano shared the considerable expense of commissioning a helicopter to transport the injured person to a hospital in Boa Vista.

fortnight-long walk back out of the *garimpo* was the only alternative option available to the famished workforce, they set to the task of building the airstrip. On 6 August, less than two months after the initial strike was made, the airstrip was completed. Thus, semi-mechanized mining in Jatapú was not preceded by an extended period of manual extraction, which characterizes the development of most remote *garimpos*.

These internal dynamics had a profound effect on the economic changes brought to the surrounding area. Before the airstrip was built all *garimpo* traffic had passed through Entre Rios and the commerce of this isolated agricultural settlement had benefited accordingly. But this situation altered dramatically as soon as the first aircraft touched down on the *garimpo's* new airstrip. As it was now easier to service the site by air direct from Boa Vista, the village of Entre Rios experienced a sharp decline in its previously expanding economy. Soon there were few hints that a gold mine existed nearby, save the occasional drone of a passing aircraft, or the sporadic arrival of *garimpeiros* who could not afford to fly into the mine.

Even so, the rush was probably the most significant event in the history of Entre Rios since its inception in 1983. In spite of being a short-term phenomenon, it certainly did leave some longer-term legacies. A number of *garimpeiros* bought land nearby from smallholder entrepreneurs and a handful of others stayed on in the area to join the local agricultural labour force. But perhaps the most prominent manifestation of Entre Rios' brief contact with the mining economy is the 'Bar dos *garimpeiros*' – a wooden grain store that was hastily converted into a ramshackle boozer.

Events like these have been occurring throughout the Amazon during the 1980s. In the Yanomami Reserve alone more than 200 *garimpos* sprung up between 1986 and 1992. Clearly, all of them have their own idiosyncrasies, which come to define the relationship between the mine and its hinterland. Recognizing what is happening in the *garimpo* itself is therefore the first step in any evaluation of its impact. Even so, at a more general level, a number of observations can be made about the consequences of informal-sector mining as it is currently practised in Amazonia. I will start with the environmental repercussions of the activity, before examining its social impacts.

# THE SOCIAL AND ENVIRONMENTAL IMPACTS OF INFORMAL-SECTOR MINING IN AMAZONIA

### Sedimentation and deforestation

As most mining operations are situated on or next to watercourses, they do have a disproportionately large impact on the riverine eco-system. In fact some researchers[5] have argued that sedimentation

*Mining Amazonian style: a garimpo in Northern Roraima.*

---

5. See, for example, Douroujeanni and Padua (1992) p 103.

of watercourses is the most significant of all the environmental costs attributable to *garimpagem*. Scientists estimate that two cubic metres of sediments enter the watercourses for every gram of gold extracted from the *garimpo*s.[6] Although geological variations ensure that this proportion will change between different mining areas, they do indicate that the sedimentation caused by Amazonian mineral extraction may be measured in billions of tons. This not only interferes with the reproduction of fish, which is an important source of protein in the region, but also accelerates the rate at which the reservoirs of certain hydroelectric projects silt up.[7]

The changes to the aquatic ecosystem may well be more significant in ecological terms than the alterations inflicted upon the terrestrial environment by mining. For, although deforestation is often perceived to be one of its worst side effects, the significance of vegetation clearance associated with *garimpagem* is perhaps exaggerated. Mining, unlike most other land uses, is concentrated in relatively small areas and so does not contribute directly to widespread deforestation. Ranching, agriculture and logging are much worse culprits in this respect. Having said that, the vegetation clearance associated with mining is often important in a local context (especially if it is in a forest area that offers a livelihood to local people). Furthermore, because it involves such a major disruption of the soil, it is very difficult to reforest patches of land that have been affected by *garimpagem*. Scientists trying to recuperate degraded mining sites are forced to rebuild soil profiles that have been completely destroyed.

Even so, by only considering the deforestation directly caused by mining *in situ*, a large proportion of the degradation caused by the activity is overlooked. Any comprehensive assessment of this issue should also evaluate how much forest clearance in other areas is financed by profits from the *garimpo*. Here it is worth contemplating the relationship between gold mining and ranching, which was discussed in Chapter 4. Evidence that gold from Roraima was being invested in the ranches of southeastern Pará suggests that mining incomes may be driving the beef economy in this area now that many of the government subsidies for ranching have been withdrawn. Clearly, *garimpagem* is only one of a range of activities from which income is tapped and channelled into ranching. But the considerable wealth generated by mining, together with its tendency

---

6. Ibid.
7. See Uhl et al (1992).

towards spatial and social concentration, hints at significant financial exchanges between the mineral and ranching sectors in certain parts of the region. In this way *garimpagem* may have important repercussions on patterns of deforestation, land tenure and agrarian violence, which extend far beyond the site of mineral extraction itself.

### Mercury contamination and its public-health implications

The public health implications of widespread mercury contamination is of particularly concern over the medium to long term. Although *garimpeiro*s are increasingly aware that mercury is highly toxic, it is still common to see a group of people huddled around wherever the gold–mercury amalgam is torched. This is, after all, the first opportunity they have to assess the fruit of their labour and hence evaluate their pay. Mineral traders in nearby urban areas will subsequently perform the same ritual when purchasing gold (as this ensures that they are not inadvertently buying mercury as well). But even though they may burn more gold than the *dono*s in the *garimpo*s, they are typically exposed to smaller amounts of mercury vapour. This is because the *dono*s will have burnt almost all the toxic metal from the gold at the site of production before taking it to the gold dealer in the city.

People who inhale mercury from the burning process absorb the metal in an inorganic form through the mucous membranes of the nose and lungs. While undoubtedly toxic, mercury in this inorganic state may be flushed out of the body and discharged with the urine.[8] Consequently, *dono*s and mineral traders who are contaminated by mercury vapour in this way can be treated quite effectively by removing them from the source of pollution. In extreme cases, drugs may be administered to increase the rate at which the mercury is discharged from the body through the urine.

A second and potentially more serious channel of mercury contamination is via the consumption of polluted fish. With the constant flow of water and sediments, some of the mercury placed behind the riffles in the *garimpeiro*s' sluice-boxes is washed into the local watercourses. It settles amongst the sediments of riverbeds, where it is joined by mercury that has been condensed out of the atmosphere with rainfall, following the burning process described above. Ground-feeding fish and other organisms absorb the

---

8. Personal communication with D Cleary during 1993.

mercury on the river bottoms and they, in turn, are eaten by carnivorous fish. In the course of these events the mercury is transformed from an inorganic to an extremely toxic organic state, called methyl-mercury, through a process known as methylation.

Unlike inorganic mercury, methyl-mercury is not easily discharged from the body. It therefore accumulates in the tissues of organisms at the higher end of the food chain (like large carnivorous fish, caymans and, eventually, people). Riverine communities in close proximity to the *garimpo*s are at greatest risk from mercury contamination through fish consumption. As the limnology and biochemical processes operating in Amazonian rivers are poorly understood, it is difficult to know what time lapses are involved in this chain of events. While research into the subject gathers momentum, the health of riverine communities is being monitored and affected populations are being warned about the consequences of eating carnivorous fish. Meanwhile, attempts are being made to introduce new technologies, such as portable mercury condensers (known as *retentor*s) and sluice attachments into the *garimpo*s, so that mercury discharges are reduced.

To date, most of the research on mercury pollution is concerned with identifying which societies are at greatest risk from contamination. Such was the objective of a collaborative research project between Imperial College, London and the Federal University of Rio de Janeiro, which is one of the most authoritative sources of information on the public health implications of mercury contamination.[9] By analysing the blood and urine of people living either in or next to the Tapajós gold fields, this research showed that gold burners in the *garimpo*s tended to have higher levels of mercury in their urine than gold traders in the cities. It also found that riverine dwellers living close to the principal mining areas have high levels of organic mercury in their bloodstreams, acquired through eating contaminated fish. Despite these worrying observations, the project recorded low levels of mercury contamination among the population of Itaituba, the nearest city. This finding does give rise to some optimism. This suggests that the Amazon's massive urban population is unlikely to be as severely affected by mercury poisoning as had once been feared. Essentially the majority of urban dwellers are insulated from the two sources of contamination noted above. Vapour pollution is low, as only a fraction of total mercury

9. The results of initial research are presented in an unpublished document to the European Commission. See Brussels (1991).

burning occurs within the confines of the city. And the threat of organic contamination is reduced because urban diets are much more diverse than rural ones, which tend to be based around fish.

Even so, there is no room for complacency, especially as so little is known about the subject. Most research on mercury pollution has focused on the Tapajós and Madeira rivers, where *garimpagem* has been practised intensely since the 1960s. Clearly, it makes sense to collect data from these areas, where mercury use has been most profligate. But, there is still a need to gather basic information from the less accessible parts of Amazonia, where gold mining also occurs. Virtually nothing is known about the extent and likely consequences of mercury use in Roraima, the Cabeça do Cachorro and Amapá. For, although less mercury has been discharged into the watercourses of these more recently-mined areas, hydrological differences and variations in local diets mean that the health implications of mercury pollution in one part of Amazonia cannot be directly extrapolated from data gathered elsewhere. In the longer term, therefore, a need exists to extend the monitoring of mercury pollution from the Madeira and Tapajós rivers to other parts of the Amazon, and to integrate this with appropriate data on the dietary habits of exposed populations.

## The repercussions for indigenous communities

It is particularly unfortunate that the geology of Amazonia encourages prospectors to enter the very watersheds that provide the ultimate refuge for some of the world's most isolated Indian societies. The arrival of *garimpeiros* on the lands of groups like the Yanomami tends to be particularly destructive. On the one hand, the Indians have minimal resistance to 'Old World' diseases, which the miners inadvertently bring with them. On the other, the Indians' livelihoods, which are often dependent on the healthy functioning of the ecosystem, may be severely disrupted when the miners start work. In this way, Indian groups can find themselves bearing the full brunt of any environmental problems, whilst simultaneously being smitten by disease. All this occurs within a social and economic context that is not only profoundly disorientating, but may be compounded by violent conflict with the invading *garimpeiros*.

The massacre of 16 Yanomami from the village of Hashimu, in August 1993, is one desperate incident that stands out in a prolonged conflict between Roraima's Indians and *garimpeiros*. In analysing events that led to this clash, the social anthropologist, Bruce Albert, emphasizes the significance of cultural misunderstanding. He explains that on entering Indian reserves, the *garimpeiros*, who are initially scared of the Indians, and in the minority, seek to pacify their indigenous hosts by offering them gifts. But as more *garimpeiros* arrived, the balance of power between the groups started to change and the miners no longer had to maintain their initial generosity:[10]

> The Indians begin to feel the rapid deterioration of their health and means of subsistence caused by gold mining. The rivers are polluted, hunting game is scared away by the noisy machinery, and many Indians die in constant epidemics of flu, malaria, etc, all of which tends to destroy the social and economic fabric of their communities. Due to this situation the Indians come to see the food and goods given by the miners as vital and indisputable compensation for the destruction they have caused. When this is refused, a feeling of explicit hostility wells up within them.
>
> Thus they arrive at a deadlock: the Indians become dependent upon the prospectors just when the latter no longer need to buy the former's goodwill. ... From there the possibility of minor incidents degenerating into open violence increases. And since the disparity in force between the prospectors and the Indians is enormous, the scales always tip against the Yanomami.

In other areas, notably where the Indian group concerned has previous experience of dealing with wider Brazilian society, problems often arise from the way mineral extraction is organized and controlled. As we have seen, there are examples of indigenous communities benefiting from *garimpagem* when it is practised on their terms. But, unfortunately, amicable relationships between Indians and *garimpeiros* are quite rare and tend to be particularly elusive whenever the deposits in question are very valuable. Even the Kayapó, who were exceptional in regulating mining activity on their lands, were forced to make certain trade-offs with the *garimpeiros*. These and other examples suggest that the negative impacts sustained by indigenous communities from *garimpos* on their lands, tops any list of the direct social costs associated with the activity. Here, despite its limitations, there is no obvious alternative to rigorous government intervention in policing indigenous reserves.

---

10. Albert (forthcoming) p 3.

## *... and for the rest of Amazonian society ...*

In contrast, for many of Amazonia's non-indigenous populations, the benefits of *garimpagem* probably outweigh the social and environmental costs it inflicts. This, however, partly reflects a widespread ignorance of the consequences of mercury pollution and a failure to associate mining with the changing pattern of disease transmission. But it does nonetheless point to the significance of an activity that brings economic growth to remote parts of the region. The spin-offs for rural areas may be considerable, especially if the *garimpo* leads to improvements in transport. For example, the Transgarimpeira highway in the Tapajós, which was built to gain access to the region's gold fields, has stimulated agriculture, ranching and timber extraction in its hinterland.

Even so, the infrastructural changes associated with *garimpagem* are minimal in comparison to those made by the formal mining sector. For example, in the mid-1980s the mineral corporation, CVRD, constructed a 900-kilometre railway to transport iron ore from the Serra do Carajás to a deep water port at São Luis. Likewise Paranapanema has built roads into the Waimiri–Atroari reserve to gain access to the Pitinga cassiterite mine. *Garimpeiros* are never responsible for such large-scale developments, but even so their impact on the regional economy and local society is probably much greater than that of the formal mining sector. This is because, quite apart from being capital intensive and therefore employing fewer people, any profits made by the corporate mining sector tend to be removed from the region and invested elsewhere. In contrast, *garimpeiros* receive a respectable proportion of the income they generate and, more significantly, they spend it locally in all sectors of the Amazonian economy. Thus the *garimpo* has a much higher 'multiplier effect' than the formal mining sector, and the considerable demand for goods, services and land that this generates often brings radical transformations at both a local and regional level.

Nowhere is this more clearly visible than in the rapid expansion of cities like Santarém, Marabá, Porto Velho and Boa Vista. Throughout the 1980s, rapid urbanization in Amazonia has been closely associated with the expansion of the regional mining economy. This has been a massive boon to anybody employed in either the formal or informal sectors of the urban economy. Indeed, the very considerable investments made by *garimpeiros* in urban enterprises have been especially significant at a time when state funding was on the ebb. In contrast to many government projects aimed at stimulating the urban economy, these private-sector investments have tended to percolate down to all sectors of urban society.

## ... *drugs and prostitution*

Even so, economic growth is not necessarily synonymous with progress. While there is clear evidence of *garimpagem* bringing a variety of benefits to city dwellers, such sudden urban expansion is not without its social costs. Drug use, prostitution and violent crime have all become part of life in the Amazonian boom towns. There are two ways in which the mining economy stimulates the demand for drugs and prostitution in its hinterland. First, men who migrate large distances to work in the *garimpo*s for extended periods may abandon their households after a while and experience isolation (although some cope with that by running dual households). Secondly, having created desires in this way, miners are one of the very few social groups in the Amazon who are wealthy enough to satiate them. As a result, informal-sector gold mining supports two thriving rackets which are often characterized by exploitation and violence.

The *garimpo*s provide fertile ground for anyone involved in the Latin American drugs trade. Cocaine and marijuana are both readily available and widely consumed, though more by the professional *garimpeiro*s than the seasonal workers. It is common for divers working on the rafts (*balsa*s) to smoke a mixture of cocaine and grass before starting their shift on the riverbed. Mining operations themselves offer a convenient cover for the distribution, and occasionally the processing, of drugs. Cocaine traders prefer to deal in gold, because, unlike American dollars, it cannot be traced. This, together with the relative ease with which firearms and gunmen can be obtained in the *garimpo*s, helps cement a close working relationship between the gold mining and drugs industries of the Amazon.

Prostitution is as much of a problem. Research in the *garimpo*s of Pará has uncovered an extensive network of Amazonian prostitution in which women are sometimes kept in conditions of slavery.[11] Women interviewed in the brothels of Cuiu-Cuiu, one of the most established *garimpo*s of the Tapajós, explained that they were lured into prostitution under false pretences and threatened

---

11. See Dimenstein (1992); SEICOM (1993).

with violence if they refused to work.[12] Like many of the prostitutes in Roraima, they were recruited from the same poverty-stricken areas of Maranhão and Pará from which most of the *garimpeiros* originate. Given the considerable strain intense regional migration places on personal relationships, it is possible that many of them are female heads of households seeking an income after having been deserted by their partners. Others are significantly younger and child prostitution is not uncommon in a region in which great status is placed on virginity. In most cases women are transported to the brothels of the gold camps by intermediaries. They arrive owing the middlemen the cost of their passage and are obliged to repay it from their earnings. Clearly it is in the brothel keeper's interest to charge the women high prices for food, clothing and keep, so that they are barely able to repay their debts.

The large, isolated, yet stable, *garimpos* of the Tapajós lend themselves to these forms of debt-bondage. But in more fragmented, volatile mining areas (like those of western Roraima) prostitution is less centralized because it is more difficult for one person to exert the same degree of control. Here, unlike Cuiu-Cuiu, there are few large brothels within the *garimpos* and, as a result, prostitutes tend to have greater autonomy. Women are typically employed in the gold mines as cooks and earn extra income by working as prostitutes for the mining crews for whom they cater. As they have often acquired their job through being a friend of the *dono de máquina* or *dono de garimpo*, they may enjoy a relatively privileged position in the mine.

While there is undoubtedly exploitation in many of the Amazon's brothels, prostitutes working in the urban areas are probably better able to escape from tyrannical employers and gain other work. Even so, conditions are far from ideal. In Boa Vista the brothels are clustered along the banks of the Rio Branco in a violent part of town that floods seasonally. Most of the women come from Maranhão, Pará and Goiás, though a number are local Macuxi seeking independence in the city. The man buys the key to the woman's room from the barman and, once the brothel keeper has deducted the cost of 'overheads', the prostitute receives a percentage of the

---

12. Following a series of articles published by Dimenstein in the *Folha de São Paulo* in February 1992, the brothels of Cuiu-Cuiu were raided by the police. They released 74 prostitutes who had been held against their will and arrested 10 brothel owners; 20 of the women who were released were minors. See Sutton (1994).

money earned from the trade she has generated. Condoms are usually available with the key, but they are seldom requested, for miners regard them as an affront to their virility. Clearly this favours the spread of sexually transmitted diseases. Syphilis is common and, although no official statistics exist, it is likely that AIDS is also rife.

## DISCUSSION

Thus, *garimpagem* is a very influential agent of change in contemporary Amazonia, affecting the health, welfare and environment of many of the region's inhabitants. As we have seen here, the strong flows of labour and capital associated with the activity ensure that the impacts of informal-sector mining extend far beyond the confines of the *garimpo* itself. Indeed, they can extend for thousands of kilometres.

For example, close links between the Brazilian northeast and the *garimpos* of Amazonia mean that fluctuations in the regional mining economy may have considerable repercussions on the fortunes of smallholders in Maranhão. Remittances from the region's gold mines and brothels presumably affect the livelihoods of thousands of northeastern households. Not only does this determine levels of disposable income and hence investment decisions, but it also influences migratory strategies, which in turn affect patterns of disease transmission and gender divisions of labour in the household.

In spite of this, the long-term migration stimulated by the gold rush is something of an unknown quantity. For, while there is now a comprehensive literature on population movements from the northeast to Amazonia related to the search of land, virtually nothing is known about the patterns of migration stimulated by the expansion of the regional mining economy. Do smallholders just go into the Amazon looking for land and enter the *garimpos* if they cannot obtain it, or is the pull of the *garimpos* sufficiently powerful to stimulate migration in its own right? It is an important question. For if the gold rush is actually drawing large numbers of migrants into the Amazon, this will further increase an already considerable pressure on the region's fragile ecosystem.

In fact, the real nub to this question lies in distinguishing temporary excursions to the *garimpos* from long-term interregional migration. For, while it is possible that the gold rush encourages large numbers of households from the northeast to pack up their bags and head into the Amazon permanently, it could well be that the opposite is true, namely that the mining boom does not accelerate long-term migration at all, but actually slows it down. If remittances from temporary excursions to the *garimpo*s are sufficient, northeastern peasant households may be able to resist the pre-existing economic and social pressures that have traditionally fuelled Amazonian migration – and stay put.

# Chapter 8

# Placing the Amazon Gold Rush in Perspective

*Gold dealers' shops in Boa Vista.*

By now it should be clear that the 1980s' gold rush is a highly significant phenomenon in the history of Amazonia. But it would be a shame to stop this book right there. For this glance at events in the Amazon provides us with an opportunity to glimpse one or two revealing insights into how the whole mining world works. In discussing some of these wider issues in this final chapter, I probe what is driving mineral exploration both in Latin America and beyond. Starting with an evaluation of why Amazonians go mining, I go on to consider how mineral extraction is likely to fare in relation to other sectors of the regional economy before standing back one step further to look at the future role of mining in the tropics.

## MOTIVES FOR MINING

One of the most interesting questions surrounding gold rushes relates to why some people go mining more than others. Throughout this book we have seen certain social groups drop virtually everything to go mining whilst others appear to be scarcely interested. Clearly gold fever does not grip everybody to the same degree. But does this mean that different societies value gold or the acquisition of material wealth in different ways?

Probably not. For one thing it is quite misleading to think in terms of a distinct set of values being held by any one society. Within any social group there are as many different perspectives as there are members of the society. For this reason some Yanomami became experienced miners with a keen eye for gold, while others could appreciate no value for the metal at all. But quite apart from this, it is not difficult to find evidence to challenge grandiose assumptions about 'social mind sets'. The case of the *caboclos* is illustrative. Whereas virtually nobody from Roraima's riverine communities went mining, one does not need to look beyond the neighbouring states of Pará and Amazonas to find *caboclos* who did. Clearly there is nothing intrinsic about being a *caboclo*, an Indian, or, for that matter, anything else, that prevents people mining.

All of this suggests that people's involvement, or disinterest, in mining relates more to personal circumstances than to any socially-defined system of values. This is not to say that it is easily understood. Personal circumstances are themselves related to constantly changing social, economic and political factors. The objective here is not to come up with some magical formula with which to explain each person's behaviour. Rather it is to try and identify what common elements underlie the decisions they take. This is worth exploring in some depth because any of the policies currently being formulated to try and manage informal-sector mining are bound to fail unless they take account of the motives behind people's participation in *garimpagem*.[1] On one level, mining appears to unite a diversity of social groups in the quest for material wealth. However, this common interest eclipses a whole range of non-economic factors that also draw people into the *garimpos*.

Many of the smallholders (especially single men) are attracted to the adventure of mining, but groups like the Macuxi appear to be looking for something completely different. To them one of the most valuable products of *garimpagem* may be gaining prestige and identity among a different society. Politicians perhaps see mining as a vehicle through which to strengthen their political support and maintain their local hegemony. For thousands of others, most notably the professional *garimpeiros*, it is purely a means of surviving economically.

Even though it means different things to different people, certain statements can be made about why some groups go mining more than others. Interestingly enough, the distance between one group of people and the *garimpo* appears not to be a dominant factor in shaping their behaviour. City dwellers and smallholders travelled thousands of miles from the northeast to extract gold in Roraima, while *caboclos* did not even venture into the headwaters of the very rivers on which they lived to go mining. Similarly, while people with previous experience of *garimpagem* are able to make more informed migratory decisions, it is difficult to predict their likely response to a mineral rush purely on the basis of their life histories. As has been noted, the Macuxi are amongst Roraima's most experienced *garimpeiros*, yet only a minority of them left their villages to join the gold rush.

A more relevant consideration is the ease with which mining can be integrated into other activities. The seasonal nature of *garimpagem* ensures that timing is all important for those seeking to combine it with alternative forms of employment. While this seldom poses a problem for urban dwellers, it is fundamental to rural people whose livelihood strategies usually vary markedly throughout the year. The case of the Macuxi is illustrative; for them, the peak gold-mining period clashes with the best time for hunting, fishing and diamond mining on the savannah. Many of the Macuxi

---

1. Following the clash between *garimpeiros* and Yanomami, which led to the massacre at Hashimu in August 1993, the Brazilian government commissioned an interparliamentary report, which set out new policies in an attempt to exert more control over informal-sector gold mining in Amazonia.

obviously felt that gold mining was not an attractive proposition, but at the same time other groups of rural producers, most notably smallholders, were flocking to the *garimpo*s. As there is virtually no demand for labour on colonist holdings during the summer months, mining dovetails neatly with agriculture. Thus, the seasonality of different activities dictates the opportunity costs of gold production.

The social networks that underpin different livelihoods also influence the ways in which groups respond to the opportunities presented to them. Although anybody can enter and leave *garimpo*s as they wish, social networks do nonetheless shape the movement of labour and capital within the informal-mining economy. This is certainly the case in remote areas like western Roraima and the Tapajós, where access to the gold fields is usually by plane and transport to the *garimpo*s is often monopolized or 'closed'. Under these circumstances, air-taxi operators and the *donos de garimpo* may fulfil a role as gatekeepers to the mining areas. As numerous people in these positions are competing with one another on a commercial basis, there is no group control over access. But even so, these more powerful individuals may still represent an obstacle that prevents certain people reaching the *garimpo*. Members of the Amazonian peasantry are generally wary of working in an alien environment precisely because their only insurance against economic exploitation is rooted in social networks. It is probably true that such a philosophy is more deeply ingrained among residents of tighter and more remote communities than it is among urban dwellers, colonist farmers or ranchers. Thus, when trying to understand why certain people are more willing to go mining than others, the extent of their social contacts merits attention.

Hence, the seasonality of an individual's employment and the extent of his or her social networks determine the ease with which gold mining can be tailored to other jobs. In this way, an individual's involvement in mining can only be truly understood if it is evaluated in relation to his or her other activities. Indeed, if *garimpagem* is considered to be one element in a range of possibilities that constitute a living, then decisions made in this sphere are probably influenced by wider livelihood strategies. Involvement in mining may, for example, reflect risk-management behaviour on a higher level. One standard argument is that the peasantry spreads risk by engaging in a wide variety of economic activities.[2] But while this

2. For example, see Sawyer (1990) p 14.

suggests that people might be on the lookout for new options, it is strange that they should embrace a high-risk venture like *garimpagem* so enthusiastically. An alternative thesis argues that Amazonians might actively seek out high-risk activities in order to keep pace with high inflation.[3] From this perspective, a short-term gamble like *garimpagem* makes greater economic sense than the gradual accumulation of capital over a long period. Obviously such a strategy only becomes feasible once an individual has other options, like agriculture, to fall back on. In this context landownership becomes highly significant, for it allows people to underwrite the inherent risks of mining against the security of their holdings – whether they be ranches, colonist plots or rubber trails.

Both theories support the notion that economic success is closely related to the efficiency with which different activities can be complemented. It is here that social networks provide the crucial lubrication; knowing the right people in the right places becomes important when moving between various sectors of the economy. In this way, social networks can acquire a clearly-defined economic significance. For example, a mining trip is most appealing to those whose absence threatens no other aspect of their livelihood and who have good contacts in the *garimpo*s. These more experienced friends will usually keep an eye on them, offer them tips and maybe even arrange employment for them in the mining camps. The very same venture is probably least attractive to those who have no contacts in the mining world, have no previous experience in the activity, and whose absence from alternative enterprises incurs high opportunity costs. Obviously, these factors are weighed up against a whole range of other considerations when evaluating the option presented by the *garimpo*. But the point to recognize is that social networks come to fulfil a central role in this decision-making process because they actually reduce many of the practical risks associated with *garimpagem*.

It is possible to evaluate the ease with which mining may be incorporated into the livelihood practices of different social groups. In broad terms, it probably fits conveniently into the portfolios of city dwellers, colonist farmers and ranchers, for these groups usually have the necessary contacts and are sufficiently footloose to enter the *garimpo*s whenever an opportunity arises. Interestingly enough, as urban employees are often obliged to quit a job with no guarantee of future employment, *garimpagem* could represent a

---

3. See Cleary (1993).

greater gamble for them than for rural producers, who always have their land to return to. At the other end of the spectrum are people with insecure land rights who derive a large proportion of their income over the summer months and who have little contact with *garimpeiros*.

Thus, to a large extent people go mining because they can move with relative ease between jobs. Indeed, the impressive occupational mobility of Amazonians is emerging as one of the recurring themes of this book. People switch occupations with such dexterity that a close look at *garimpeiros* reveals not simply gold miners but smallholders, Indians and even ranchers. This can be confusing. For although individuals may have various forms of employment, they are labelled according to only one of their professions at any one time. It is therefore important to recognize the limitations of using terms like *garimpeiro*, *caboclo* and *fazendeiro* in this context, for they accord a false impression of occupational stability to what is a highly mobile population.

This high degree of flux also accounts for the enormous difficulties in quantifying the informal mining sector. Estimates for the total number of *garimpeiros* vary wildly precisely because the word is so vaguely defined. Do only those engaged in mineral extraction qualify? Or should anybody in the *garimpo* at any particular moment (traders, carpenters, mechanics, cooks and prostitutes) be included? And what about that percentage of miners who are taking a break from the *garimpo* for a couple of weeks to spend their earnings in the city? Or, for that matter, the investors who provide the capital but never set foot in the *garimpo*? Are they *garimpeiros* too? The ambiguities stem from trying to quantify a highly dynamic interaction of activities from only one perspective. Indeed, the relevance of such an exercise is questionable. By focusing on individuals only when they are in the guise of *garimpeiros* it is easy to lose sight of the very processes that create and sustain such a large mining population in the first place.

## THE WIDER AMAZONIAN PICTURE

Because the *garimpo* is so much a product of wider processes affecting other spheres of Amazonian life, the trends observed here are by no means restricted to the informal mining sector alone. Far from it, by looking at what is going on in the *garimpo* we come face to face with many of the dominant forces operating throughout the region. The occupational fluidity, if not instability, mentioned above is a case in point. Migrants cover thousands of miles on the strength of poorly founded rumours, cities mushroom in a few months as new opportunities arise, people switch jobs and move between rural and urban areas at the drop of a hat, and capital jumps from one speculative venture to another. In short, contemporary settlement processes in the Brazilian Amazon appear to be far from settled.

This is the product of both social and economic factors. First, migration, both inter- and intraregional, is intense. During the 1980s inter-urban population movements became increasingly important relative to rural–urban migration. This was fuelled, perhaps more than anything else, by the periodic boosts that informal-sector mining gave to the urban economy. Even though over half the Amazonians now live in cities, their livelihoods are not guaranteed by a stable and diversified urban economy. Because rapid urban growth is founded upon the short-term exploitation of mineral resources, it offers no long-term security of employment. People have to move frequently, either between jobs or between cities, in order to survive. Transience prevails. Simultaneously, the population influx from other regions of Brazil appears to be slowing, so internal movement accounts for an increasing proportion of total migration. Even so, as employment prospects for the region's poor are likely to remain insecure, there is little evidence that the Amazonian population will become any less mobile in the immediate future. An authoritative forecast of regional demographic change suggests that intense population mobility will continue at least until 2010.[4]

Secondly, the movement of capital appears to be equally volatile. Investments are typically short term; capital is withdrawn from productive activities in one sphere the instant a more attractive opportunity arises elsewhere. Although not easily quantified, it is likely that an increasing proportion of the capital invested in Amazonia is being generated within the region itself. This is because the gold rush increased local wealth whilst economic stagnation at a national level, coupled with fiscal changes, simultaneously reduced the incentives for external producers to channel corporate funds into the region. The net result is that, in common with the dynamics of the labour market, Amazonian capital flows are increasingly defined by intrinsic and not external factors. Again, there are few indications that this situation will change over the short term, particularly as an increasingly impotent federal government can no

---

4. Sawyer (1990) p 19.

longer provide either the infrastructure or the incentives usually required to entice capital into the region. Even massively subsidized projects like the Grande Carajás Programme may not provide satisfactory returns to potential investors; this was demonstrated by the withdrawal of a consortium of Japanese aluminium producers from the ALUNORTE (Alumínio do Norte) project at Bararena near Belém in 1987.[5]

On the other side of this equation new investment opportunities that fall neatly into the hands of the local entrepreneurial class are emerging to supersede the gold rush, which is itself already showing signs of slowing up. Timber production has been growing during the early 1990s, particularly in Pará and Rondônia, and, with the global supply of hardwoods from Southeast Asia and West Africa diminishing because of unsustainable, short-term management practices, the market is set to continue expanding.[6] As these areas have commanded the attention of the international trade for so long, the Amazonian timber industry has been left mainly in the hands of domestic companies, many of which are owned by regional entrepreneurs. Even so, they are likely to face growing competition from larger concerns seeking to make an entrance in Amazonian timber production.

Given that inflation shows no sign of abating it is likely that investors will continue to hunt out short-term high-risk ventures in Amazonia. Here the expanding cocaine industry looks set to generate investment opportunities similar to those offered by both the speculative land markets of the late 1970s and the gold economy of the 1980s. As governments clamp down on Colombian and Bolivian production, the Brazilian Amazon is acquiring a new significance in the Latin American drugs economy. Gold mining undoubtedly contributed to the expansion of the regional cocaine industry during the 1980s. A glance at a map of the Amazon reveals that Brazil's *garimpeiros* inadvertently established a network of airstrips along international frontiers, which are strategically important to the drugs trade. The *garimpos* of Rondônia, Cabeça do Cachorro, and Roraima all have the main Bolivian and Colombian cocaine-producing areas on one side of them and their export routes along the Caribbean coast on the other, suggesting that 'the western

---

5. Hall (1989) p 56.
6. See Johnson and Cabarle (1993).

Brazilian Amazon ... will become more deeply involved in the international drugs trade as time goes on'.[7]

This impermanence of both labour and capital in productive activities has important repercussions for the use of land. Not surprisingly, labourers and investors are reluctant to commit themselves to any particular venture under such circumstances, and so short-term management is usually the order of the day. But this tendency to keep one eye on the job in hand while the other continually appraises alternative options ensures that any one sector of the economy always remains particularly sensitive to changes elsewhere. For this very reason land management practices are highly responsive to external socioeconomic stimuli. Indeed it is easy to get the impression that land-use decisions are more often a response to changes in other sectors of the economy than they are to the productive economics of the land use itself. For example, fluctuations in the price of gold, not rice, are what frequently determine the labour investments made by smallholders on their plots. Exactly the same process is at work when ranchers are observed slaughtering productive heifers to raise short-term venture capital for mining investments. Clearly, it is only by understanding the rationale behind such decision-making that we begin to recognize the true forces that dictate the use of Amazonian land.

These insights have all been gained by looking at how different social groups, managing different ecosystems, respond to changing socioeconomic circumstances. And this is where we can make a contribution to a wider global debate on conservation and development. The point is that none of the processes that have been scrutinized here are exclusively Amazonian. All over the world different societies are constantly adapting to macro-level changes defined by forces completely beyond their control. This book simply takes one such stimulus – a sudden increase in the price of gold – and illustrates how it comes to have a series of far-reaching social and environmental consequences. Perhaps one of the most disturbing aspects of the global economy is that the true costs of changing commodity values, in both human and ecological terms, are seldom recognized and virtually never accounted for.

## LOOKING BEYOND BRAZIL

Brazil is only one part of this puzzle. The rising price of gold at the

---

7. Cleary (1993) p 18.

start of the 1980s sparked gold rushes throughout Latin America, especially in Colombia, Peru, Venezuela and the Dominican Republic, but also in Chile, Ecuador, Argentina, Guyana, Mexico and Nicaragua.[8] Further afield, Papua New Guinea, Zimbabwe, the Philippines and Ghana have emerged as important gold producers during the decade, with much of their output coming from the informal sector. In many countries, particularly in the southern hemisphere, the rural poor has kindled a new interest in gold mining. In all these states, mineral exploration will have influenced patterns of land use and settlement in much the same way as in Amazonia.

Given that many areas of the humid tropics show considerable geological potential, fluctuations in the international mineral markets will continue to shape the occupation and development of the world's last remaining rain forests. This is certainly true of Papua New Guinea, Malaysia, parts of West Africa (notably the Ivory Coast, Ghana and Zaire) and, above all, Amazonia. The Amazon's northern watershed, which still boasts vast tracts of natural forest and is home to many of the region's Indian groups, is a case in point. The recent surge of *garimpagem* in this remote area is perhaps only the first step in a more protracted process of occupation driven principally by the quest for mineral wealth. One has to remember that the *garimpeiros* themselves were only working the most accessible secondary deposits and that these are by no means exhausted. As any metals analyst will vouch, the geological potential of northern Amazonia is certainly not being overlooked by the world's mining industry:[9]

> Countries in Central and Southern America have recently attracted more mining producers and exploration work is being done in Venezuela and Argentina by both senior and junior companies. A large precambrian greenstone belt which extends from French Guyana in the east, through Surinam, Guyana, Venezuela, northern Brazil and into Colombia in the west, offers very good mineral potential and is the focus of most exploration in the region.

In evaluating the development pressures faced by parts of the humid tropics, specialists could do worse than deepen their under-

---

8. See Green (1982).
9. The statement below comes from a consultative document to fund managers and potential investors interested in the mining industry. RBC Dominion Securities (1993) p 49.

standing of international mineral markets and relate that knowledge to local geology. The prices of most base metals can be forecast with some degree of accuracy because they are defined by changing patterns of supply and demand (for use), like any other commodity. Speculation on the metals markets may cause some unpredictable fluctuations in the short term, but medium and long-term trends are relatively easy to decipher as they are shaped by structural processes.

Gold is the one notable exception because it is not just priced as a commodity, but also has what is known as a 'currency value'. In essence, gold is a bastion of global economics providing a yardstick against which currencies can be valued. The gold standard, which was introduced in the wake of the Napoleonic wars and maintained in various forms right up to 1971 (albeit with a brief interlude during the First World War), fixed the value of paper money and coins in circulation to gold reserves held in banks. Since the collapse of the gold standard in 1971, currencies tend not to be directly linked to the metal and are more often pegged against one another. But people, and particularly governments, are unwilling to shake off their confidence in gold and regulate its value to that of any other commodity. Thus, central banks continue to hold vast gold reserves (35,000 tons in 1992),[10] there is still a tendency for investors to look to gold as a security in difficult times, and the metal maintains its currency value as a result.

Whilst analysts can predict trends in the commodity value of gold with some degree of confidence, they have considerable difficulty forecasting its changing currency value. This is because it is often, but not always, sensitive to events that cause economic insecurity on a global scale. For example, even though the gold price had been rising sharply throughout the mid-1970s due to free trading in the wake of the defunct gold exchange standard (which had held the gold price artificially low at US $15 an ounce), its value was further boosted by two political events at the very end of the decade. The United State's decision to freeze Iran's assets and Russia's invasion of Afghanistan were primarily responsible for pushing gold to its peak value of US $850 on 21 January 1980.[11] Of equal significance is that a decade later Iraq's invasion of Kuwait

---

10. Ironically, these vast reserves mean that the economy of the developed world, which actually produces only a limited amount of gold, benefits tremendously from any increases in the price of the metal.
11. Green (1981) p 2.

and the ensuing Gulf War had virtually no impact on the price of the metal. This led some analysts to suggest that gold no longer maintains its currency value, but others who base their opinion on the metal's 6000 year-old economic history are less sure.[12] Even though the relatively stable price of gold during the early 1990s suggests that its commodity value dominates at the moment, its currency value has not disappeared altogether and may well rise suddenly (as it has done in the past) in response to unpredictable events that threaten global economic security. The surprising thing is that this inherent volatility does nothing to diminish gold's role as economic bedrock. On the contrary, investors' confidence in gold is confirmed every time they rush to it when other ventures look shaky.[13] Thus, investors and gold have a strange relationship in which instability appears to breed security.

As a rule, changes in the world's mineral markets influence the economics of any mining operation. But even so, it is by no means clear how different producers will react to changes in price. Generally speaking, mineral companies tend to be more sensitive than informal-sector miners to price changes. During the late 1980s and early 1990s larger producers have been struggling to restrict gold output as the price of the metal has fallen. Responding to both this and increasingly stiff environmental legislation in Canada and the USA, North American mining companies have looked abroad in search of low-cost mines. Expanding operations in less developed countries provide them with an opportunity to reduce productive overheads and diversify out of gold into other metals.

Simultaneously, the governments of many less developed countries are privatizing their minerals sector to attract more foreign investment. This movement has been led by Ghana and Zaire in Africa and by Mexico, Chile, Peru and Venezuela in Latin America. The shift from North to South America is particularly impressive. In 1992 the proportion of total exploration funds spent in the USA by North American mining companies declined from 71 per cent in 1989 to 63 per cent, while Latin America's share rose from 6 to 15

---

12. Nesbitt (1993) p 1. See also *The Mining Journal* (1993) pp 440–3.
13. For example, in April 1993 a bear gold market turned bullish overnight when a couple of powerful investors (George Soros and Sir James Goldsmith) moved into gold. Many other investors followed suit and, in the space of six weeks, the price of the metal rose from US $327 to $380 per ounce (*Sunday Times*, 23 May 1993).

per cent.[14] Venezuela is emerging as an important recipient of this venture capital. A site known as Kilometro 88, situated near the Brazilian border, has generated considerable interest among North American gold-mining companies. In 1993 they were clamouring to gain prospecting rights in this area, which is part of the greenstone belt mentioned above. Even though the same geological formation extends over the border, it has not stimulated the same activity because foreign investment in Brazil's mineral economy is currently restricted by the country's tough mining laws. This situation might well change in 1994, when the constitution is being revised, for a growing free-market lobby is urging the government to relax this legislation.

This situation suggests that poor and rich countries tend to respond in different ways to changing mineral prices. Without large amounts of capital to fall back upon, poor countries are less able to restrict or diversify production when prices fall. Very often they are desperate to acquire hard currency. So, instead of reducing output and sitting on their deposits until more favourable prices prevail, they try to maintain production. Rightly or wrongly, attracting foreign investment is seen by many governments as one way of achieving this.[15]

Even though informal-sector miners often have alternative subsistence options available to them, they tend to be even less responsive than the corporate sector is to price falls. With non-existent production costs, and minimal opportunity costs, informal-sector mining can still makes good economic sense if prices are low or in decline. *Garimpeiros* working in the Yanomami Reserve actually increased production of tin and gold during 1988 and 1989 when the prices of these metals were falling. Thus, while the behaviour of formal-sector mineral companies is essentially demand led, informal-sector production is driven by other, more immediate concerns. Here, forecasting is not so difficult. Poverty and people's struggle against it have a permanence that guarantees informal-sector mining a continued role in the resource conflicts of

14. The Gold Institute (1993) p 1. By 1993 South America was receiving 19 per cent out of a total US $1700 million spent by the world's mining companies on mineral research. *The Mining Journal* (1993) p 440.
15. This is precisely the argument presented by Gilberto Mestrinho, governor of the state of Amazonas, Brazil, when he addressed a public lecture in Glasgow in November 1992. He stated that, in response to falling mineral prices, Brazil, and particularly Amazonia, should be trying to increase mineral production so as to maintain the same level of income.

the humid tropics.

*The garimpeiro: assured of a place in the future of Amazonia.*

# Bibliography

Abers, R N (1992) 'Urbanization and city–ward migration on a resource frontier: the Amazon gold rush and the case of Boa Vista, Roraima', MA thesis, Department of Urban Planning, University of California, Los Angeles

Abers, R N and A C L Pereira (1992) 'Gold, geopolitics and hyperurbanization in the Brazilian Amazon: the case of Boa Vista, Roraima', in G Fadda (ed) *La Urbe Latinoamericana ante el Nuevo Milenio*, Fondo Editorial Acta Científica Venezolana, Caracas

*Ação Pela Cidadania* (1989) 'Roraima o aviso da morte', CCPY/CEDI/CIMI

— (1990) 'Yanomami a todos os povos da terra', CCPY/CEDI/ CIMI/NDI

Albert, B (ed) (1990) *Brésil: Indiens et développement en Amazonie*, Révue de Survival International (France), pp 11–12, Survival International, Paris

— (1992) 'Indian lands, environmental policy and military geopolitics in the development of the Brazilian Amazon: the case of the Yanomami', *Development and Change*, vol 23, pp 35–70

— (1993) 'Desenvolvimento militar e o *garimpo* no norte Amazônico: Os indios Yanomami face o projeto *Calha Norte*', *Anthropologia e Indigenismo*, vol 2, Museo Nacional, Rio de Janeiro

— (forthcoming) *The massacre of the Yanomami of Hashimu*. Part of the official report for the Federal Police, FUNAI and the Attorney General's Office. Due to be published by CCPY

Allen, E (1992) 'Calha Norte: military development in Brazilian Amazonia', *Development and Change*, vol 23, pp 71–99

Amparro, P P do (forthcoming) 'Sustainable development in Brazil', PhD thesis, Heriot Watt University, Edinburgh

Anderson, A B and D Posey (1989) 'Management of a tropical scrub savanna by the Gorotire Kayapó of Brazil', in D Posey and W Balée (eds), qv, pp 159–73

Andrade, M C de (1989) *A Cassiterita nas regiões Norte e Nordeste do Brasil*, CNP, Brasília

ATPC (1991) *Proceedings of the thirteenth session of the Executive Committee of Tin Producing Countries*, Canberra, Australia, 15–18 October

Ayres, D de M L (1992) 'The social category *Caboclo*: history, social organisation, identity and outsider's social classification of the rural population of an Amazonian region (the middle Solimões)', PhD thesis, King's College, University of Cambridge

Baines, S G (1991) *É a FUNAI que sabe – a frente de atração Waimiri–Atroari*, Museo Paraense Emilio Goeldi, Col Eduardo Galvão, Belém, Pará

Bakx, K (1987) 'Planning agrarian reform: Amazonian settlement projects, 1970–1986', *Development and Change*, vol 18, pp 533–55

Balée, W (1989) 'The culture of Amazonian forests', in D Posey and W Balée (eds), qv, pp 1–21

Barbira Scazzochio, F (ed) (1980 *Land, people and planning in contemporary Amazônia*, Centre of Latin American Studies, University of Cambridge, Occasional Publications no 3

Barros, N C de (1992) 'Paisagem, homem e natureza no vale do Rio Branco, Roraima, Brasil', unpublished manuscript

Bogue, D and Y Butts (1989) *International Amazonia: its human side*, Social Development Centre, Chicago

Bourne, R (1978) *Assault on the Amazon*, Victor Gollancz, London

Brussels (1991) 'Mercury contamination in the Brazilian Amazon: a report for the European Commission DG1/environment', unpublished document

Bunker, S (1985) *Underdeveloping the Amazon: extraction, unequal exchange and the failure of the modern state*, University of Illinois Press, Urbana

Burkhalter, S B and R S Murphy (1989) 'Trappers and sappers: rubber, gold and money amongst the Mundurukú', *American Ethnologist*, 16 February, pp 100–16

Butler, J (1985) 'Land, gold, and farmers: agricultural colonization and frontier expansion in the Brazilian Amazon', PhD dissertation, Department of Anthropology, Gainesville, University of Florida

— (1990) *'garimpeiros* and the placer mining sector', Annex IV of *Brazil; an analysis of environmental problems in the Amazon*, World Bank report 94104–BR, Washington DC, unpublished

Carvalho, J P F de (1982) *Waimiri–Atroari a história que ainda não foi contada*, independently published, Brasília

Castro, M B, B Albert and W C Pfeiffer (1991) 'Mercury levels in Yanomami Indians' hair from Roraima, Brazil', Paper presented at the international conference on heavy metals in the environment in Edinburgh, September

CCPY (1985) UHIRI no 1

— (1989) UHIRI no 11

— (1991) UHIRI no 14

# Bibliography

CEDI/CONAGE (1988) *Empresas de mineração e terras indígenas na Amazonia*, CEDI, São Paulo

CIDR (1992) 'Relatório das violências contra os Índios em Roraima', May 1992, Assessoria Juridica da Diocese de Roraima, e Conselho Indigena de Roraima

CIR (1992) 'Relatório da situação fundiaria da area indígena Raposa/Serra do Sol realizado pelo Conselho Indigena de Roraima de Agosto a Decembro de 1991', unpublished report, Boa Vista, Roraima

Clara da Silva, M (1991) 'Ecológia de subsistência de uma população cabocla na Amazônia Brasileira', MSc, INPA/FUA

Clay, J W (1988) 'Indigenous peoples and tropical forests: models of land use and land management from Latin America', *Cultural Survival Report*, 27, MA, USA

Cleary, D (1990) *Anatomy of the Amazon gold rush*, Macmillan Press in association with Saint Antony's College Oxford, Basingstoke

— (1991) *The Brazilian rainforest: politics, finance, mining and the environment*, The Economist Intelligence Unit, special report no 2100, 66pp

— (1993) 'After the frontier: problems with political economy in the modern Brazilian Amazon', *Journal of Latin American Studies*, vol 25, pp 331–49

Coelho, M C N and R G Cota (1986) 'Relações entre o *garimpo* e a estrutura fundiária: o exemplo de Marabá', *Pará Desenvolvimento*, no 19, June, pp 20–4

*Correio do Garimpo* (1988) November

Couto, R C de S (1990) 'Condições de saude nos *garimpo*s de ouro da Amazônia', in Hacon et al (eds) *Riscos e consequencias do uso do mercúrio*, Fiesp, Rio de Janeiro, pp 54–69

Cowell, A (1990) *The decade of destruction*, Hodder & Stoughton in association with Headway, London

Coy, M (1987) 'Rondônia: frente pioneira e programma POLONOROESTE, O processo de diferenciação sócio-econômica na periferia e os limites do planejamento público', in G Kohlhep and A Schrader (eds), *Homen e Natureza na Amazônia*, Universität Tubingen, Tubingen, pp 253–70

— (1989) 'Relações entre campo e cidade em areas de colonização governamental e particular. Os exemplos de Rondônia e do Norte Matogrossense', *Actas Latinoamericanas de Varsovia*, vol 7, Warsaw, pp 43–67

— (1991) *The frontier in North Mato Grosso: soybean production, timber extraction and goldmining*. Nijmegen Studies on Cultural Anthropology, Nijmegen

CPI (1992) *Informe Juridico*, nos 21 and 22, Comissão Pro-Índio, São Paulo

Crowson, P (1992) *Minerals Handbook 1990–1991*, M Stockton Press

Cruz, S A S (1980) 'O Garimpo do Tepequém: aspectos geológico e geoeconômico', Boa Vista, unpublished manuscript

Cruz, S A S and P M S Costa (1989) 'Garimpo uma realidade no contexto da Amazonia', São Paulo, August, unpublished manuscript

Cunha, M C de (1992) *História dos indios do Brasil*, FAPESP/SMC/Companhia das Letras, São Paulo

CVRD (1980) p/ext–116/80 of 28 February 1980 from CVRD to DNPM

Dimenstein, G (1992) *As meninas da noite*, Editora Atica, São Paulo

DNPM (1975) *Levantamento de recursos naturais*, vol 8 Folha NA 20; *Boa Vista e Parte das Folhas*, NA 21; *Tumucumaque*, NB 20; *Roraima*, NB 21, Ministério das Minas e Energia, Rio de Janeiro

— (1978) *Projeto Molibidénio em Roraima*, Ministério das Minas e Energia, Brasília

— (1982a) *Projeto Catrimani–Uraricoera*, Ministério das Minas e Energia, Brasília

— (1982b) *Os maiores mineradores do Brasil*, vol III, Brasília

— (1984) *Projeto Rio Branco*, Ministério das Minas e Energia, Brasília

— (1987–1990) *Súmario mineral*, Ministério das Minas e Energia, Brasília

— (1990) 'O Projeto Ouro Gemas', Manaus, unpublished manuscript

Dourojeanni, M and M T Padua (1992) *Ecology in Brazil, myths and reality*, FUNATURA/FACTO, Rio de Janeiro

Eden, M J (1990) *Ecology and land management in Amazonia*, Belhaven Press, London

Environmental Defense Fund (1992) 'Brazilian forest policy in the Collor government', June, 6pp manuscript, Washington DC

Eusebi, L (1991) *A barriga morreu: o genecidio dos Yanomami*, Edições Loyola, São Paulo, Brazil

Fagar (1991) 'Associação da Frente de Apoio ao *garimpeiro* de Roraima', unpublished map

Falesi, I C (1976) 'Ecossistema de pastagem cultivada na Amazônia brasileira', *EMBRAPA Bóletim Técnico*, Belém, no 1, pp 1–193

Farage, N (1991) *As Muralhas das Sertões: Os povos indigenas no Rio Branco e a Colonização*, Paz e Terra/ANPOCS, Rio de Janeiro

Farage, N and P Santilli (1992) 'Estado de sítio: territórios e identidades no vale do Rio Branco', in M C Cunha (ed), qv, pp 267–78

# Bibliography

Fearnside, P M (1980) 'Land use allocation of the Transamazonian highway: colonists of Brazil and its relation to human carrying capacity', in F Barbira Scazocchio (ed), qv, pp 114–38

— (1984) 'Brazil's Amazon settlement schemes', *Habitat International*, vol 8, no 1, pp 45–61

— (1985) 'Environmental change and deforestation in the Brazilian Amazon', in J Hemming (ed) *Change in the Amazon Basin*, vol 1, *Man's impact on forests and rivers*, Manchester University Press, Manchester, pp 70–89

— (1986) *Human carrying capacity of the Brazilian rainforest*, Columbia University Press, New York

— (1989) 'A ocupação humana de Rondônia: impactos, limites e planejamento', Programa POLONOROESTE, *Relatório de Pesquisa*, no 5, SCT/PR CNP, Assessoria Editorial e Divulgaçao Científica, Brasília, 76pp

— (1991a) *A situação da cobertura vegetal no Brasil, con enfase na situação da Amazônia*, Subsídio tecnico para a Relatório Nacional do Brasil para UNCED 1992

— (1991b) *Pressões antrópicas sobre os ecossistemas amazônicos: situação atual e perspectivas de conservação*, Subsídio tecnico para a Relatório Nacional do Brasil para UNCED 1992

Feijão, A J and Pinto, J A (1990) *garimpeiros activities in South America: the Amazon gold rush*, USAGAL/BMF, Pará ms, 15pp

Fernandes, F R C (1987) *O subsolo brasileiro*, MCT/CNP, Brasília

Fernandes, F R C and I C de M Portela (1991) *Recursos minerais da Amazônia: alguns dados sobre situação e perspectivas*, CETEM–CNP, Brasília

Ferri, P (1990) *Achados ou perdidos? A imigração indígena em Boa Vista*, MLAL, Goiânia, Goias, 96pp

Filho, A P (1984) 'A Miséria do colono e o ouro no Araguaia e Amazônia', in G A Rocha (ed) *Em Busca de Ouro, garimpos e garimpeiros no Brasil*, Marco Zero Books, Rio de Janeiro

*Financial Times* (1993) 'Christine Lamb: A lost Eden?' 20 March

Freitas, L A Soares de (1991) *Políticas públicas e administrativas de territórios federais do Brasil*, Editora Boa Vista, Boa Vista

FUNAI/CIMI/INESC/NDI (1991) *Porque demarcar as terras indigenas?* 4 pp, December

FUNATURA (1992) *Cost of implantation of conservation units in Legal Amazonia*, SCT/PR PNUD, Brasília

Furley, P A (ed) (1993) *The forest frontier: settlement and change in Brazilian Roraima*, Routledge, London

Gallois, D (1990) 'L'or et la boue: cosmologie et orpaillage waiapi', in B Albert (ed) qv, pp 50–5

Gama de Silva, R (1991) *O Entreguismo dos Minérios*, Tché, São Paulo

Gaspar, E dos S (1990) 'Os bamburrados do Tapajós', Msc thesis, Universidade Federal de Paraiba, Campina Grande

Gianluppi, D (1991) 'Pecuária em Roraima', unpublished document, 5pp

Gold Institute (1993) *The search for gold: US producers look abroad*, The Gold Institute, London, February

Good, K (1992) *Into the Heart*, Penguin, Harmondsworth

Goodland, R J A (1980) 'Environmental ranking of Amazonian development projects in Brazil', *Environmental Conservation*, vol 7, no 1, pp 9–26

Goodman, D and A Hall (eds) (1990) *The future of Amazonia: destruction or sustainable development?* Macmillan Press, Basingstoke

Goodman, D and M Redclift (eds) (1991) *Environment and development in Latin America: the politics of sustainability*, Manchester University Press, Manchester

Gray, A (1986) *And after the gold rush? human rights and self development among the Amarakaeri of southeastern Perú*, IWGIA Document 55, Copenhagen

Green, T (1982) *The new world of gold: the inside story of the markets, the politics, the investors*, Weidenfeld & Nicholson, London

Hall, A (1989) *Developing Amazonia: deforestation and social conflict in Brazil's Carajás Programme*, Manchester University Press, Manchester

Hecht, S B (1982) 'Cattle Ranching in the eastern Amazon: evaluation of a development strategy', PhD thesis, University of California, Berkeley

— (1987) 'Contemporary dynamics of Amazonian development: reanalysing colonist attrition', Los Angeles, unpublished manuscript

Hecht, S B and A Cockburn (1989) *The fate of the forest*, Verso, London

Hemming, J (ed) (1985) *Change in the Amazon Basin*, 2 vols, Manchester University Press, Manchester

— (1990a) *Roraima : Brazil's northernmost frontier*, Institute of Latin American Studies Research Papers 20, London

— (1990b) 'How Brazil acquired Roraima', *Hispanic American Historical Review*, vol 70, no 2

Hine, J (1991) 'Peasants politics and agrarian transition in the eastern Amazon: the case of peasant organisation in Marabá and the Poligano das Castanhais', PhD thesis, Department of Sociology, University of Liverpool

# Bibliography

Hugh-Jones, S (1992) 'Yesterday's luxuries, tomorrow's necessities: business and barter in northwest Amazonia', in C Humphrey and S Hugh-Jones (eds) *Barter exchange and value: an anthropological approach*, Cambridge University Press, Cambridge, pp 42–74

IBASE (1990) *Politica de desenvolvimento regional na Amazonia, 20 anos de SUDAM*, IBASE, Rio de Janeiro

IBDF (1984) *Alteração da cobertura vegetal natural do território de Roraima*, Anexo Relatório Técnico, IBDF, Ministério da Agricultura, Brasília, 79pp

IBGE (1980–84)

— (1983) *Censo Demográfico IX Recenseamento Géral do Brasil 1980*, Instituto Brasileiro de Geografía e Estatística, Rio de Janeiro

— (1986) *Anuário Éstatístico do Brasil*, Instituto Brasileiro de Geografía e Estatística, Rio de Janeiro

— (1990) *Censos econômicos de 1985 censo* agropecuária: Numero 5–Roraima, Fundaçao Instituto Brasileiro de Geografía e Estatística, Rio de Janeiro

— (1992) *Roraima: Censo demográfico 1991, Resultados Preliminares*, Janeiro 1992, Instituto Brasileiro de Geografía e Estatística, Boa Vista

IBGE/Governo do Território Federal de Roraima (1981) *Atlas de Roraima*, Fundaçao Instituto Brasileiro de Geografía e Estatística, Rio de Janeiro

IDB/UNDP/TCA (1992) *Amazonia without myths*, Commission on Development and Environment for Amazonia, IDB/UNDP/TCA, Washington

Jardim, W de F (1988) Contaminação por mercúrio; fatos e fantasías, Ciencia Hoje, vol 7, no 41, pp 78–9

Johnson, N and B Cabarle (1993) *Surviving the cut: natural forest management in the humid tropics*, World Resources Institute, Washington DC

Kelsey, T F (1972) 'The beef cattle industry in the Roraima savannas: a potential supply for Brazil's north', PhD dissertation, University of Florida

Lazarin, M A and Vessani, L A (1987) *Xiriana, Indios que garimpam: relatório de pesquisa na area Yanomami*, University of Goias/CNP, Brasília

Levi-Strauss, C (1974) *Triste Tropiques*, Athaneum, New York

Liu, C C, P Hernandez Filho and A T Tardin (1990) *Deteção de atividades de mineração na reserva do groupo Yanomami atraves de imagens TM/LANDSAT*, São José dos Campos, INPE–S182–RPE/638

Lobato de Azevedo, A L (1991) *Levantamento da atividade de mineração em areas indigenas*, CETEM, Rio de Janeiro

MacMillan, G J (1993a) 'Gold mining and land use change in the Brazilian Amazon', PhD thesis, University of Edinburgh

— (1993b) 'Ouro e agricultura na Amazônia', *Ciência Hoje*, vol 15, no 88, April, pp 9–11

— (1993c) 'Land-use pressures at the start of the 1990s', in P A Furley (ed), qv

Maennling, C (1987) El boom del oro en Madre de Dios, Peru: aspectos socioeconomicos, conflitos sociales y la persistencia del pequeno agro-minero', in G Kohlhep and A Schrader (eds) *Homen e natureza na Amazonia*, Universität Tubingen, Tubingen, pp 433–43

Magalhães, D de (1987) *Roraima informações históricas*, Graphos, Rio de Janeiro

Mahar, D J (1989) *Government policies and deforestation in Brazil's Amazon region*, The World Bank, Washington DC

Malm, O, W C Pfeiffer, C M M Souza and R Reuther (1990) 'Mercury pollution due to gold mining in the Madeira river basin, Brazil', *Ambio*, vol 19, no 1, February

Martine, G (1990) 'Rondônia and the fate of small producers', in D Goodman and A Hall (eds) qv, pp 23–48

MCT/CNP (1987) *A questão mineral da Amazonia*, MCT/CNP, Brasília

Migliazza, E (1978) *The integration of the indigenous peoples of the Territory of Roraima, Brazil*, IWGIA Document 32, Copenhagen

Miller, D (1985) 'Replacement of traditional elites: an Amazon case study', in J Hemming (ed) *Change in the Amazon Basin*, vol 2, *The frontier after a decade of colonisation*, Manchester University Press, Manchester, pp 158–71

Milliken, B (1991) 'Tropical Deforestation, Land Degradation, and Society in Rondônia Brasil', in S Hecht and J Nations (eds) *The social dynamics of deforestation in Latin America*, Cornell University Press, Ithaca NY

Mining Journal (1991) *Metals and minerals annual review 1990*, London

— (1993) 'The mining industry in 1993', *The Mining Journal*, vol 321, no 8256, 24–31 December, pp 440–3

Monbiot, G (1992) *Amazon watershed*, Target Books, London

Moran, E F (1989) 'Models of native and folk adaptation in Amazonia', in D Posey and W Balée (eds), qv, pp 22–9

Nesbitt Research (1993) *North American gold producers quarterly review*, Sunlife Tower, Toronto

Nugent, S L (1979) 'Society economy and national integration; an anthropological study of Santarém', PhD thesis, University of London

— (1991) 'The limitations of environmental management: forest utilization in the lower Amazon', in D Goodman and M Redclift (eds), qv, pp 141–54

Parker, E P (1989) 'A Neglected human resource in Amazonia: the Amazon *caboclo*', in D Posey and W Balée (eds), qv, pp 249–59

Pereira, A C L (1990) 'Garimpo e a fronteira Amazônica: as transformações dos anos 80', MSc thesis, Universidade Federal de Minas Gerais, Belo Horizonte

Porantins (1991) *Area indigena Raposa/Serra do Sol: os garimpos continuam matando*, May edition

Posey, D and W Balée (eds) (1989) *Resource management in Amazonia: indigenous and folk strategies*, vol 7, *Advances in economic botany*, New York Botanic Gardens, New York

Ramos, A R and K I Taylor (1979) *The Yanomama in Brazil*, IWGIA Document 37, Copenhagen

Ramos, A R, M A Lazarin and G G Gomes (1985) *Yanomami em tempo de ouro: relatório de pesquisa*, Serie Antropologica no 51, Universidade de Brasília, Brasília

RBC Dominion Securities (1993) *Annual precious metals and diamonds review 1993*, Royal Bank of Canada Dominion Securities

Ribeiro, B G and Kenhiri, T (1989) 'Rainy seasons and constellations: the Desana economic calendar', in D Posey and W Balée (eds), qv, pp 97–114

Richards, M (1992) *Review of the impacts of the commercialization of extractive forest products on welfare and resource use in Amazonia, and implications for sustainable forest management*, Natural Resources Institute, Chatham, Kent

Rivière, P (1972) *The forgotten frontier: ranchers of northern Brazil*, New York

Roosevelt, A C (1992) 'Arqueologia Amazônica', in M C de Cunha (ed), qv

Roraima, Governo de (1991) *Manifestação e declaração de princípios dos governadores da Amazônia occidental sobre o desenvolvimento auto-sustentado, integração continental e abertura de novos mercados*, Boa Vista

— (1992) *Diagnóstico técnico fundiário do Estado de Roraima*, Boa Vista

— SEPLAC (1980) *Informações estatísticas*, vol 1, nos 1–2, SEPLAC, Boa Vista

— SEPLAN–RR (1989) *Perfil econômico do Estado de Roraima*, Secretária de Planejamento e Coordenação, Boa Vista, 53pp

Santilli, M (1990) 'Projet *Calha Norte*: politique indiginiste et frontières nord-amazoniennes', in B Albert (ed), qv, pp 111–15

Sawyer, D (1990) 'Population growth and migration in the Brazilian Amazon', Annex I of *Brazil: an analysis of environmental problems in the Amazon*, World Bank report no 9104–BR, unpublished

Schmink, M (1985) 'Social change in the *garimpo*', in J Hemming (ed), qv, vol 2, *The frontier after a decade of colonisation*, pp 185–99

— (1992) 'Building institutions for sustainable development in Acre, Brazil' unpublished document

Schmink, M and C H Wood (1985) *Frontier expansion in Amazonia*, University of Florida Press, Gainesville, Florida

— (1992) *Contested frontiers in Amazonia*, Columbia University Press, NY

SEICOM (1993) *As mulheres de ouro: a força de trabalho nos garimpos do Tapajós*, Governo do Pará

Silbergeld, E K (1989) 'Report on travel to Brazil', unpublished document

Silva et al, A R B de (1986) 'Como repensar o *garimpo* na Amazônia?' *Pará Desenvolvimento*, no 19, June, pp 25–6

Silveira, I M de and M Gatti (1988) 'Notas sobre a ocupação de Roraima, migração e colonisação', *Bóletim do Museu Paraense Emilio Goeldi*, Sér Antropológia, no 41, pp 43–64

Sizer, N C (1991) 'Extractivism in the Jaú National Park, Amazonia', unpublished manuscript, Botany School, University of Cambridge

Smith, N J H (1982) *Rainforest corridors: the Transamazon colonization scheme*, University of California Press, Berkeley

Smole, W J (1989) 'Yanoama horticulture in the Parima highlands of Venezuela and Brazil', in D Posey and W Balée (eds), qv, pp 115–28

SUCAM (1991) 'Malária dados epidemiologicos de Roraima, 1888–1990', unpublished

SUDAM (1984) *O fenómeno migratório e a ação articulada dos programas de desenvolvimento de comunidade e migrações internas no território federal de Roraima*, SUDAM, Belém

SUDAM/OEA/PROVAM (1991) *Atualização dos estudos basicos do Vale do Rio Branco*, PR–SDR/SUDAM/SAP, June, Belém

*Sunday Times* (1993) 'Gold set to break through the US $400 barrier' by J Bethell, 23 May

SUPLAN (1980) *Aptidão agrícola das terras de Roraima*, Secretária Nacional de Planejamento Agrícola, Ministério de Agricultura, Brasília DF, 78pp

Sutton, A (1994) 'Prostitution in mining camps', in Anti-Slavery International, *Amazonian slavery: a link in the chain of Brazilian development*, Anti-Slavery International, London

Taylor, K I (1979) 'Development against the Yanomama: the case of mining and agriculture', unpublished document

Texeira de Carvalho, W (1992) 'Indiens et *garimpeiros*', in B Albert (ed), qv, pp 43–9

# Bibliography

Torres, H (1988) 'Desistêngia e substituiçaõ de colonos em projetos de colonizaçaõ de Amazônia; o caso de Machadino', Centro de Desenvolvimento Regional (CEPLAR), Universidade Federal de Mias Gerais (UFMG). Unpublished manuscript

Torres, H and G Martins (1991) *Amazonian extractivism: prospects and pitfalls*, Doc de Trabalho 5, ISPN, Brasília

Uhl, C, M M Mattos, J D Verissimo, Z Brandino, R Tarifa and, I Viera (1991) *Wood as a catalyst for ecological change in Amazonia*, research document, IMAZON, Belém, Brazil

Uhl, C, O Bezerra and A Martini (1992) *An ecosystem perspective on threats to biodiversity in eastern Amazonia*, research document, IMAZON, Pará state

*Veja* (1983) 'A fronteira do futuro', aviso pelo governo do Roraima, *Veja*, 13 April

Wagley, C H (1953) *Amazon town: a study of man in the tropics*, Oxford University Press, Oxford (reprinted 1976)

Weinstein, B (1983) *The Amazon rubber boom 1850–1920*, Stanford University Press, Stanford

Wesche, H and T Bruneau (1990) *Integration and change in Brazil's middle Amazon*, University of Ottawa Press, Ottawa

Wright, R (1990) 'Guerres de l'or sur le haut Rio Negro: strategies indiennes', in B Albert (ed), qv, pp 38–42

# Suggested Further Reading

This list offers a few comments on a handful of principal texts which the author recommends to anybody seeking a deeper understanding of the material covered in this volume.

Excellent discussions of *contemporary developments in the Amazon* are to be found in: Schmink and Wood (1992) and Hecht and Cockburn (1989). Both volumes offer impressive scholarship in an easily digestible form. Monbiot (1992) provides a similarly readable overview which, among other topics, follows the migratory trail of smallholders from the Brazilian northeast into the gold camps of Roraima. In addition to these volumes, other deep insights into post-war regional change can be gleaned from Cowell (1990), which, like the outstanding documentary films produced by the same author, paints a vivid picture of life on the frontier.

On *mining*, Hall (1989) provides a very thorough analysis of *corporate sector* mineral extraction in the Eastern Amazon. While Cleary (1990) offers a brilliant ethnography of the *informal sector* alternative. To put these developments into perspective consult Green (1982).

For those interested in different Amazonian societies, Wagley (1953) remains the classic text on *coboclo culture and society*. Equally timeless and beautifully written is Levi Strauss (1974) on *Brazilian indigenous populations* and the pressures facing them, while the relationship between these societies and the forest is explored in a fascinating collection of essays edited by Posey and Balee (1989). Finally, for an immediate account, not to mention a gripping read about life with the *Yanomami* try Good (1992).

# Index

*Manual mining in the Gurupi.*